LUCIANI

MENIPPUS ET TIMON

T0371569

LUCIANI
MENIPPUS ET TIMON

EDITED BY

E. C. MACKIE, B.A.

RECTOR OF STOCKTON-ON-THE-FOREST, YORKSHIRE,
LATE CLASSICAL MASTER AT HEVERSHAM GRAMMAR SCHOOL

CAMBRIDGE:
AT THE UNIVERSITY PRESS
1904

CAMBRIDGE UNIVERSITY PRESS
Cambridge, New York, Melbourne, Madrid, Cape Town,
Singapore, São Paulo, Delhi, Mexico City

Cambridge University Press
The Edinburgh Building, Cambridge CB2 8RU, UK

Published in the United States of America by Cambridge University Press, New York

www.cambridge.org
Information on this title: www.cambridge.org/9781107620032

© Cambridge University Press 1892

First edition 1892
First published 1892
Reprinted 1900, 1904
First paperback edition 2013

A catalogue record for this publication is available from the British Library

ISBN 978-1-107-62003-2 Paperback

PREFACE.

IN preparing these two dialogues for the press, I have used the text of Dindorf (1858), without any alterations in the *Menippus*, and with only a few in the *Timon*, duly noted. A few sentences have been omitted in *Timon* §§ 16, 17, as being scarcely suitable for class translation. I have also had by me Abbott's *Selections from Lucian*, Sommerbrodt's text, Yonge's *Scriptores Graeci*, and a Dublin edition of some of Lucian's dialogues by Wheeler (Walker). I am also greatly indebted to Heitland's little book in the Pitt Press Series, and, in writing the introduction, to Müller and Donaldson's *Literature of Ancient Greece*, and Collins' *Lucian* in his *Ancient Classics for English Readers*. When the notes were nearly ready for the press, I was, by the courtesy of the Cambridge University Librarian, enabled to consult Faber's notes on the *Timon*, and Hemsterhuis on both dialogues; and I can only express my regret that I had not the opportunity of seeing them before. Hemsterhuis is *facile princeps* among editors of Lucian. He was commissioned by the publisher Wetstein to edit the whole of Lucian; but after many years of laborious research he had only covered one-sixth of his ground,—believing in thoroughness rather than speed,— and Wetstein impatiently handed over the task to T. F. Reitz, a man of whom Dindorf says, "hominem si quem alium suscepto negotio imparem" (A.D. 1743). My thanks are also due to Mr G. M. Edwards, of Sidney Sussex College, Cambridge, for many kind suggestions, and to my brother the Head Master of Godolphin School, for corrections in the *Menippus*, and the Introduction.

All the quotations from Dante are from Cary's translation.

E. C. MACKIE.

BOLTON PERCY,
   Oct. 20, 1891.

PREFACE TO SECOND EDITION.

IN this edition, a few corrections and emendations have been made, suggested for the most part in reviews: by the Classical Review, the Educational Review, and the Athenæum.

E. C. M.

GLAISDALE VICARAGE.
   Feb. 3, 1900.

CONTENTS.

INTRODUCTION.

LIFE OF LUCIAN.

OUR chief source of knowledge with regard to the life and
work of Lucian (or Lycinus, as he often calls himself) is
found in the references which he makes to himself and his
family in his various works. The "inimitable Lucian," as
Gibbon calls him, was born at Samosata[1], the chief town of the
Syrian province of Commagene on the bank of the Euphrates[2].
The date of his birth is uncertain. Suidas says it was ἐπὶ τοῦ
Καίσαρος Τραϊανοῦ (A.D. 98—117); but by Lucian's own state-
ments this seems to be false, unless by Trajanus Suidas means
Trajan Hadrian. Probably A.D. 120 is about the time. His
parentage was humble, though his father's profession is not
known. His mother's family were chiefly sculptors, both his
uncles and his grandfather having followed that occupation[3].
After a family council, held to consider what was the best
thing to do with the lad, Lucian was, at the age of 15 or 16[4],
handed over to one of his uncles to follow the profession of a
statuary, it being settled that a liberal education was too ex-
pensive for the family resources. The plan seemed the more
likely to succeed, as this uncle was very celebrated in his art,

[1] *de hist. consc.* § 24, τὴν ἐμὴν πατρίδα τὰ Σαμόσατα.
[2] *Pisc.* § 19, πατρὶς δέ; Σύρος, τῶν Ἐπευφρατιδίων. Cf. *de Syr.
dea* § 1, γράφω δὲ Ἀσσύριος ἐών.
[3] *Somn.* § 7, ὅ τε γὰρ πάππος λιθοξόος ἦν, καὶ τὼ θείω ἀμφοτέρω.
[4] *Somn.* § 1, πρόσηβος ὤν, § 16, ἀντίπαις ἔτι ὤν, *bis acc.* § 27,
κομιδῇ μειράκιον.

ἄριστος ἑρμογλύφος καὶ λιθοξόος ἐν τοῖς μάλιστα εὐδόκιμος[1], and
Lucian himself had from earliest years shewn no little aptitude
for modelling in wax. However it was not to be: the very
first slab of marble entrusted to him he broke; and in a few
minutes he had fled from his irascible uncle, smarting under
the blows which he had got for his pains.

That very night he had a dream, wherein "Sculpture" and
"Education" appeared as two women, each using the most
persuasive words and demeanour to induce Lucian to follow her
lead. Needless to say, without hesitation he chose the latter[2],
and from that day devoted himself to literature. How he found
the means, he does not tell us[3]: but we find him trained as a
rhetorician, and before the age of 20, travelling into Ionia, and
from thence into Greece, practising first as an advocate at
Antioch, where he can hardly have failed to meet either in his
professional duties or in his private life with the Christians[4],
and then as an itinerant professor of rhetoric. In this way he
visited Syria, Phoenicia, Egypt, Greece, Italy and Gaul, picking
up much information on his way about the manners and customs,
the philosophy and geography, and the religious beliefs of the
different nations; and being, as Lucian undoubtedly was, a
man of shrewd observation, quick to recognize the salient
features of nature and men, he laid up no ordinary store of
knowledge in his retentive memory, ready to be reproduced as
occasion needed in his oral lectures or his written works.

At Rome he fell in with Nigrinus the philosopher, with
whom he had formed a friendship in Greece. Nigrinus tried to
persuade him to give up rhetoric and take to philosophy, but he
found the former too lucrative to be cast aside for the present. It

[1] *Somn.* § 2.
[2] *Somn.* § 14, τὴν ἄμορφον ἐκείνην καὶ ἐργατικὴν ἀπολιπὼν μετέβαινον
πρὸς τὴν Παιδείαν μάλα γεγηθώς.
[3] In *Somn.* § 18 he hopes the young men of his native town will
take heart of grace by reason of his example remembering, οἷος μὲν ὢν
πρὸς τὰ κάλλιστα ὥρμησα καὶ παιδείας ἐπεθύμησα μηδὲν ἀποδειλιάσας
πρὸς τὴν πενίαν τὴν τότε.
[4] Cf. Acts 11. 26, "The disciples were called Christians first in
Antioch."

was not till his 40th year that he gave his last rhetorical lecture
at Thessalonica[1], and returned to his native town. It would
seem that it was at this point of his life that he wrote the
Dream, intended probably to be an incentive to the youth of
his native town to follow his own example[2]. Finding his
father alive he first removed him and his family to Greece[3],
and a year after followed them himself, A.D. 165.

On this journey he very nearly lost his life through the evil
machinations of the impostor Alexander[4], and travelled on into
Greece with Peregrinus, who shortly after burned himself alive
at Olympia, Lucian being himself a spectator of this very extraordinary scene, as he tells us in his treatise on that pseudo-
Christian's death. From the year of his settlement at Athens,
he gave up all thoughts of rhetoric and devoted himself to
philosophy, not so much to one particular school of thought,
but rather employing all his energies in exposing the fallacies
of the different forms of philosophy so rampant at the time.
It was here that he wrote his chief satires, and in these
Lucian is to be seen at his best, for he is never so happy
as when following in the footsteps of his great master
Aristophanes. Probably no three dialogues can be found of
more striking humour and caustic wit, than the *Vitarum
Auctio*, or Sale of Philosophers' Lives, the *Piscator*, or " The
Philosophers come to life again," and *The Timon*. Nor did
Lucian forget to continue the careful study of the best masters
of Greek thought and style. Homer, Thucydides, Demosthenes,
Xenophon, Plato, Euripides, Aristophanes were his chief guides;
and the more one reads Lucian's writings the more one is
astonished at the high pitch of excellence to which he attained.

At the close of his life Lucian's means apparently became
much straitened once again, and he found himself compelled to
resort to the old profession of his youth for a livelihood. He

[1] *Bis accus.* § 32, καλῶς εἶχέ μοι ἀνδρὶ ἤδη τετταράκοντα ἔτη σχεδὸν
γεγονότι θορύβων μὲν ἐκείνων καὶ δικῶν ἀπηλλάχθαι.
[2] Heitl. Introd. § 8.
[3] *Alex.* § 56, τὸν πατέρα καὶ τοὺς ἐμοὺς εἰς Ἄμαστριν προὐκπεπομφώς.
[4] v. *Alex.* §§ 55, 56, 57.

was, however, saved from the misery of an impecunious old age through the offer of a lucrative appointment in the law-courts at Alexandria by the Roman Emperor[1]. His duties seem to have been those of clerk and registrar of the supreme court, president of the courts of justice and keeper of the records[2]. The acceptance of such a post placed him in a somewhat awkward dilemma, as he had only recently published a short treatise "on those who let themselves out for hire." However, as he says[3], future prospects seemed otherwise so black, and a man will do anything to run away from poverty; and he wisely quiets his conscience with the thought that there is a sufficiently wide difference between being the dependent of a private individual in a private house, "suffering all that I set forth in my pamphlet," and being the public servant of the Crown in a post of no mean distinction[4]. The post was of such emolument as to enable him to pass the close of his life in affluence[5]. But he was not left in undisturbed enjoyment of his good luck, as it is reasonable to infer from his many allusions to the gout, that he had much experience of this painful malady toward the close of his life[6].

Of the attitude of Lucian toward Christianity, a subject which has been the battlefield of much controversy, it does not seem needful to speak here, as there is nothing in either of these dialogues to raise the question. Suffice it to say that it seems most natural that Lucian should have looked upon

[1] Authorities are divided as to who the Emperor was: *Marcus Aurelius* (Collins, &c.), *Commodus* (Wieland), *Severus* (M. and D.).

[2] In L.'s own words, *Apol.* § 12, τὰς δίκας εἰσάγειν καὶ τάξιν αὐταῖς τὴν προσήκουσαν ἐπιτιθέναι καὶ τ. πραττομένων καὶ λεγομένων ἀπαξαπάντων (misprinted in M. and D.) ὑπομνήματα γράφεσθαι.

[3] *Apol.* § 10.

[4] *Apol.* § 11, ἐννόησον ὡς πάμπολυ διαφέρει εἰς οἰκίαν τινὸς πλουσίου ὑπόμισθον παρελθόντα δουλεύειν καὶ ἀνέχεσθαι ὅσα μοι φησι τὸ βιβλίον, ἢ δημοσίᾳ πράττοντά τι τῶν κοινῶν καὶ ἐς δύναμιν πολιτευόμενον ἐπὶ τούτῳ παρὰ βασιλέως μισθοφορεῖν.

[5] *Apol.* § 12, ὁ μισθὸς οὐ μικρὸς ἀλλὰ πολυτάλαντος.

[6] He describes this affliction as part of the punishment of the wicked : cf. *Men.* § 11, ὠχροὶ καὶ προγάστορες καὶ ποδαγροί. He wrote two short serio-comedies in which he makes Ποδάγρα the chief

Christianity as akin to the many forms of religious worship
that he had come across in his travels : and one sees no
reason to believe that he was more opposed to Christianity
than to the forms of Eastern superstition with which he had
been led to class the history of our Saviour. Assuredly, if
Lucian thought Peregrinus a fair specimen of a Christian, one
cannot wonder at his severity against the sect.

Lucian lived on into the 3rd century, some averring that
he was 100 years old at his death. Under any circumstances,
surely even 80 years (the minimum estimate), assisted by τὴν
ἀκίνητον δεσπότιν πόνων Ποδάγραν, would be quite enough to
account for his death by natural decay without the extraordinary assertion of Suidas, which deserves to be quoted *in
extenso*, as a notable specimen of Christian charity when a
man allows himself to be overmastered by his prejudices:

"Lucian of Samosata, nicknamed the Blasphemer or Slan-
derer, because in his dialogues he makes even what is told
about divine things a subject-matter for ridicule ...... is reported to have met his death at the hands of dogs for raving
against the truth; for in his *Life of Peregrinus* he carps at
Christianity, and blasphemes Christ Himself. Wherefore for
his madness he paid an ample penalty in this life, and in the
life to come he shall be an inheritor with Satan of everlasting
fire."

dramatis persona, and puts into the mouth of Ποδαγρὸς these strong
words as the opening lines of one of them :—

> ὦ στυγνὸν οὔνομ᾽, ὦ θεοῖς στυγούμενον,
> Ποδάγρα πολυστένακτε, Κωκυτοῦ τέκνον.

His epigram (*Anth. Pal.* 11, 403) "To Gout" seems also the pro-
duction of one who could write feelingly :—

> Μισόπτωχε θεά, μούνη πλούτου δαμάτειρα,
> ἡ τὸ καλῶς ζῆσαι πάντοτ᾽ ἐπισταμένη.
> εἰ δὲ καὶ ἀλλοτρίοις ἐπιζομένη ποσὶ χαίρεις,
> ὁπλοφορεῖν τ᾽ οἶδας, καὶ μύρα σοι μέλεται·
> τέρπει καὶ στέφανός σε καὶ Αὐσονίου πόμα Βάκχου.
> ταῦτα παρὰ πτωχοῖς γίγνεται οὐδέποτε.
> τοὔνεκά νυν φεύγεις πενίης τὸν χάλκεον οὐδόν,
> τέρπῃ δ᾽ ἐς πλούτου πρὸς πόδας ἐρχομένη.

LUCIAN'S STYLE.

There is nothing more worthy of admiration in Lucian than the astonishing ability he displays in his imitations of the great Greek masters, whose style he set before himself as an ideal. "He evinces a perfect mastery over a language as wonderful in its inflexion as in its immense and varied vocabulary; and it is a well merited praise of this author to say that to a good scholar the pages of Lucian are almost as easy and entertaining as an English or French novel[1]." To the tyro equally with the "good scholar," Lucian is "easy and entertaining." One forgets that he is an Asiatic, living in the age of the Antonines. His Attic dialect is so pure, its blemishes so few, that one could almost fancy him a contemporary of the great writers, whom he knows so thoroughly and quotes so frequently, instead of living in a century whose greatest writers after himself were Marcus Aurelius, Herodian, Hermogenes, Celsus, Galen, Pausanias, Appian, Aelian. It was only close study and much determination that could bring him to such a pitch of excellence. His works, like every good writer's, are stamped with his own individuality. There are but few traces of mannerism, and no remnant of the vernacular, which he confesses clung to him for many years: and what failings he had may be put down very largely to the carrying out of his own rule, "Sacrifice most of all to grace and clearness[2]."

Lucian is elegant, witty and sarcastic; of abundant resource, and fertile in imagination. As one of his earliest editors says, he is grammarian, rhetorician, physician, advocate, historian, poet, philosopher and politician rolled into one, and there is no author who can with greater advantage be placed in the hands of one fresh to the Greek language. Simple and straightforward as his construction is, he is yet full of interest. Here he is wise, there witty, here grave and there gay, here gentle,

---

[1] Prof. Paley. Art. sub v. in *Encyc. Brit.*
[2] *Lexiph.* § 23, μάλιστα δὲ χάρισι καὶ σαφηνείᾳ θῦε (cf. M. and D. 229).

there severe; Protean in his many changes, and like a chameleon in the variety of his colouring.

MENIPPUS, THE DIALOGUE.

Editors **are** divided as to the genuineness **of** this little brochure. Hemsterhuis and Dindorf accept it; Solanus rejects it; Müller and Donaldson dismiss it summarily with the remark:—"Menippus, or the oracle of the dead, seems to be the work of some imitator of Lucian, and is full of passages taken *verbatim* from his genuine works (adding in a footnote): According to Diogenes of Laërte (162 D), Menippus wrote a Νέκυια, and Solanus has accordingly supposed that he is the author of the 'Menippus' of Lucian." I will take each of these objections separately.

A. *Solanus* is clearly not very decided in his opinion. At one place he writes "*if Lucian wrote* this dialogue, it must have been in A.D. 163." At another, "*if it is genuine*, it is clear that it must have been written when Lucian was still quite young." How Solanus professes to make these remarks tally I cannot say", unless he considers 38 to 43 years of age as "quite young"! Solanus also takes exception to certain phrases occurring in the book:—

a. τελῶναι, § 11, placed between μοιχοὶ and κόλακες, and says " Lucian is not wont to inveigh against such." And yet, though I cannot find that he uses the noun elsewhere, in *Pseudol.* § 30 Lucian places the *verb* in almost as bad company, viz. among beggars and clothes-stealers! εἴ τις ἀναισχύντως αἰτεῖ, μᾶλλον δὲ προσαιτεῖ καὶ λωποδυτεῖ καὶ τελωνεῖ.

b. He complains in this work *quosdam igne torreri,* "which is stooping too low for Lucian." It is not quite clear what argument against its genuineness Solanus means to base on this. He is evidently referring to § 14, οἰμωγὴ τῶν ἐπὶ τοῦ πυρὸς ὀπτωμένων, but this very phrase occurs also in the *Vera Hist.* II. § 29, κνῖσα δὲ πονηρὰ καὶ ἀφόρητος ὥσπερ ἀπ᾽ ἀνθρώπων ὀπτωμένων

...ἠκούομεν δὲ καὶ μαστίγων ψόφον καὶ οἰμωγὴν ἀνθρώπων πολλῶν[1].
Would Solanus think this spurious?

c. "*reges stipem colligentes*," § 17, he thinks is "omnino
puerilia et Luciano indigna." This is a matter of opinion:
the λέγω of Ξέρξας λέγω, and the phrase κατὰ κορρῆς παιόμενος
are quite Lucianic (cf. *Inf. Dial.* 20. 2, *Tyr.* § 11, *Gall.* 29).
Does it seem too mean an office for Philip of Macedon to be
mending shoes? And yet it is well to remember that Lucian
had no very high opinion of this king. In *Inf. Dial.* 14. 3 he
makes Philip's own son, Alexander the Great, charge him with
vices of no very light hue; and the attack though not direct is
manifestly implied. Alexander says: οὐδὲ προδοσίαις ὠνούμενος
τὰς νίκας ἐκράτουν αὐτῶν· οὐδ' ἐπιώρκησα πώποτε ἢ ὑποσχόμενος
ἐψευσάμην ἢ ἄπιστον ἔπραξά τι τοῦ νικᾶν ἕνεκα. I cannot think
that this third objection is any strong argument against the
whole piece.

d. The fact that Menippus had written a Νέκυια is surely a
very lame reason for ascribing this work to him. Can anyone
carefully read it through from beginning to end, full as it is of
Lucian's phraseology and favourite words and idioms, and then
ascribe it to a man who died two or three centuries before
Lucian was born?

B. The assumption that it is by some imitator of Lucian,
as Müller and Donaldson say, is at least more worthy of consideration than the theory of Solanus. And yet after carefully
reading and studying the piece as a whole, I cannot help feeling
that its author was no other than Lucian. A few excrescences
may have grown on to it, but even that is doubtful. I believe
no one could copy so minutely and exactly as this. It is above
all most unsafe to reject anything ascribed to Lucian, because it
appears to be taken in great part from some work that no one
doubts to be his. Lucian is continually repeating himself. It
is this which forms the chief drawback to his literary style. He
palls on one at last. As Heitland says (Introd. A. 7), "In his
matter and style alike there is a sort of sameness which is

[1] Cf. too *Phal.* 8 and *Fug.* 1.

rather wearisome to the reader. The same old simile, quotation
and even turn of phrase reappears more often than is palatable."
It is true that large pieces of chap. 15 are from the *Inf. Dial.*,
and § 16 is just like *Nigrinus* § 20, and § 4 is like *Pisc.* § 11
and so on. But this is Lucian's usual plan[1]. It would require
no great labour to prove the *Timon* spurious too for similar
reasons. To the student of Lucian his continual readjustment
of the same old thoughts is so well known that there is no
need to dwell on the point. I append one specimen from the
Timon, and for others refer the student to the notes.

Tim. §§ 54, 55, 56.	*Pisc.* §§ 34, 35.
τὸν πλησίον παραγκωνιζόμενος ...κυνηδὸν ἐμφορούμενος...μεμψί-μοιρος ἀεί...λόγοι πολλοὶ ἐπὶ τῇ κύλικι...ὑπὸ τοῦ ἀκράτου πονηρῶς ἔχων...Τὸ χρυσίον μὲν γὰρ οὐδὲν τιμιώτερον τῶν ἐν τοῖς αἰγιαλοῖς ψηφίδων μοι δοκεῖ.	ἀλλήλους παραγκωνιζόμενοι... φορτικῶς ἐμφορούμενοι...μεμψί-μοιροι φαινόμενοι καὶ ἐπὶ τῆς κύλικος...φιλοσοφοῦντες καὶ τὸν ἄκρατον οὐ φέροντες...τί γὰρ τὸ χρυσίον ἢ ἀργύριον οὐδὲν τῶν ἐν τοῖς αἰγιαλοῖς ψηφίδων διαφέρον;

I am confirmed in my opinion by the appearance throughout the whole dialogue of Lucian's own peculiar idiosyncrasies.

a. We have his own favourite phrases running through it.
οὐκ οἶδ᾽ ὅπως—ἅτε—ἀγαθῇ τύχῃ—καὶ δὴ—μονονουχὶ—οὐμενοῦν—
καὶ ταῦτα—μικροῦ δεῖν, and the epithet in predicate.

b. Lucian's "slips" and non-atticisms abound: the misplaced ἄν, the heavy use of καί, e.g. (taken at random) § 4,
22 times in 31 lines; § 12, 12 in 23; § 11, 15 in 20; § 14, 20 in
17; § 18, 14 in 15 lines; μή for οὐ; the heavy perfect and plu-
perfect forms.

c. The following too bespeak the pen of Lucian, I think.
The introduction of eastern soothsayers, Zoroaster &c.; the
πῶς οἴει inserted § 14 (v. note); the τί γὰρ ἂν πάθοι τις § 3,
as in *Tim.* § 39 and *Char.* § 2; the introduction of his old
enemy the gout, § 11, ποδαγροί: the ever-recurring Tantalus,
Sisyphus and Ixion, Pyriphlegethon, Minos, Nireus, Thersites,

---

[1] One might as well say that S. Paul's Epistle to the Colossians
is spurious, because it is in places worded verse for verse like the
Ephesians.

&c. and other minor points too numerous to mention. Hemsterhuis also at § 18, where Nestor and Palamedes are represented as being companions of Socrates, reminds us that the same three are "congerrones" in *V. H.* II. 17; which is also a small undesigned coincidence.

This internal evidence of minute correspondence in detail is a safer argument for its genuineness, than is the repetition of lines and ideas from other works for its spuriousness.

It needs not many words to explain the object of the *Menippus.* It was doubtless written partly as a satire on the vast influx of Eastern peoples and customs, their religious, social and moral influence, but more especially, as in the case of the *Dialogues of the Dead,* to show the uncertainty of human life, the follies of many of the old tales still credited, and the ridiculous superstitions of the age. On this subject Bacon writes, "It was no mean apprehension of Lucian, who says of Menippus, that in his travels through hell he knew not the kings of the earth from other men, but only by their louder cryings and tears; which was fostered in them through the remorseful memory of the good days they had seen, and the fruitful havings which they so unwillingly left behind them. He that was well seated looked back at his portion and was loth to leave his farm; and others minding marriages, pleasures, profit or preferment, desired to be excused from death's banquet; they had made an appointment with earth, looking at the blessings, not the hand that enlarged them, forgetting how unclothedly they came hither, or with what naked ornaments they were arrayed[1]."

MENIPPUS THE PHILOSOPHER.

Modern editors are of one mind in acknowledging this famous mouthpiece of Lucian to be the well-known philosopher, the pupil of Diogenes. Philostratus, a noted sophist, of the 2nd and 3rd centuries A.D., says that Lucian throughout his works

---

[1] *Essay on Death,* Vol. II. pp. 474, 5.

means another Cynic philosopher, named Menippus, who lived
near to his own time; and Olearius, the chief editor of Philostratus' works, upholds the same theory, bringing to bear on the
question the words placed by Lucian in the mouth of Diogenes
at the end of the 1st Dialogue of the Dead where he asks Polydeuces to rebuke the Lacedaemonians for falling away from their
former simplicity and discipline, and Olearius thinks this fits in
with the times of the later rather than the earlier Menippus.
Few scholars will assent to this argument, for surely no period
in the history of Sparta more marks the decadence of that
famous city than the time of Diogenes the Cynic and his successors, the fourth and beginning of the third centuries B.C.,
when Athens was captured at the close of the Peloponnesian
War, and Lysander first introduced vast sums of gold and silver
into the treasury, when effeminacy and luxury took the place of
that hardihood, endurance and rigorous simplicity of living,
which had always been associated with the Spartan race.

Menippus was a native of Gadara in Palestine; a pupil, as
has been said, of Diogenes the celebrated Cynic of the time of
Alexander the Great, and so we are continually finding them
coupled together by Lucian[1]; and Lucian is never tired of employing the nickname κύων, in allusion to the snarling nature of
the Cynic school in general, and Menippus in particular[2]. He
seems to have been born a Phoenician slave, but in some way

[1] The Dialogues of the Dead open with a request by Diogenes to
Polydeuces (Castor's twin-brother) that, if he happens to see Menippus,
"the dog," he will let him know that absurd and ridiculous as things
are on earth, they are nothing by the side of what he will find to be the
case in the lower world. In the 21st Dialogue Cerberus says that
Menippus and Diogenes alone of all men had met death in a manner
creditable to the canine race. In *Fugit.* § 11 Antisthenes, Diogenes,
Crates and Menippus are found together.
[2] Cf. note *Men.* § 1, the opening lines. In *Bis acc.* § 33 "Dialogue"
complains of the way in which Lucian is always bringing in Menippus:
τελευταῖον δὲ καὶ Μένιππόν τινα τῶν παλαιῶν κυνῶν μάλα ὑλακτικόν, ὡς
δοκεῖ, καὶ κάρχαρον ἀνορύξας καὶ τοῦτον ἐπεισήγαγέ μοι φοβερόν τινα ὡς
ἀληθῶς κύνα καὶ τὸ δῆγμα λαθραῖον, ὅσῳ καὶ γελῶν ἅμα ἔδακνε. So
in *Vit. Auc.* § 7 his master Diogenes is spoken of as a good "watch-dog,"
cf. *Pisc.* § 26; Varro speaks of M. as "nobilem canem."

or other to have obtained his freedom, and found his way to Greece, where he gained a living as a money-lender. In the first Dialogue of the Dead Diogenes tells Polydeuces he is most likely to find Menippus at the Craneum at Corinth or in the Lyceum (at Athens?)[1]; in the same place Lucian describes him as "aged and bald, with an old cloak full of holes[2]." To his profession as usurer he added that of Cynic philosopher, flouting every school of thought but his own in both prose and verse. Of these writings nothing remains, but they were celebrated for their biting satire, containing indeed more of spite and malice than of wit and amusement, and herein differing widely from the compositions of Lucian[3]. There is no character Lucian is so fond of introducing as Menippus, probably for a double reason, first because he came from the East like Lucian himself, but chiefly because none treated the philosophers of every rank and thought with such caustic savagery. Thus it has come about, as Solanus puts it, that just as Socrates, while writing nothing, has become immortalized for wisdom and rectitude through the writings of Plato and Xenophon, so Menippus is far more widely known for his cynicism through Lucian than through any of his own writings. He is arbiter

---

[1] εὕροις δ' ἂν αὐτὸν ἐν Κορίνθῳ κατὰ τὸ Κράνειον ἢ ἐν Λυκείῳ. In these two places, philosophers of all schools were wont to meet for instruction and disputation; cf. (of Diogenes) *on history* § 3, ἐν ᾧ ἐτύγχανεν οἰκῶν, ἄνω καὶ κάτω τοῦ Κρανείου, and Diog. Laert. p. 158 says Διογένης ἐτύγχανε διάγων ἐν Κρανείῳ τῷ πρὸ τοῦ Κορίνθου γυμνασίῳ and the same author says of Chrysippus (VIII. p. 185), πρῶτος ἐθάρρησε σχολὴν ἔχειν ὕπαιθρον ἐν Λυκείῳ. Solanus thinks that Menippus was not born a slave, but that he lived at Athens and frequented the Lyceum there before his time of slavery.

[2] γέρων, φαλακρός, τριβώνιον ἔχων πολύθυρον, ἅπαντι ἀνέμῳ ἀναπεπταμένον καὶ ταῖς ἐπιπτυχαῖς τῶν ῥακίων ποικίλον. We must not take L. too seriously. The generality of his philosophers are old and bald, and seedy looking, v. the section on Lucian's attitude toward philosophy, and v. Index sub v. ἀναφαλαντίας.

[3] Hence Varro called his collection *Menippean Satires.* In France in 1593 A.D. there appeared a work by five authors, named Satire Menippée, a burlesque report of the meeting of the States-General, in the time of Henri Quatre, called for the purpose of supporting the League.

between Thersites and Nereus (*Inf. Dial.* 25). He is the subject of a round-robin sent to Pluto by the millionaires, for they cannot longer endure his ridicule (*Dial.* 2). He debates with Teiresias on vaticination (*D.* 28), with Trophonius and Amphilochus on oracles (*D.* 3), and in *D.* 17 he begs Tantalus to cheer up, as he is in no way worse off than others, since the dead cannot eat and drink. Besides this there are dialogues with Cheiron, Aeacus, Charon, Hermes, Cerberus, &c., while in the *Icaromenippus* he takes a voyage by way of the Moon up to Jupiter, and there discusses with his Olympian Majesty the state of philosophy and religion upon earth.

Probably, like other exorbitant money-lenders, he was not too scrupulous in his transactions, and the biter at last found himself bitten. He lost his wealth by the roguery of others, and is then said to have committed suicide[1].

TIMON THE MISANTHROPE.

Timon, the celebrated misanthrope, the son of Echecratides, remarkable, as Tanaquil Faber says, only for being the father of Timon, flourished about the time of the Peloponnesian war. He was of the deme of Colyttus (v. note, §§ 7, 44). The town Colyttus lay at the foot of Mt Hymettus; hence the appropriateness of Zeus' question (§ 7) τίς οὗτός ἐστιν, ὦ Ἑρμῆ, ὁ κεκραγὼς ἐκ τῆς Ἀττικῆς παρὰ τὸν Ὑμηττόν; Faber does his best to whitewash the character of Timon. He says: "There is no need to say aught about this man's dis-

---

[1] Lucian alludes to this in *Inf. Dial.* 10, 11, where the philosopher asks: σὺ γάρ, ὦ Μένιππε, οὐκ ἄχθη ἀποθανών; to which M. replies πῶς, ὃς ἔσπευσα ἐπὶ τὸν θάνατον, καλέσαντος μηδενός; So in *Inf. Dial.* 21, 2 Cerberus, in answer to this question ἐγὼ δὲ πῶς σοι κατελήλυθέναι ἔδοξα; says μόνος, ὦ Μένιππε, ἀξίως τοῦ γένους, καὶ Διογένης πρὸ σοῦ, ὅτι μὴ ἀναγκαζόμενοι εἰσήειτε μηδ' ὠθούμενοι, ἀλλ' ἐθελούσιοι...Diogenes' death was caused by swallowing a raw polypus (*Vit. Auc.* 10) but M.'s is uncertain. Diog. Laert. 162 B says it was by hanging himself: ὑπ' ἀθυμίας βρόχῳ τὸν βίον μεταλλάξαι, but the scholiast in a note on *Inf. D.* 1, 1 says, ὠμὰ φαγὼν ᾠὰ τέθνηκεν.

position, for Plutarch has done this in his life of Antony. I will merely add that Timon had been a good man, of such known excellence toward mankind, that no creature of a more kindly disposition (χρηστότερον) ever existed. For men to nick-name him 'misanthrope' is most emphatically wrong. One may just as well apply the epithet ἄθεος to a man who refuses to believe in the existence of Mercury, Venus, Sylvanus and other follies of that stamp, as call Timon μισάνθρωπος. You will ask 'how so?' Because it was not men but wild beasts that he hated, with which that age abounded." And he brings forward pseudo-Plato to bear him out[1].

Hemsterhuis disagrees with this, and modern readers will probably see little to excuse, and very little to admire, in the sour and resentful spirit of the misanthrope. Hemsterhuis says the epistles of Plato are not to be taken too seriously; and against this testimony we have the whole weight of antiquity. In Aristophanes[2] we have in more than one place a strong allusion to the unnatural disposition of Timon, and two passages from Cicero[3] bear equal testimony.

Pliny (*N. H.* VII. 19) also, in referring to Timon, says: "hunc quidem etiam in totius odium generis humani evectum." Diogenes Laertius, in writing of the life of Timon of Phlius, the well-known philosopher, speaks disparagingly of

---

[1] συνέγνων ὅτι Τίμων οὐκ ἦν ἄρα μισάνθρωπος, μὴ εὑρίσκων μέντοι ἀνθρώπους, οὐκ ἠδύνατο θηρία φιλεῖν (Epis. 24 as collated by Leo Allatius).

[2] Τίμων ἦν τις ἀΐδρυτος ἀβάτοισιν ἐν | σκώλοισι τὰ πρόσωπα περιειργμένος | Ἐρινύος ἀπορρὼξ | οὗτος ἄρ' ὁ Τίμων ᾤχεθ' ὑπὸ μίσους [εἰς ἀγρὸν ἔρημον] | πολλὰ καταρασάμενος ἀνδράσι πονηροῖς (*Lysist.* 808—815). So in *Aves* 1549, Peithetaerus says to Prometheus: νὴ τὸν Δί' ἀεὶ δῆτα θεομισὴς ἔφυς, to which Prom. replies Τίμων καθαρός, "Yes, a Timon to the back-bone."

[3] Cf. *de Amic.* 23, 87, "si quis ea asperitate est et immanitate naturae, congressus ut hominum fugiat atque oderit, qualem fuisse Athenis Timonem nescio quem accepimus." So in *Tusc. Disp.* IV. 11, 25, "But those feelings, which are the contrary of these, are supposed to have fear for their foundation...or the hatred of the whole human species, as Timon is reported to have had, whom they called the Misanthrope"; and a little lower down § 27, "the hatred of the human species like that displayed by Timon."

our Timon in a passage the more interesting as informing us that Timon was "fond of gardening" (φιλόκηπος), which adds a piquancy to Lucian's representation of him digging with smock-frock and spade.

Even more important than these is the well-known passage from Plutarch, alluded to above. "Antony in the meantime forsook the city and the society of his friends, and retired to a small house which he had built himself near Pharos, on a mound he had cast up in the sea. In this place, sequestered from all commerce with mankind, he affected to live like Timon, because there was a resemblance in their fortunes. He had been deserted by his friends, and their ingratitude had put him out of humour with his own species.

"This Timon was a citizen of Athens, and lived about the time of the Peloponnesian War, as appears from the comedies of Aristophanes and Plato, in which he is exposed as the hater of mankind. Yet, though he hated mankind in general, he caressed the bold and impudent boy Alcibiades, and being asked the reason of this by Apemantus, who expressed some surprise at it, he answered that it was because he foresaw that he would plague the people of Athens. Apemantus was the only one he admitted to his society, and he was his friend in point of principle. At the feast of sacrifices for the dead, these two dined by themselves, and when Apemantus observed that the feast was excellent, Timon answered, 'It would be so if you were not here.' Once in an assembly of the people, he mounted the rostrum, and the novelty of the thing occasioned a universal silence and expectation; at length he said, 'People of Athens, there is a fig tree in my yard, on which many worthy citizens have hanged themselves; and, as I have determined to build upon the spot, I thought it necessary to give this public notice, that such as choose to have recourse to this tree for the aforesaid purpose may repair to it before it is cut down'[1]."

[1] Plutarch in *Alcib.* p. 948, Langhorne's translation. So Strabo (17, 745) says Antony, when conquered by Augustus, called his palace

Hemsterhuis, after alluding to this story, adds "what greater proof could one wish for to show the man's harshness of manner? Howbeit, this temper seems to have been brought about by the behaviour of his friends, whose ingratitude after so many kindnesses received drove Timon into such an estimate of the world at large, that he defined the highest happiness of life to consist in the universal hatred of mankind."

Something more on this point may be found under the section on "Timon, the Dialogue." Few will deny that the brooding spirit of malice is one of the worst of bad characters; it ever finds itself out of joint with all the world, and sees nothing but its "seamy side"; and we can feel more sympathy with the "dog" Menippus, who snarls and bites, and in the nether world "lies on his back and laughs" at the follies of men than with the narrow-minded pessimist, who bides his time, and nurses the smouldering embers of bitter hatred in his heart against the possible day of retribution. Callimachus has an epigram on Timon:

Τίμων (οὐ γὰρ ἔτ' ἐσσὶ) τί τοι, φάος ἢ σκότος ἐχθρόν;
Τὸ σκότος, ὑμέων γὰρ πλείονες ἐν Ἀΐδῃ.

Plutarch says that "he was buried at Halae near the sea, and the water surrounded his tomb in such a manner that he was even then inaccessible to mankind." Plutarch also adds two epitaphs[1], the former by Callimachus:

Τίμων μισάνθρωπος ἐσοικέω· ἀλλὰ πάρελθε·
Οἰμώζειν εἴπας πολλά, πάρελθε μόνον·

the latter said to be Timon's own:

Ἐνθάδ' ἀπορρίψας ψυχὴν βαρυδαίμονα κεῖμαι·
Τοὔνομα δ' οὐ πεύσεσθε, κακοὶ δὲ κακῶς ἀπόλοισθε.

Timonium, hereafter in this intending to follow his example, viz., to have no more intercourse with mankind but to live in seclusion.

[1] Shakspere seems to have joined these two in his paraphrase of the epitaph. Alcibiades [reads]:

Here lies a wretched corse, of wretched soul bereft:
Seek not my name. A plague consume you wicked caitiffs left!
Here lie I, Timon; who, alive, all living men did hate:
Pass by and curse thy fill; but pass and stay not here thy gait.

TIMON, THE DIALOGUE.

The *Timon*, on whose genuineness no one casts the slightest doubt, is almost universally acknowledged to be Lucian's master-piece. Tanaquil Faber, who has devoted his talents and critical acumen to the elucidation of this dialogue in particular, speaks of it in the highest terms:

"However, I deem this dialogue to be so elegant and chaste, that I have no hesitation in placing it among the most finished of Lucian. It is written in so clever and easy a style, that no comedy can be compared with it. Here, if anywhere, you will find speech of such purity, that nothing can surpass it. Its beginning is, it is true, somewhat vehement and bordering on the tragic; but so exactly adapted to the circumstances and character of the man, that nothing more befitting can possibly be conceived."

Solanus also says:—"This is deservedly placed among the best efforts of Lucian. You have here a comedy of high ex-cellence, in which the conduct and intrigues of more than one kind of flatterer are presented in an extremely picturesque form, and (with many other points bearing on wealth) are handled with consummate skill. If you compare this little work with the *Plutus* of Aristophanes, you will, if you are of my opinion, feel bound to give the palm to our author, for many reasons too numerous to specify."

Aristophanes wrote much that was better than his *Plutus;* but still this is high praise, and few will be found to dispute its justice. In the *Plutus* we have clear signs of the decadence of ancient comedy ; there is no longer that keenness of wit and abundance of personal · satire which mark the best works of Aristophanes; but the *Timon* abounds in satirical humour and in many an elegant turn of phrase and original situation—in a word, in all those chief characteristics which have given Lucian such a high position in the favour of critics. There is indeed a dramatic fitness about the whole piece with its five Acts.

I. Timon leaning solitarily with one hand on his spade, and the other stretched toward heaven, half cursing Zeus for his indifference, and half imploring him to come and help him.

II. Zeus, Hermes and Plutus in deep consultation, and the well-told hesitation of the last-named to go to a man who will turn him out as soon as he arrives.

III. Timon discovered, surrounded by Poverty, Want, Toil, Wisdom, &c. as his body-guard; the disgust of Poverty, and the unwillingness of Timon to have any more to do with such a fellow as Plutus.

IV. Timon once more alone; discovers Gold. "Now will I pay them back in their own coin—henceforth I am Misanthrope."

V. The news spreads. The toadies hasten to the gold, as moths to the light, and one seems to see the surly misanthrope wielding his spade, and laughing in his sleeve as each goes off with a broken head. The curtain falls upon him as he stands with stones all round, and his hands full, ready to give a warm reception to the next applicant.

After the *Plutus* of Aristophanes, which Lucian no doubt had in his thoughts when he wrote this dialogue, as the number of references to that play of his favourite master abundantly proves, one naturally seeks to compare the *Timon* with Shakspere's play. It looks at times as if Shakspere knew of Lucian's piece, though the *Timon of Athens* is acknowledged to be founded chiefly on the twenty-eighth novel in Painter's *Palace of Pleasure*. Shakspere's aim is not the same as Lucian's. He introduces us to Timon in the opening scenes as still in the height of his popularity and luxuriousness; we see men flocking to his riches, and surrounding him with all the flattery and toadyism which time out of mind have attended on wealth. We see the first advent of his poverty, the miserable way in which each so-called friend finds excuse for not holding out a helping hand; and there is a feeling of no slight pity in one's heart for the philanthropic Timon, as the fourth Act opens and shows him outside the walls of Athens, soliloquizing, and ending his stinging satire with the lines:

"Timon will to the woods; where he will find
The unkindest beast more kinder than mankind.
The gods confound (hear me, ye good gods all!)
The Athenians both within and out that wall!
And grant, as Timon grows, his hate may grow
To the whole race of mankind, high and low.
Amen."

The faithfulness of Flavius to his old master, the arrival of
Senators (in the fifth Act) from Athens, begging the Misanthrope
to come back to the city, the suicide of Timon, and the con-
cluding words of the play spoken by Alcibiades:

> "Dead
> Is noble Timon; of whose memory
> Hereafter more"—

all help to increase the feeling of compassion for Timon; and
this was clearly Shakspere's aim, his satire in the main being
directed at the "trencher-friends," and the hollowness of human
friendship.

But Lucian's design was much wider :

(1) To cast ridicule upon the foolish teaching of ancient
Greece about religion.

(2) To show up several sorts of parasites and sycophants.

(3) To rouse disgust against men, like Timon, who were so
utterly incapable of choosing fitting friends; against those who
spent all their substance upon these unworthy creatures. As
Dr Abbott says (p. 151), "It is not till we bring Timon, no less
than his flatterers, into the sphere of satire, that the full signifi-
cance of such a story is reached. That one of the noblest of
Athenians in Athens' noblest time should spend his substance
in giving banquets to parasites and sycophants, and seek to
obtain by such means the friendship of such men, is a fitter
subject for ridicule than the fickleness of wretches, who know not
where to look for a meal."

That Lucian did not really think much of the character of
Timon seems fairly clear from the only other passage in which
he mentions him. In the *Vera Historia* he is represented as
being the guardian of the narrow pass which runs between
the various rivers of Acheron, surrounding the abode of the

damned[1]. It is no doubt a sort of "half-way house"; but Lucian evidently could not find it in his heart to allow the surly cross-grained pessimist a home in any higher settlement.

PARASITISM.

The flattery and toadyism of the parasite or hanger on, the boorishness of the wealthy snob toward his humbler brethren, the extraordinary fascination to the neglected and over-worked plebeian of an annual dinner "under his patron's mahogany," have been such obvious subjects of satire from days long before Lucian that it scarcely seems necessary to allude to them. All satirists from Lucilius, Juvenal and Horace, down to Dryden, Swift and Dr Johnson, have loved to dwell upon the humiliating snubs doled out by the rich patrician to the poor dependent. How often the latter has to be contented with

> "Black mouldy fragments which defy the saw,
> The mere despair of every aching jaw,
> While manchets of the finest flour are set
> Before your lord."
>
> GIFFORD, *Juv.* v. 68.

It seems necessary, therefore, only to add a few remarks on the other two main subjects of satire in these two dialogues— the existing philosophy and the decaying theology; the former so humorously pourtrayed in the *Menippus*, and the latter in the *Timon*.

LUCIAN'S ATTITUDE TOWARDS GREEK RELIGION.

It is impossible within the narrow limits of an Introduction like this to discuss at all fully the position which Lucian assumed towards social and religious institutions, but a few thoughts are put together as more or less essential to the understanding of the spirit and object of these two dialogues.

---

[1] *V. H.* 2. 31, εἴσοδος δὲ μία στενὴ διὰ πάντων ἦν, καὶ πυλωρὸς ἐφειστήκει Τίμων ὁ Ἀθηναῖος.

The ridiculous absurdity of much of the heathen mythology
was too obvious to be allowed by Lucian to pass unnoticed. It
had been the butt of its own adherents. A religion which
could incorporate into its own original body the multifarious
creeds of the many nations which fell under its political sway
was clearly one which laid itself open to criticism. The
Christian apologists of Lucian's time, when they came to attack it, found their task easy because the philosophers had exposed its falseness long before. The poets had only to put in
an attractive form the disgraceful legends handed down from
antiquity; the actors in their plays exposed the gods to popular
ridicule; at the public games, the gods, in whose honour all
were assembled, were so depicted as to expose them to the
contempt and abhorrence of all. They furnished a mark for
the low wit and scurrilous jests of the comedians. When a
good hit was made, the spectators, we are told, shouted and
rose up, and the whole pit resounded with the clapping of
hands and applause. While a whisper against the king was
deemed treason, and to insult a senator a crime, the gods were
in no way guarded; about them, and them alone, anyone was
at liberty to say what he would[1].

The fact that Lucian in early life had himself been a
moulder of busts of Hermes, and had been surrounded by those
who made their living by carving gods, was not likely to increase his respect for the heathen deities. A man who has
hammered, or cast, or carved, or graven a god of marble,
wood, stone or brass is not likely to have any deep feeling
either of love or fear for that which could never have had an
existence but for himself. And Lucian felt and thought about
these things more than most men. The gods of the Greek
world, Olympian and Infernal alike, were so very material:
their birth, habits, surroundings, virtues and vices so tangible,
that the faith which men had placed, or had professed to place,
in them of old, had ceased. As Timon laments in the opening
scene, the old Zeus is gone. Once he could instil terror into

[1] Cf. Lecky's *Europ. Morals*, 177—179.

the wicked, now the scoffers and cheats get off scot free, and "the smell of the sulphur" is the most disagreeable part of the once terrible bolt of Jove. Men of thought argued that many gods destroy the perfection of deity, that while each possessed in full some art or quality, yet each was lacking entirely in something else equally or more essential. History showed too that the world existed before the Greek gods. Men gave the gods their origin, not the gods men. Lucian, in his usual sarcastic and humorous way, makes a broad caricature of all this. The absurdity of so many gods he points out in the *Concilium Deorum.* There had been such an influx of deities into Olympus that the originals were in fear of being crowded out; there were Pan, Silenus, Heracles, Asclepius and all the host of new-fangled deities from Africa and Asia, Attis, Mithras, Mên, Anubis, the bull from Memphis, and the rest, and so a decree is proposed by Momus the jester, that "when Hermes shall call you, you are all to come, each bringing clear proof and undoubted testimony to your father's and mother's names; and why you were made a god, and how; your tribe and brotherhood; and whoever does not bring sufficient proof will no longer be deemed eligible to a seat in the House, no matter how huge his temple on earth, or how high he may be held in the esteem of mortals."

In the *Dialogues of the Gods, Prometheus* and *Zeus Tragoedus*, we have a further development of the same amusing satire. Zeus is buried in Crete; how can he be immortal? He deals greatly in quotations from Homer and Euripides, and strives to copy the good Attic style of Demosthenes. Eros is a child, yet older than Zeus' grandfather. Hermes, while still a helpless babe, steals Zeus' sceptre, invents the lyre, and runs away with Hephaestus' anvil, which he hides in his cradle. The gods all leave Olympus to go down and witness an argument between two philosophers as to their own existence. There is no more telling way of ridiculing any religion than by materialistic representations of this kind; and it was quite the fault of the Greek and Roman

people that their religion was especially open to such caricaturing. And because Lucian could see nothing to attract in
this sort of religion, nor in what he personally experienced
of our own Christian faith, he has been denounced in the
bitterest terms[1]. As has been remarked elsewhere, these two
dialogues do not raise the question of Lucian's position as
regards Christianity; so into that vexed question we need not
enter. It is very true that Lucian was a puller down of
existing institutions, rather than a builder up of a new one,
but it was only because the truth was not clear to him.
The only thing manifest was that the old religion was absurd
and antiquated. But whether intentionally or not, at least "he
did the same service to the advancing forces of Christianity as
the explosion of a mine does to the storming party who are
watching in the trenches; he blew into ruins the fortifications
of pagan superstition already grievously shaken. He did not
know who was to enter in at the breach, but he had a strong
conviction that the old stronghold of falsehood ought at any
cost not to stand[2]."

LUCIAN'S ATTITUDE TOWARD PHILOSOPHY.

It has been urged that next to the absurdities of the
popular religion, the pretenders to philosophy lay most open
to the attack of the satirist; and that in holding up to
derision the charlatans and impostors who sheltered themselves under the names of the great masters of old times, who
pushed their tenets to absurdity, Lucian lays himself open to
the charge of caricaturing those venerable sages themselves[3].
This charge seems to be substantiated by his dialogue "Sale
of Philosophers' Lives" (*Vitarum Auctio*), in which several
philosophers representing the greatest schools are sold off at
prices varying from about £500 for Socrates to 3½d. for

[1] Watson calls him "a scoffer at all religions and a licentious wit."
[2] Collins, *Anc. Class. for Eng. Readers*, p. 180.
[3] *Ibid.*, pp. 90, 91.

Diogenes the Cynic; that some critics put this construction on this work seems clear from the fact that Lucian found it necessary to write an apologetic pamphlet known as "The Fisher" (*Piscator*), or "The Philosophers come to life again," which opens with a scene representing the greatest philosophers of the greatest schools chasing Lucian and pelting him, and threatening him with summary chastisement. Lucian takes this opportunity of freeing himself from any such unjust suspicions; he would like to ask Philosophy herself as to his real treatment of her, but it is hard to say where she lives just now[1]. They find her, however, most opportunely walking in the porch of the Stoics, and immediately she consents to be arbitress in the case. After much discussion, Diogenes being chief accuser, aggrieved (as well he might be) for the paltry sum he fetched in the auction, it is finally settled that Lucian's attacks had been made only against the sham exponents of philosophy. He is triumphantly acquitted and declared by all, even by Diogenes, to be the real friend of truth and "one of us[2]."

Those who read Lucian most will be the first to acknowledge the truth of this conclusion. Lucian has been termed the "Voltaire of paganism," and described as "the universal mocker and censor," but all through his writings there is a genuine ring of one who abhors shams and loves the truth[3]. That Lucian had a high appreciation of the best philosophical teachers of Greece is shown clearly enough in his own peculiar way. Socrates he sells for £500. Aristotle he describes as "moderate, upright, consistent in his life, fair and exceedingly knowing[4]." Aristippus fetches the highest price next to Socrates, viz. £80. Of Plato he speaks most highly as possessing "a marvellous loftiness of thought, a surpassing grace and the sweetest Attic

---

[1] *Pisc.* § 11, ποῦ τὴν Φιλοσοφίαν εὕροι τις ἄν ; οὐ γὰρ οἶδα ἔνθα οἰκεῖ.

[2] *Pisc.* § 38. ΔΙΟΓ. καὶ αὐτός, ὦ Φιλοσοφία, πάνυ ἐπαινῶ τὸν ἄνδρα καὶ ἀνατίθεμαι τὰ κατηγορημένα καὶ φίλον ποιοῦμαι αὐτὸν γενναῖον ὄντα.

ΦΙΛ. εὖγε...ἀφίεμέν σε τῆς αἰτίας...καὶ τὸ λοιπὸν ἴσθι ἡμέτερος ὤν.

[3] *Pisc.* § 20, φιλαλήθης τε γὰρ καὶ φιλόκαλος καὶ φιλαπλοϊκὸς καὶ ὅσα τῷ φιλεῖσθαι συγγενῆ.

[4] *Vit. Auc.* § 26.

diction [1]," while elsewhere [2] he seems to favour Epicurus more
than any other philosopher. But he never ceases to raise his
voice and pen against that vast army of pseudo-philosophers [3]
whom he naturally thought it was proper to consult when a man
is in doubt as to the best mode of life; but having himself made
trial of them, he can only call it jumping out of the frying-pan
into the fire. No two men gave the same advice; their arguments were most specious, but the conclusions contradictory.
It was impossible to say where the truth lay, and not a single
one of them attempted to carry out in practice what he taught
in theory [4].

Having once made up his mind to lampoon these miserable
self-constituted pretenders, Lucian, as might be expected, takes
no half measures. It needs nothing but a bit of a "make up" to
change an ordinary man into a philosopher. His garb must
include a cloak and wallet; he must have his staff in his right
hand and possibly a book in his left [5]. A long flowing beard
and a solemn demeanour is indispensable, and an elevation of
the eyebrows [6], to give a look of superiority. His complexion [7] is
sallow, his voice harsh, his temper hot; he is a cheat [8], juggler,

[1] *Pisc.* § 22.
[2] *Alex.* § 47.
[3] *Pisc.* § 20, μισαλαζών εἰμι καὶ μισογόης καὶ μισοψευδὴς καὶ μισό-
τυφος καὶ μισῶ πᾶν τὸ τοιουτῶδες εἶδος τῶν μιαρῶν ἀνθρώπων.
[4] Cf. a passage from Lactantius, *Div. Inst.* III. 15, "who is there
who does not see those men are not teachers of virtue who are themselves destitute of virtue? for if anyone should diligently inquire into
their character, he will find they are passionate, covetous, lustful,
arrogant, wanton, and concealing their devices under a show of
wisdom, doing those things at home which they had censured in the
schools."
[5] *Bis acc.* § 6.
[6] Passages in support of the above abound. It may be well to note
a few of the Greek terms. The stick is βακτήριον or ξύλον, the
wallet πήρα, the cloak τρίβων, or τριβώνιον, or πορφυρίς, the fashion
of wearing it, ἀναβολή. His strut is βάδισμα. τὸν βαθὺν πώγωνα
καθειμένος or ἐν βαθεῖ γενείῳ is a common phrase for the beard.
[7] His looks σεμνὸς—βρενθυόμενος—τὰς ὀφρῦς ἐπηρκώς, or ἀνατείνας.
Complexion, ὠχρὸς, ὕπωχρος, Voice τραχύφωνος, Temper ὀργίλος.
[8] He is a γόης, ἀλάζων, κόλαξ, ἐπίτριπτος, τεράτων μέστος. His
talk λῆρος, ὕθλος, μικρολογία. His qualities ἀμαθία, ἔρις, κενοδοξία,
ψεῦδος, ἡδυπάθεια, μαλακία, τῦφος, ἀσελγεία, ὕβρις, καὶ μυρία ἄλλα.

mountebank, rascal. His talk is nothing but drivelling twaddle; and he is a store-house of flattery, ignorance, wrangling, lying, vanity, luxury, effeminacy, vulgarity, discontent, swagger, greed, and impudence. When Zeus wishes to hear what two philosophers are disputing about, he passes for a philosopher at once by donning a cloak and beard and using his elbows[1]. When Hermotimus declares that he will eschew philosophy, he says, "You say well, Lucian, so I will off at once and change my dress; you shall see me soon without any shaggy and thick beard; I will lay aside my cloak that all may know I no longer have aught to do with this nonsense[2]." When Socrates first meets Menippus in the shades and asks him what the latest news is from Athens, Menippus replies that "many of the young men *say* they are philosophers; and so far as external appearance and swagger go, they are consummate philosophers[3]." With Lucian, too, the philosophers are open to bribes and extortion; they stand open-mouthed at the chance of silver, they are "more snarling than little dogs, more cowardly than hares, greedier than cats, more quarrelsome than fighting-cocks, and can no more attain to true philosophy than a vulture can to the voice of a nightingale[4]." Is it to be wondered at, that ordinary people despised philosophy and blamed philosophy herself rather than her false exponents[5]?

If Thackeray's dictum be true, "if fun is good, truth is better, and love is best of all," Lucian, though he knew little of the last, certainly is unsurpassed in the first, and was a striver after the truth. Different people will regard Lucian in different ways, according to their standard of judgment. While some may blame him for his uncontrolled mirth, others will only look upon him as a "very good fellow," who has no wish to wound unnecessarily, but who has such a horror of shams and

---

[1] *Jup. Trag.* § 16.
[2] *Hermot.* § 86.
[3] *Inf. Dial.* 20. 5.
[4] Cf. *Pisc.* §§ 34—37, νῦν δὲ θᾶττον ἂν γὺψ ἀηδόνα μιμήσαιτο ἢ οὗτοι φιλοσόφους: cf. description of Thrasycles below, *Tim.* §§ 54, 55.
[5] *Fug.* § 21.

such a love of truth, that to keep silence is impossible; such at least will agree that we are the richer for his writings, and that in his life he did a noble work, and left behind him at his death an example of honest straightforward plain-speaking, which many would do well to imitate[1].

[1] Cf. Müller and Donaldson, III. 228.

LIST OF READINGS IN DINDORF'S TEXT NOT ADOPTED IN THIS BOOK. (Leipzig 1858.)

Menippus.

None.

Timon.

§ 6.   Οἴτης for Αἴτνης.

§ 10. [τινας] omitted.

§ 24. παρ' αὐτὸν, no brackets.

§ 27. πρὸς after ἀμβλυώττοντες.

§ 38. πρὸς, before οὕτω...κατηγορηθέντα.

§ 43. ἑκὰς ὢν τῶν ἄλλων.

§ 44. ἐν after ἐπεψήφισεν.

§ 55. omit [ἤ].

ΜΕΝΙΠΠΟΣ Η ΝΕΚΥΟΜΑΝΤΕΙΑ.

The scene opens in Lebadeia (v. last note of dialogue). Menippus appears, with his head full of quotations, having just returned from a journey to the lower world, and a talk with Homer and Euripides; he meets his friend Philonides, who begs him to cease quoting poetry, and to explain the reason of his descent.

ΜΕΝΙΠΠΟΣ ΚΑΙ ΦΙΛΩΝΙΔΗΣ.

1. ΜΕΝ. ᾿Ω χαῖρε μέλαθρον πρόπυλά θ᾿ ἑστίας
ἐμῆς,
ὡς ἅσμενός σ᾿ ἐπεῖδον ἐς φάος μολών.

ΦΙΛ. Οὐ Μένιππος οὗτός ἐστιν ὁ κύων; οὐ μὲν
οὖν ἄλλος, εἰ μὴ ἐγὼ παραβλέπω· Μένιππος ὅλος. τί 5
οὖν αὐτῷ βούλεται τὸ ἀλλόκοτον τοῦ σχήματος, πῖλος
καὶ λύρα καὶ λεοντῆ; προσιτέον δὲ ὅμως αὐτῷ.
χαῖρε, ὦ Μένιππε· πόθεν ἡμῖν ἀφῖξαι; πολὺς γὰρ
χρόνος ἐξ ὅτου οὐ πέφηνας ἐν τῇ πόλει.

ΜΕΝ. ῞Ηκω νεκρῶν κευθμῶνα καὶ σκότου πύλας 10
λιπών, ἵν᾿ ῞Αδης χωρὶς ᾤκισται θεῶν.

ΦΙΛ. ῾Ηράκλεις, ἐλελήθει Μένιππος ἡμᾶς ἀποθανών, κᾆτ᾿ ἐξ ὑπαρχῆς ἀναβεβιωκώς;

ΜΕΝ. Οὔκ, ἀλλ᾿ ἔτ᾿ ἔμπνουν ῞Αιδης μ᾿ ἐδέξατο.

M. L.   I

ΦΙΛ. Τίς δ' ἡ αἰτία σοι τῆς καινῆς καὶ παρα-
δόξου ταύτης ἀποδημίας;

ΜΕΝ. Νεότης μ' ἐπῆρε καὶ θράσος τοῦ νοῦ
πλέον.

5 ΦΙΛ. Παῦσαι, μακάριε, τραγῳδῶν καὶ λέγε οὑτωσί πως ἁπλῶς καταβὰς ἀπὸ τῶν ἰαμβείων, τίς
ἡ στολή; τί σοι τῆς κάτω πορείας ἐδέησεν; ἄλλως
γὰρ οὐχ ἡδεῖά τις οὐδὲ ἀσπάσιος ἡ ὁδός.

ΜΕΝ. Ὦ φιλότης, χρειώ με κατήγαγεν εἰς Ἀΐδαο,
10 ψυχῇ χρησόμενον Θηβαίου Τειρεσίαο.

ΦΙΛ. Οὗτος, ἀλλ' ἢ παραπαίεις; οὐ γὰρ ἂν οὕτως
ἐμμέτρως ἐρραψῴδεις πρὸς ἄνδρας φίλους.

ΜΕΝ. Μὴ θαυμάσῃς, ὦ ἑταῖρε· νεωστὶ γὰρ
Εὐριπίδῃ καὶ Ὁμήρῳ συγγενόμενος οὐκ οἶδ' ὅπως
15 ἀνεπλήσθην τῶν ἐπῶν καὶ αὐτόματά μοι τὰ μέτρα
ἐπὶ τὸ στόμα ἔρχεται.

*Woe betide the usurers, perjurers, et hoc genus omne: terri-
ble laws have lately been passed in the nether world.
" But I must not reveal such secrets," says M.   " You
can to a friend, and one of the initiated," replies Ph.,
" so tell me the reason of your going, who showed you
the way, and what you saw and heard."*

2. ἀτὰρ εἰπέ μοι, πῶς τὰ ὑπὲρ γῆς ἔχει καὶ τί
ποιοῦσιν οἱ ἐν τῇ πόλει;

ΦΙΛ. Καινὸν οὐδέν, ἀλλ' οἷα καὶ πρὸ τοῦ ἁρπά-
20 ζουσιν, ἐπιορκοῦσι, τοκογλυφοῦσιν, ὀβολοστατοῦσιν.

ΜΕΝ. Ἄθλιοι καὶ κακοδαίμονες· οὐ γὰρ ἴσασιν
οἷα ἔναγχος κεκύρωται παρὰ τοῖς κάτω καὶ οἷα κε-
χειροτόνηται τὰ ψηφίσματα κατὰ τῶν πλουσίων, ἃ
μὰ τὸν Κέρβερον οὐδεμία μηχανὴ τὸ διαφυγεῖν αὐτούς.

ΦΙΛ. Τί φής; δέδοκταί τι νεώτερον τοῖς κάτω
περὶ τῶν ἐνθάδε;

ΜΕΝ. Νὴ Δία, καὶ πολλά γε· ἀλλ' οὐ θέμις
ἐκφέρειν αὐτὰ πρὸς ἅπαντας οὐδὲ τὰ ἀπόρρητα ἐξαγορεύειν, μὴ καί τις ἡμᾶς γράψηται γραφὴν ἀσεβείας 5
ἐπὶ τοῦ Ῥαδαμάνθυος.

ΦΙΛ. Μηδαμῶς, ὦ Μένιππε, πρὸς τοῦ Διός, μὴ
φθονήσῃς τῶν λόγων φίλῳ ἀνδρί· πρὸς γὰρ εἰδότα
σιωπᾶν ἐρεῖς, τά τ' ἄλλα καὶ πρὸς μεμυημένον.

ΜΕΝ. Χαλεπὸν μὲν ἐπιτάττεις τοὐπίταγμα καὶ 10
οὐ πάντῃ ἀσφαλές· πλὴν ἀλλὰ σοῦ γε ἕνεκα τολ-
μητέον. ἔδοξε δὴ τοὺς πλουσίους τούτους καὶ πολυ-
χρημάτους καὶ τὸ χρυσίον κατάκλειστον ὥσπερ τὴν
Δανάην φυλάττοντας—

ΦΙΛ. Μὴ πρότερον εἴπῃς, ὦγαθέ, τὰ δεδογμένα, 15
πρὶν ἐκεῖνα διελθεῖν, ἃ μάλιστ' ἂν ἡδέως ἀκούσαιμί
σου, τίς ἡ ἐπίνοιά σου τῆς καθόδου ἐγένετο, τίς δὲ ὁ
τῆς πορείας ἡγεμών, εἶθ' ἐξῆς ἅ τε εἶδες ἅ τε ἤκουσας
παρ' αὐτοῖς· εἰκὸς γὰρ δὴ φιλόκαλον ὄντα σε μηδὲν
τῶν ἀξίων θέας ἢ ἀκοῆς παραλιπεῖν. 20

*Well, I suppose I must. The stories which Homer and
Hesiod tell us about the gods have always puzzled me :
their conduct is quite at variance with what the laws
lay down. So my first step was to consult the so-
called professors of philosophy as to the proper mode of
living. But here I was worse off than ever. Each
school told me differently.*

3. ΜΕΝ. Ὑπουργητέον καὶ ταῦτά σοι· τί γὰρ
ἂν καὶ πάθοι τις, ὁπότε φίλος ἀνὴρ βιάζοιτο; καὶ δὴ
πρῶτά σοι δίειμι τὰ περὶ τῆς γνώμης τῆς ἐμῆς καὶ

ὅθεν ὡρμήθην πρὸς τὴν κατάβασιν· ἐγὼ γάρ, ἄχρι
μὲν ἐν παισὶν ἦν, ἀκούων Ὁμήρου καὶ Ἡσιόδου πολέμους καὶ στάσεις διηγουμένων οὐ μόνον τῶν ἡμιθέων,
ἀλλὰ καὶ αὐτῶν ἤδη τῶν θεῶν, ἔτι δὲ καὶ μοιχείας
5 αὐτῶν καὶ βίας καὶ ἁρπαγὰς καὶ δίκας καὶ πατέρων
ἐξελάσεις καὶ ἀδελφῶν γάμους, πάντα ταῦτα ἐνόμιζον
εἶναι καλὰ καὶ οὐ παρέργως ἐκνώμην πρὸς αὐτά· ἐπεὶ
δὲ εἰς ἄνδρας τελεῖν ἠρξάμην, πάλιν αὖ ἐνταῦθα
ἤκουον τῶν νόμων τἀναντία τοῖς ποιηταῖς κελευόντων,
10 μήτε μοιχεύειν μήτε στασιάζειν μήτε ἁρπάζειν. ἐν
μεγάλῃ οὖν καθειστήκειν ἀμφιβολίᾳ, οὐκ εἰδὼς ὅ τι
χρησαίμην ἐμαυτῷ· οὔτε γὰρ ἄν ποτε τοὺς θεοὺς μοι-
χεῦσαι καὶ στασιάσαι πρὸς ἀλλήλους ἡγούμην, εἰ μὴ
ὡς περὶ καλῶν τούτων ἐγίγνωσκον, οὔτ' ἂν τοὺς νομο-
15 θέτας τἀναντία τούτοις παραινεῖν, εἰ μὴ λυσιτελεῖν
ὑπελάμβανον.

4. Ἐπεὶ δὲ διηπόρουν, ἔδοξέ μοι ἐλθόντα παρὰ
τοὺς καλουμένους τούτους φιλοσόφους ἐγχειρίσαι τε
ἐμαυτὸν καὶ δεηθῆναι αὐτῶν χρῆσθαί μοι ὅ τι βού-
20 λοιντο καί τινα ὁδὸν ἁπλῆν καὶ βέβαιον ὑποδεῖξαι
τοῦ βίου. ταῦτα μὲν δὴ φρονῶν προσῄειν αὐτοῖς,
ἐλελήθειν δ' ἐμαυτὸν εἰς αὐτό, φασί, τὸ πῦρ ἐκ τοῦ
καπνοῦ βιαζόμενος· παρὰ γὰρ δὴ τούτοις μάλιστα
ηὕρισκον ἐπισκοπῶν τὴν ἄγνοιαν καὶ τὴν ἀπορίαν
25 πλείονα, ὥστε μοι τάχιστα χρυσὸν ἀπέδειξαν οὗτοι
τὸν τῶν ἰδιωτῶν βίον· ἀμέλει ὁ μὲν αὐτῶν παρῄνει
τὸ πᾶν ἥδεσθαι καὶ μόνον τοῦτο ἐκ παντὸς μετιέναι·
τοῦτο γὰρ εἶναι τὸ εὔδαιμον· ὁ δέ τις ἔμπαλιν, πονεῖν
τὰ πάντα καὶ μοχθεῖν καὶ τὸ σῶμα καταναγκάζειν
30 ῥυπῶντα καὶ αὐχμῶντα καὶ πᾶσι δυσαρεστοῦντα καὶ
λοιδορούμενον, συνεχὲς ἐπιρραψῳδῶν τὰ πάνδημα

ἐκεῖνα τοῦ Ἡσιόδου περὶ τῆς ἀρετῆς ἔπη καὶ τὸν
ἱδρῶτα καὶ τὴν ἐπὶ τὸ ἄκρον ἀνάβασιν· ἄλλος καταφρονεῖν χρημάτων παρεκελεύετο καὶ ἀδιάφορον οἴεσθαι τὴν κτῆσιν αὐτῶν· ὁ δέ τις ἔμπαλιν ἀγαθὸν
εἶναι καὶ τὸν πλοῦτον αὐτὸν ἀπεφαίνετο· περὶ μὲν 5
γὰρ τοῦ κόσμου τί χρὴ καὶ λέγειν; ὅς γε ἰδέας καὶ
ἀσώματα καὶ ἀτόμους καὶ κενὰ καὶ τοιοῦτόν τινα
ὄχλον ὀνομάτων ὁσημέραι παρ' αὐτῶν ἀκούων ἐναυ-
τίων. καὶ τὸ πάντων ἀτοπώτατον, ὅτι περὶ τῶν ἐναν-
τιωτάτων ἕκαστος αὐτῶν λέγων σφόδρα νικῶντας καὶ 10
πιθανοὺς λόγους ἐπορίζετο, ὥστε μηδὲ τῷ θερμὸν τὸ
αὐτὸ πρᾶγμα λέγοντι καὶ ψυχρὸν ἀντιλέγειν ἔχειν,
καὶ ταῦτα εἰδότα σαφῶς ὡς οὐκ ἄν ποτε θερμὸν εἴη
τι καὶ ψυχρὸν ἐν ταὐτῷ χρόνῳ· ἀτεχνῶς οὖν ἔπασχον
τοῖς νυστάζουσι τούτοις ὅμοιον, ἄρτι μὲν ἐπινεύων, 15
ἄρτι δὲ ἀνανεύων ἔμπαλιν.

*Moreover, the most ridiculous thing of all was that not one
of them attempted to practise what he preached.*

5. Πολλῷ δὲ τούτων ἐκεῖνο ἀλογώτερον· τοὺς
γὰρ αὐτοὺς τούτους ηὕρισκον ἐπιτηρῶν ἐναντιώτατα
τοῖς αὐτῶν λόγοις ἐπιτηδεύοντας· τοὺς γοῦν καταφρονεῖν παραινοῦντας χρημάτων ἑώρων ἀπρὶξ ἐχομέ- 20
νους αὐτῶν καὶ περὶ τόκων διαφερομένους καὶ ἐπὶ
μισθῷ παιδεύοντας καὶ πάντα ἕνεκα τούτων ὑπομέ-
νοντας, τούς τε τὴν δόξαν ἀποβαλλομένους αὐτῆς
ταύτης χάριν τὰ πάντα καὶ πράττοντας καὶ λέγοντας,
ἡδονῆς τε αὖ σχεδὸν ἅπαντας κατηγοροῦντας, ἰδίᾳ δὲ 25
μόνῃ ταύτῃ προσηρτημένους.

*So I came away in disappointment and disgust. However,
one day it struck me that I would go to Babylon and
ask one of the followers of Zoroaster to show me the
way down to the lower world, where I might find that
famous old blind soothsayer, Teiresias of Bœotia; no
sooner had I formed this resolve than I went and
found one Mithrobarzanes, who fixed his own charge,
and agreed to act as my guide.*

6. Σφαλεὶς οὖν καὶ τῆσδε τῆς ἐλπίδος ἔτι μᾶλλον
ἐδυσχέραινον ἠρέμα παραμυθούμενος ἐμαυτόν, ὅτι
μετὰ πολλῶν καὶ σοφῶν καὶ σφόδρα ἐπὶ συνέσει διαβεβοημένων ἀνόητός τέ εἰμι καὶ τἀληθὲς ἔτι ἀγνοῶν
5 περιέρχομαι· καί μοί ποτε διαγρυπνοῦντι τούτων
ἕνεκα ἔδοξεν ἐς Βαβυλῶνα ἐλθόντα δεηθῆναί τινος
τῶν μάγων τῶν Ζωροάστρου μαθητῶν καὶ διαδόχων,
ἤκουον δ᾽ αὐτοὺς ἐπῳδαῖς τε καὶ τελεταῖς τισιν ἀνοίγειν τε τοῦ ῞Αδου τὰς πύλας καὶ κατάγειν ὃν ἂν
10 βούλωνται ἀσφαλῶς καὶ ὀπίσω αὖθις ἀναπέμπειν.
ἄριστον οὖν ἡγούμην εἶναι παρά τινος τούτων διαπραξ-
άμενον τὴν κατάβασιν ἐλθόντα παρὰ Τειρεσίαν τὸν
Βοιώτιον μαθεῖν παρ᾽ αὐτοῦ, ἅτε μάντεως καὶ σοφοῦ,
τίς ἐστιν ὁ ἄριστος βίος καὶ ὃν ἄν τις ἕλοιτο εὖ
15 φρονῶν· καὶ δὴ ἀναπηδήσας ὡς εἶχον τάχους ἔτεινον
εὐθὺ Βαβυλῶνος. ἐλθὼν δὲ συγγίγνομαί τινι τῶν
Χαλδαίων σοφῷ ἀνδρὶ καὶ θεσπεσίῳ τὴν τέχνην,
πολιῷ μὲν τὴν κόμην, γένειον δὲ μάλα σεμνὸν καθει-
μένῳ, τοὔνομα δὲ ἦν αὐτῷ Μιθροβαρζάνης· δεηθεὶς
20 δὲ καὶ καθικετεύσας μόγις ἐπέτυχον παρ᾽ αὐτοῦ, ἐφ᾽
ὅτῳ βούλοιτο μισθῷ, καθηγήσασθαί μοι τῆς ὁδοῦ.

I had many preliminaries to go through first. Incantations and spells—ablutions and fixed diet.

7. Παραλαβὼν δέ με ὁ ἀνὴρ πρῶτα μὲν ἡμέρας
ἐννέα καὶ εἴκοσιν ἅμα τῇ σελήνῃ ἀρξάμενος ἔλουε
κατάγων ἕωθεν ἐπὶ τὸν Εὐφράτην, πρὸς ἀνίσχοντα
τὸν ἥλιον ῥῆσίν τινα μακρὰν ἐπιλέγων, ἧς οὐ σφόδρα
κατήκουον· ὥσπερ γὰρ οἱ φαῦλοι τῶν ἐν τοῖς ἀγῶσι 5
κηρύκων ἐπίτροχόν τι καὶ ἀσαφὲς ἐφθέγγετο· πλὴν
ἐῴκει γέ τινας ἐπικαλεῖσθαι δαίμονας. μετὰ δ' οὖν
τὴν ἐπῳδὴν τρὶς ἄν μου ἐς τὸ πρόσωπον ἀποπτύσας
ἐπανῄειν πάλιν οὐδένα τῶν ἀπαντώντων προσβλέ-
πων· καὶ σιτία μὲν ἡμῖν τὰ ἀκρόδρυα, ποτὸν δὲ γάλα 10
καὶ μελίκρατον καὶ τὸ τοῦ Χοάσπου ὕδωρ, εὐνὴ δὲ
ὑπαίθριος ἐπὶ τῆς πόας. ἐπεὶ δὲ ἅλις εἶχε τῆς προ-
διαιτήσεως, περὶ μέσας νύκτας ἐπὶ τὸν Τίγρητα ποταμὸν ἀγαγὼν ἐκάθηρέ τέ με καὶ ἀπέμαξε καὶ περιήγνισε
δᾳδίοις καὶ σκίλλῃ καὶ ἄλλοις πλείοσιν ἅμα καὶ τὴν 15
ἐπῳδὴν ἐκείνην ὑποτονθορύσας, εἶτα ὅλον με καταμαγεύσας καὶ περιελθών, ἵνα μὴ βλαπτοίμην ὑπὸ
τῶν φασμάτων, ἐπανάγει ἐς τὴν οἰκίαν, ὡς εἶχον, ἀναποδίζοντα, καὶ τὸ λοιπὸν ἀμφὶ πλοῦν εἴχομεν.

*I was then decked out with a cap like Odysseus, a lion's
skin like Heracles, and a lyre like Orpheus, and
strictly enjoined if I was asked my name to give one of
these names and not Menippus.*

8. Αὐτὸς μὲν οὖν μαγικήν τινα ἐνέδυ στολὴν τὰ 20
πολλὰ ἐοικυῖαν τῇ Μηδικῇ, ἐμὲ δὲ τουτοισὶ φέρων
ἐνεσκεύασε, τῷ πίλῳ καὶ τῇ λεοντῇ καὶ προσέτι τῇ
λύρᾳ, καὶ παρεκελεύσατο, ἤν τις ἔρηταί με τοὔνομα,

Μένιππον μὲν μὴ λέγειν, Ἡρακλέα δὲ ἢ Ὀδυσσέα ἢ
Ὀρφέα.

ΦΙΛ. Ὡς δὴ τί τοῦτο, ὦ Μένιππε; οὐ γὰρ
συνίημι τὴν αἰτίαν οὔτε τοῦ σχήματος οὔτε τῶν ὀνο-
5 μάτων.

ΜΕΝ. Καὶ μὴν πρόδηλον τοῦτό γε καὶ οὐ παν-
τελῶς ἀπόρρητον· ἐπεὶ γὰρ οὗτοι πρὸ ἡμῶν ζῶντες
εἰς Ἅιδου κατεληλύθεσαν, ἡγεῖτο, εἴ με ἀπεικάσειεν
αὐτοῖς, ῥᾳδίως ἂν τὴν τοῦ Αἰακοῦ φρουρὰν διαλαθεῖν
10 καὶ ἀκωλύτως παρελθεῖν ἅτε συνηθέστερον τραγικῶς
μάλα παραπεμπόμενον ὑπὸ τοῦ σχήματος.

On the 30th day at dawn we went down to the river
Euphrates—where everything had been prepared for
the voyage—and landed at a certain place, where my
guide sacrificed with much bawling to all the nether
gods.

9. Ἤδη δ᾽ οὖν ὑπέφαινεν ἡμέρα, καὶ κατελθόντες
ἐπὶ τὸν ποταμὸν περὶ ἀναγωγὴν ἐγιγνόμεθα· παρε-
σκεύαστο δ᾽ αὐτῷ καὶ σκάφος καὶ ἱερεῖα καὶ μελίκρα-
15 τον καὶ ἄλλ᾽ ὅσα πρὸς τὴν τελετὴν χρήσιμα. ἐμ-
βαλόμενοι οὖν ἅπαντα τὰ παρεσκευασμένα οὕτω δὴ
καὶ αὐτοὶ
βαίνομεν ἀχνύμενοι, θαλερὸν κατὰ δάκρυ χέοντες.

καὶ μέχρι μέν τινος ὑπεφερόμεθα ἐν τῷ ποταμῷ, εἶτα
20 δ᾽ εἰσεπλεύσαμεν ἐς τὸ ἕλος καὶ τὴν λίμνην, εἰς ἣν ὁ
Εὐφράτης ἀφανίζεται· περαιωθέντες δὲ καὶ ταύτην
ἀφικνούμεθα ἔς τι χωρίον ἔρημον καὶ ὑλῶδες καὶ ἀνή-
λιον, εἰς ὃ δὴ ἀποβάντες—ἡγεῖτο δὲ ὁ Μιθροβαρζάνης—βόθρον τε ὠρυξάμεθα καὶ τὰ μῆλα ἐσφάξαμεν
25 καὶ τὸ αἷμα περὶ αὐτὸν ἐσπείσαμεν. ὁ δὲ μάγος ἐν

τοσούτῳ δᾷδα καομένην ἔχων οὐκέτ᾽ ἠρεμαίᾳ τῇ φωνῇ,
παμμέγεθες δέ, ὡς οἷός τε ἦν, ἀνακραγὼν δαίμονάς τε
ὁμοῦ πάντας ἐπεβοᾶτο καὶ Ποινὰς καὶ Ἐρινύας,
   καὶ νυχίαν Ἑκάτην καὶ ἐπαινὴν Περσεφόνειαν.
παραμιγνὺς ἅμα καὶ βαρβαρικά τινα καὶ ἄσημα 5
ὀνόματα καὶ πολυσύλλαβα.

*Suddenly a rumbling was heard, and in a moment the
rivers of hell, the watch-dog, and all the realm of
Pluto was revealed. Charon taking me to be
Heracles was polite enough to row us over and
show us which path to take.*

10. Εὐθὺς οὖν ἅπαντα ἐκεῖνα ἐσαλεύετο καὶ ὑπὸ
τῆς ἐπῳδῆς τοὔδαφος ἀνερρήγνυτο καὶ ἡ ὑλακὴ τοῦ
Κερβέρου καὶ πόρρωθεν ἠκούετο καὶ τὸ πρᾶγμα
ὑπερκατηφὲς ἦν καὶ σκυθρωπόν.   10

Ἔδδεισεν δ᾽ ὑπένερθεν ἄναξ ἐνέρων Ἀϊδωνεύς·
κατεφαίνετο γὰρ ἤδη τὰ πλεῖστα, καὶ ἡ λίμνη καὶ
ὁ Πυριφλεγέθων καὶ τοῦ Πλούτωνος τὰ βασίλεια.
κατελθόντες δ᾽ ὅμως διὰ τοῦ χάσματος τὸν μὲν
Ῥαδάμανθυν ηὕρομεν τεθνεῶτα μικροῦ δεῖν ὑπὸ τοῦ 15
δέους· ὁ δὲ Κέρβερος ὑλάκτησε μέν τι καὶ παρεκίνησε, ταχὺ δέ μου κρούσαντος τὴν λύραν παρα-
χρῆμα ἐκηλήθη ὑπὸ τοῦ μέλους. ἐπεὶ δὲ πρὸς τὴν
λίμνην ἀφικόμεθα, μικροῦ μὲν οὐδ᾽ ἐπεραιώθημεν·
ἦν γὰρ πλῆρες ἤδη τὸ πορθμεῖον καὶ οἰμωγῆς ἀνά- 20
πλεων, τραυματίαι δὲ πάντες ἐπέπλεον, ὁ μὲν τὸ
σκέλος, ὁ δὲ τὴν κεφαλήν, ὁ δὲ ἄλλο τι συντετριμ-
μένος, ἐμοὶ δοκεῖν, ἔκ τινος πολέμου παρόντες. ὅμως
δ᾽ οὖν ὁ βέλτιστος Χάρων ὡς εἶδε τὴν λεοντῆν, οἰηθείς με τὸν Ἡρακλέα εἶναι, εἰσεδέξατό με καὶ διε- 25

πόρθμευσέ τε ἄσμενος καὶ ἀποβᾶσι διεσήμηνε τὴν
ἀτραπόν.

*Before long we reached the judgment seat of Minos; aveng-
ing deities stood all around, while each culprit was
brought up in turn for judgment; each man being
convicted or condoned on the evidence of his own
shadow!*

11. Ἐπεὶ δὲ ἦμεν ἐν τῷ σκότῳ, προῄει μὲν ὁ
Μιθροβαρζάνης, εἱπόμην δ᾽ ἐγὼ κατόπιν ἐχόμενος
5 αὐτοῦ, ἕως πρὸς λειμῶνα μέγιστον ἀφικνούμεθα τῷ
ἀσφοδέλῳ κατάφυτον, ἔνθα δὴ περιεπέτοντο ἡμᾶς
τετριγυῖαι τῶν νεκρῶν αἱ σκιαί· κατ᾽ ὀλίγον δὲ προϊ-
όντες παραγιγνόμεθα πρὸς τὸ τοῦ Μίνω δικαστήριον,
ἐτύγχανε δὲ ὁ μὲν ἐπὶ θρόνου τινὸς ὑψηλοῦ καθήμε-
10 νος, παρειστήκεσαν δὲ αὐτῷ Ποιναὶ καὶ ἀλάστορες
καὶ Ἐρινύες· ἑτέρωθεν δὲ προσήγοντο πολλοί τινες
ἐφεξῆς ἁλύσει μακρᾷ δεδεμένοι, ἐλέγοντο δὲ εἶναι
μοιχοὶ καὶ πορνοβοσκοὶ καὶ τελῶναι καὶ κόλακες καὶ
συκοφάνται καὶ ὁ τοιοῦτος ὅμιλος τῶν πάντα κυκών-
15 των ἐν τῷ βίῳ· χωρὶς δὲ οἵ τε πλούσιοι καὶ τοκογλύφοι προσῇεσαν ὠχροὶ καὶ προγάστορες καὶ ποδαγροί,
κλοιὸν ἕκαστος αὐτῶν καὶ σκύλακα διτάλαντον ἐπικείμενος. ἐφεστῶτες οὖν ἡμεῖς ἑωρῶμέν τε τὰ γιγνό-
μενα καὶ ἠκούομεν τῶν ἀπολογουμένων· κατηγόρουν
20 δὲ αὐτῶν καινοί τινες καὶ παράδοξοι ῥήτορες.

ΦΙΛ. Τίνες οὗτοι, πρὸς Διός; μὴ γὰρ ὀκνήσῃς
καὶ τοῦτο εἰπεῖν.

ΜΕΝ. Οἶσθά που ταυτασὶ τὰς πρὸς τὸν ἥλιον
ἀποτελουμένας σκιὰς ἀπὸ τῶν σωμάτων;

25 ΦΙΛ. Πάνυ μὲν οὖν.

MEN. Αὗται τοίνυν, ἐπειδὰν ἀποθάνωμεν, κατη-
γοροῦσί τε καὶ καταμαρτυροῦσι καὶ διελέγχουσι τὰ
πεπραγμένα ἡμῖν παρὰ τὸν βίον, καὶ σφόδρα τινὲς
ἀξιόπιστοι δοκοῦσιν ἅτε ἀεὶ συνοῦσαι καὶ μηδέποτε
ἀφιστάμεναι τῶν σωμάτων.   5

*The wealthy and powerful amongst mankind were the
special subjects of wrath ; and we could see them count-
ing over their past blessings and misused opportunities
upon their fingers.   Dionysius of Syracuse was pardoned, however, because of his kindly patronage of
literature.*

12. Ὁ δ' οὖν Μίνως ἐπιμελῶς ἐξετάζων ἀπέ-
πεμπεν ἕκαστον ἐς τὸν τῶν ἀσεβῶν χῶρον δίκην ὑφέξοντα κατ' ἀξίαν τῶν τετολμημένων, καὶ μάλιστα
ἐκείνων ἥπτετο τῶν ἐπὶ πλούτοις τε καὶ ἀρχαῖς τετυ-
φωμένων καὶ μονονουχὶ καὶ προσκυνεῖσθαι περιμε- 10
νόντων, τήν τε ὀλιγοχρόνιον ἀλαζονείαν αὐτῶν καὶ
τὴν ὑπεροψίαν μυσαττόμενος, καὶ ὅτι μὴ ἐμέμνηντο
θνητοί τε ὄντες αὐτοὶ καὶ θνητῶν ἀγαθῶν τετυχηκό-
τες· οἱ δὲ ἀποδυσάμενοι τὰ λαμπρὰ ἐκεῖνα πάντα,
πλούτους λέγω καὶ γένη καὶ δυναστείας, γυμνοὶ κάτω 15
νενευκότες παρειστήκεσαν ὥσπερ τινὰ ὄνειρον ἀναπεμπαζόμενοι τὴν παρ' ἡμῖν εὐδαιμονίαν· ὥστε ἔγωγε
ταῦθ' ὁρῶν ὑπερέχαιρον καὶ εἴ τινα γνωρίσαιμι αὐτῶν,
προσιὼν ἂν ἡσυχῇ πως ὑπεμίμνησκον οἷος ἦν παρὰ
τὸν βίον καὶ ἡλίκον ἐφύσα τότε, ἡνίκα πολλοὶ μὲν 20
ἔωθεν ἐπὶ τῶν πυλώνων παρειστήκεσαν τὴν πρόοδον
αὐτοῦ περιμένοντες ὠθούμενοί τε καὶ ἀποκλειόμενοι
πρὸς τῶν οἰκετῶν· ὁ δὲ μόγις ἄν ποτε ἀνατείλας
αὐτοῖς πορφυροῦς τις ἢ περίχρυσος ἢ διαποίκιλος εὐ-

12 ΛΟΥΚΙΑΝΟΥ [12—14

δαίμονας ᾤετο καὶ μακαρίους ἀποφαίνειν τοὺς προσει-
πόντας, ἢ τὸ στῆθος ἢ τὴν δεξιὰν προτείνων καταφιλεῖν. ἐκεῖνοι μὲν οὖν ἡνιῶντο ἀκούοντες.

13. Τῷ δὲ Μίνῳ μία τις καὶ πρὸς χάριν ἐδικά-
5 σθη· τὸν γάρ τοι Σικελιώτην Διονύσιον πολλὰ καὶ
ἀνόσια ὑπό τε Δίωνος κατηγορηθέντα καὶ ὑπὸ τῆς
σκιᾶς καταμαρτυρηθέντα παρελθὼν Ἀρίστιππος ὁ
Κυρηναῖος — ἄγουσι δ᾽ αὐτὸν ἐν τιμῇ καὶ δύναται
μέγιστον ἐν τοῖς κάτω — μικροῦ δεῖν τῇ Χιμαίρᾳ πα-
10 ραδοθέντα παρέλυσε τῆς καταδίκης λέγων πολλοῖς
αὐτὸν τῶν πεπαιδευμένων πρὸς ἀργύριον γενέσθαι
δεξιόν.

*From the judgment-hall we moved on into the place of
punishments ; really, the sight was most heartrending
—every instrument of torture was in use ; and all
classes from kings to beggars ; even the fabulous Sisyphus, and his crew.*

14. Ἀποστάντες δ᾽ ἡμεῖς τοῦ δικαστηρίου πρὸς
τὸ κολαστήριον ἀφικνούμεθα. ἔνθα δή, ὦ φίλε, πολλὰ
15 καὶ ἐλεεινὰ ἦν καὶ ἀκοῦσαι καὶ ἰδεῖν· μαστίγων τε
γὰρ ὁμοῦ ψόφος ἠκούετο καὶ οἰμωγὴ τῶν ἐπὶ τοῦ
πυρὸς ὀπτωμένων καὶ στρέβλαι καὶ κύφωνες καὶ τρο-
χοί, καὶ ἡ Χίμαιρα ἐσπάραττε καὶ ὁ Κέρβερος ἐδάρ-
δαπτεν, ἐκολάζοντό τε ἅμα πάντες, βασιλεῖς, δοῦλοι,
20 σατράπαι, πένητες, πλούσιοι, πτωχοί, καὶ μετέμελε
πᾶσι τῶν τετολμημένων. ἐνίους δὲ αὐτῶν καὶ ἐγνω-
ρίσαμεν ἰδόντες, ὁπόσοι ἦσαν τῶν ἔναγχος τετελευτη-
κότων· οἱ δὲ ἐνεκαλύπτοντο καὶ ἀπεστρέφοντο, εἰ δὲ
καὶ προσβλέποιεν, μάλα δουλοπρεπές τι καὶ κολα-
25 κευτικόν, καὶ ταῦτα πῶς οἴει βαρεῖς ὄντες καὶ ὑπερ-

ὅπται παρὰ τὸν βίον; τοῖς μέντοι πένησιν ἡμιτέλεια
τῶν κακῶν ἐδίδοτο, καὶ διαναπαυόμενοι πάλιν ἐκολά-
ζοντο. καὶ μὴν κἀκεῖνα εἶδον τὰ μυθώδη, τὸν Ἰξίονα
καὶ τὸν Σίσυφον καὶ τὸν Φρύγα Τάνταλον καὶ τὸν
γηγενῆ Τιτυόν, Ἡράκλεις ὅσος· ἔκειτο γοῦν τόπον 5
ἐπέχων ἀγροῦ.

Passing through here, we reached the plain of Acheron—
where dwell the heroes and heroines and general mass
of mankind—not that it was possible to distinguish
individuals even with the most careful scrutiny.   The
Egyptians were in the best state of preservation.   But
with the Greeks there was no telling the most hand-
some from the ugliest; or the highest born from the
meanest beggar.

15. Διελθόντες δὲ καὶ τούτους ἐς τὸ πεδίον
ἐσβάλλομεν τὸ Ἀχερούσιον, εὑρίσκομέν τε αὐτόθι
τοὺς ἡμιθέους τε καὶ τὰς ἡρῴνας καὶ τὸν ἄλλον ὅμιλον
τῶν νεκρῶν κατὰ ἔθνη καὶ κατὰ φῦλα διαιτωμένους, 10
τοὺς μὲν παλαιούς τινας καὶ εὐρωτιῶντας καί, ὥς
φησιν Ὅμηρος, ἀμενηνούς, τοὺς δ᾽ ἔτι νεαλεῖς καὶ
συνεστηκότας, καὶ μάλιστα τοὺς Αἰγυπτίους αὐτῶν
διὰ τὸ πολυαρκὲς τῆς ταριχείας. τὸ μέντοι διαγιγ-
νώσκειν ἕκαστον οὐ πάνυ τι ἦν ῥᾴδιον· ἅπαντες γὰρ 15
ἀτεχνῶς ἀλλήλοις γίγνονται ὅμοιοι τῶν ὀστῶν γεγυμ-
νωμένων· πλὴν ἀλλὰ μόγις τε καὶ διὰ πολλοῦ ἀνα-
θεωροῦντες αὐτοὺς ἐγιγνώσκομεν. ἔκειντο δ᾽ ἐπ᾽ ἀλλήλοις ἀμαυροὶ καὶ ἄσημοι καὶ οὐδὲν ἔτι τῶν παρ᾽
ἡμῖν καλῶν φυλάττοντες. ἀμέλει πολλῶν ἐν ταὐτῷ 20
σκελετῶν κειμένων καὶ πάντων ὁμοίων φοβερόν τι καὶ
διάκενον δεδορκότων καὶ γυμνοὺς τοὺς ὀδόντας προ-

φαινόντων, ἠπόρουν πρὸς ἐμαυτὸν ᾧτινι διακρίναιμι
τὸν Θερσίτην ἀπὸ τοῦ καλοῦ Νιρέως ἢ τὸν Ἶρον ἀπὸ
τοῦ Φαιάκων βασιλέως ἢ Πυρρίαν τὸν μάγειρον ἀπὸ
τοῦ Ἀγαμέμνονος· οὐδὲν γὰρ ἔτι τῶν παλαιῶν γνωρι-
5 σμάτων αὐτοῖς παρέμενεν, ἀλλ' ὅμοια τὰ ὀστᾶ ἦν,
ἄδηλα καὶ ἀνεπίγραφα καὶ ὑπ' οὐδενὸς ἔτι διακρίνε-
σθαι δυνάμενα.

And I thought to myself:—The life of men is like a great
   procession ; and fickle Fortune is the mistress of the
   ceremonies. She decks this man in regal, and that
   one in servile, attire, just at her own caprice ; she
   sets up or pulls down according to the whim. She
   changes the costumes and status of a man, exactly like
   an actor on the stage, who now takes the part of Creon,
   or Agamemnon, and a few minutes after comes forth
   as a messenger, or slave ; and then at the close, he
   throws everything aside and goes home, no longer a
   great man, but just Polus or Satyrus, the tragedian.

16. Τοιγάρτοι ἐκεῖνα ὁρῶντι ἐδόκει μοι ὁ τῶν
ἀνθρώπων βίος πομπῇ τινι μακρᾷ προσεοικέναι, χορη-
10 γεῖν δὲ καὶ διατάττειν ἕκαστα ἡ Τύχη διάφορα καὶ
ποικίλα τοῖς πομπευταῖς τὰ σχήματα προσάπτουσα·
τὸν μὲν γὰρ λαβοῦσα, εἰ τύχοι, βασιλικῶς ἐνεσκεύασε
τιάραν τε ἐπιθεῖσα καὶ δορυφόρους παραδοῦσα καὶ
τὴν κεφαλὴν στέψασα τῷ διαδήματι, τῷ δὲ οἰκέτου
15 σχῆμα περιέθηκε, τὸν δέ τινα καλὸν εἶναι ἐκόσμησε,
τὸν δὲ ἄμορφον καὶ γελοῖον παρεσκεύασε· παντοδα-
πὴν γάρ, οἶμαι, δεῖ γενέσθαι τὴν θέαν. πολλάκις δὲ
καὶ διὰ μέσης τῆς πομπῆς μετέβαλε τὰ ἐνίων σχήματα οὐκ ἐῶσα ἐς τέλος διαπομπεῦσαι ὡς ἐτάχθησαν,

ἀλλὰ μεταμφιέσασα τὸν μὲν Κροῖσον ἠνάγκασε τὴν
οἰκέτου καὶ αἰχμαλώτου σκευὴν ἀναλαβεῖν, τὸν δὲ
Μαιάνδριον τέως ἐν τοῖς οἰκέταις πομπεύοντα τὴν τοῦ
Πολυκράτους τυραννίδα μετενέδυσε, καὶ μέχρι μέν
τινος εἴασε χρῆσθαι τῷ σχήματι· ἐπειδὰν δ' ὁ τῆς 5
πομπῆς καιρὸς παρέλθῃ, τηνικαῦτα ἕκαστος ἀποδοὺς
τὴν σκευὴν καὶ ἀποδυσάμενος τὸ σχῆμα μετὰ τοῦ σώματος ὅσπερ ἦν πρὸ τοῦ γίγνεται, μηδὲν τοῦ πλησίον
διαφέρων. ἔνιοι δὲ ὑπ' ἀγνωμοσύνης, ἐπειδὰν ἀπαιτῇ
τὸν κόσμον ἐπιστᾶσα ἡ Τύχη, ἄχθονταί τε καὶ ἀγα- 10
νακτοῦσιν ὥσπερ οἰκείων τινῶν στερισκόμενοι καὶ
οὐχ ἃ πρὸς ὀλίγον ἐχρήσαντο ἀποδιδόντες. οἶμαι δέ
σε καὶ τῶν ἐπὶ τῆς σκηνῆς πολλάκις ἑορακέναι τοὺς
τραγικοὺς ὑποκριτὰς τούτους πρὸς τὰς χρείας τῶν
δραμάτων ἄρτι μὲν Κρέοντας, ἐνίοτε δὲ Πριάμους 15
γιγνομένους ἢ Ἀγαμέμνονας, καὶ ὁ αὐτός, εἰ τύχοι,
μικρὸν ἔμπροσθεν μάλα σεμνῶς τὸ τοῦ Κέκροπος ἢ
Ἐρεχθέως σχῆμα μιμησάμενος μετ' ὀλίγον οἰκέτης
προῆλθεν ὑπὸ τοῦ ποιητοῦ κεκελευσμένος· ἤδη δὲ
πέρας ἔχοντος τοῦ δράματος ἀποδυσάμενος ἕκαστος 20
αὐτῶν τὴν χρυσόπαστον ἐκείνην ἐσθῆτα καὶ τὸ προσωπεῖον ἀποθέμενος καὶ καταβὰς ἀπὸ τῶν ἐμβατῶν
πένης καὶ ταπεινὸς περίεισιν οὐκέτ' Ἀγαμέμνων ὁ
Ἀτρέως οὐδὲ Κρέων ὁ Μενοικέως, ἀλλὰ Πῶλος Χαρι-
κλέους Σουνιεὺς ὀνομαζόμενος ἢ Σάτυρος Θεογείτονος 25
Μαραθώνιος. τοιαῦτα καὶ τὰ τῶν ἀνθρώπων πράγ-
ματά ἐστιν, ὡς τότε μοι ὁρῶντι ἔδοξεν.

"But, Menippus, what about those who have magnificent
tombs, and laudatory epitaphs, here on earth?"—
"Such things are folly, my dear fellow; I can only

*say misery seems to weigh upon them just in propor-
tion to the size of their monuments. And you would
laugh to see their menial occupations and the insults
they receive from the passers by. I saw Philip of
Macedon cobbling shoes."*

17. ΦΙΛ. Εἰπέ μοι, ὦ Μένιππε, οἱ δὲ τοὺς πολυτελεῖς τούτους καὶ ὑψηλοὺς τάφους ἔχοντες ὑπὲρ
γῆς καὶ στήλας καὶ εἰκόνας καὶ ἐπιγράμματα οὐδὲν
τιμιώτεροι παρ' αὐτοῖς εἰσι τῶν ἰδιωτῶν νεκρῶν ;

5 ΜΕΝ. Ληρεῖς, ὦ οὗτος· εἰ γοῦν ἐθεάσω τὸν
Μαύσωλον αὐτὸν — λέγω δὲ τὸν Κᾶρα, τὸν ἐκ τοῦ
τάφου περιβόητον — εὖ οἶδα οὐκ ἂν ἐπαύσω γελῶν,
οὕτω ταπεινὸς ἔρριπτο ἐν παραβύστῳ που λανθάνων
ἐν τῷ λοιπῷ δήμῳ τῶν νεκρῶν, ἐμοὶ δοκεῖν, τοσοῦτον
10 ἀπολαύων τοῦ μνήματος, παρ' ὅσον ἐβαρύνετο τηλι-
κοῦτον ἄχθος ἐπικείμενος· ἐπειδὰν γάρ, ὦ ἑταῖρε, ὁ
Αἰακὸς ἀπομετρήσῃ ἑκάστῳ τὸν τόπον—δίδωσι δὲ τὸ
μέγιστον οὐ πλέον ποδός — ἀνάγκη ἀγαπῶντα κατα-
κεῖσθαι πρὸς τὸ μέτρον συνεσταλμένον. πολλῷ δ'
15 ἄν, οἶμαι, μᾶλλον ἐγέλασας, εἰ ἐθεάσω τοὺς παρ' ἡμῖν
βασιλέας καὶ σατράπας πτωχεύοντας παρ' αὐτοῖς
καὶ ἤτοι ταριχοπωλοῦντας ὑπ' ἀπορίας ἢ τὰ πρῶτα
διδάσκοντας γράμματα καὶ ὑπὸ τοῦ τυχόντος ὑβριζο-
μένους καὶ κατὰ κόρρης παιομένους ὥσπερ τῶν ἀν-
20 δραπόδων τὰ ἀτιμότατα· Φίλιππον γοῦν τὸν Μακε-
δόνα ἐγὼ θεασάμενος οὐδὲ κρατεῖν ἐμαυτοῦ δυνατὸς
ἦν· ἐδείχθη δέ μοι ἐν γωνιδίῳ τινὶ μισθοῦ ἀκούμενος
τὰ σαθρὰ τῶν ὑποδημάτων. πολλοὺς δὲ καὶ ἄλλους
ἦν ἰδεῖν ἐν ταῖς τριόδοις μεταιτοῦντας, Ξέρξας λέγω
25 καὶ Δαρείους καὶ Πολυκράτας.

" *Why, it is almost incredible.   And Socrates, Diogenes,
&c. what of them?*"   "*Socrates goes about 'button-
holing' people as he always used to here; Diogenes
has to live side by side with Midas, and other millionaires: but he amuses himself continually by lying
on his back, and laughing or singing.*"

18.   ΦΙΛ.   Ἄτοπα διηγῇ τὰ περὶ τῶν βασιλέων
καὶ μικροῦ δεῖν ἄπιστα.   τί δὲ ὁ Σωκράτης ἔπραττε
καὶ Διογένης καὶ εἴ τις ἄλλος τῶν σοφῶν ;

ΜΕΝ.   Ὁ μὲν Σωκράτης κἀκεῖ περιέρχεται διελέγχων ἅπαντας· σύνεισι δ' αὐτῷ Παλαμήδης καὶ 5
Ὀδυσσεὺς καὶ Νέστωρ καὶ εἴ τις ἄλλος λάλος νεκρός.
ἔτι μέντοι ἐπεφύσητο αὐτῷ καὶ διῳδήκει ἐκ τῆς φαρ-
μακοποσίας τὰ σκέλη.   ὁ δὲ βέλτιστος Διογένης
παροικεῖ μὲν Σαρδαναπάλλῳ τῷ Ἀσσυρίῳ καὶ Μίδᾳ
τῷ Φρυγὶ καὶ ἄλλοις τισὶ τῶν πολυτελῶν· ἀκούων 10
δὲ οἰμωζόντων αὐτῶν καὶ τὴν παλαιὰν τύχην ἀναμε-
τρουμένων γελᾷ τε καὶ τέρπεται καὶ τὰ πολλὰ ὕπτιος
κατακείμενος ᾄδει μάλα τραχείᾳ καὶ ἀπηνεῖ τῇ φωνῇ
τὰς οἰμωγὰς αὐτῶν ἐπικαλύπτων, ὥστε ἀνιᾶσθαι τοὺς
ἄνδρας καὶ διασκέπτεσθαι μετοικεῖν οὐ φέροντας τὸν 15
Διογένην.

" *Well, but what about that decree you mentioned at the
beginning?*"   "*Thank you for reminding me!   I am
afraid I've wandered away a little; but I'll tell you.
I saw a crowd rushing along one day, so I joined in;
and heard among other business which was transacted,
the following bill proposed.*"

19.   ΦΙΛ.   Ταυτὶ μὲν ἱκανῶς· τί δὲ τὸ ψήφισμα

ἦν, ὅπερ ἐν ἀρχῇ ἔλεγες κεκυρῶσθαι κατὰ τῶν πλουσίων;

ΜΕΝ. Εὖ γε ὑπέμνησας· οὐ γὰρ οἶδ' ὅπως περὶ τούτου λέγειν προθέμενος πάμπολυ ἀπεπλανήθην
5 τοῦ λόγου. διατρίβοντος γάρ μου παρ' αὐτοῖς προὔθεσαν οἱ πρυτάνεις ἐκκλησίαν περὶ τῶν κοινῇ συμφερόντων. ἰδὼν οὖν πολλοὺς συνθέοντας ἀναμίξας ἐμαυτὸν τοῖς νεκροῖς εὐθὺς εἰς καὶ αὐτὸς ἦν τῶν ἐκκλησιαστῶν. διῳκήθη μὲν οὖν καὶ ἄλλα, τελευταῖον
10 δὲ τὸ περὶ τῶν πλουσίων· ἐπεὶ γὰρ αὐτῶν κατηγόρητο πολλὰ καὶ δεινά, βία καὶ ἀλαζονεία καὶ ὑπεροψία καὶ ἀδικία, τέλος ἀναστάς τις τῶν δημαγωγῶν ἀνέγνω ψήφισμα τοιοῦτον.

The souls of all extortioners and oppressors of the poor are to be sent into asses for 250,000 years. The bill was duly read, put to the vote, and passed.

ΨΗΦΙΣΜΑ.

20. "Ἐπειδὴ πολλὰ καὶ παράνομα οἱ πλούσιοι
15 δρῶσι παρὰ τὸν βίον ἁρπάζοντες καὶ βιαζόμενοι καὶ πάντα τρόπον τῶν πενήτων καταφρονοῦντες, δεδόχθω τῇ βουλῇ καὶ τῷ δήμῳ, ἐπειδὰν ἀποθάνωσι, τὰ μὲν σώματα αὐτῶν κολάζεσθαι καθάπερ καὶ τὰ τῶν ἄλλων πονηρῶν, τὰς δὲ ψυχὰς ἀναπεμφθείσας ἄνω ἐς τὸν
20 βίον καταδύεσθαι ἐς τοὺς ὄνους, ἄχρι ἂν ἐν τῷ τοιούτῳ διαγάγωσι μυριάδας ἐτῶν πέντε καὶ εἴκοσιν, ὄνοι ἐξ ὄνων γιγνόμενοι, καὶ ἀχθοφοροῦντες καὶ ὑπὸ τῶν πενήτων ἐλαυνόμενοι, τοὐντεῦθεν δὲ [λοιπὸν] ἐξεῖναι αὐτοῖς ἀποθανεῖν. εἶπε τὴν γνώμην Κρανίων Σκελε-
25 τίωνος Νεκυσιεὺς φυλῆς Ἀλιβαντίδος." τούτου ἀναγνωσθέντος τοῦ ψηφίσματος ἐπεψήφισαν μὲν αἱ ἀρ-

χαί, ἐπεχειροτόνησε δὲ τὸ πλῆθος καὶ ἐνεβριμήσατο
ἡ Βριμὼ καὶ ὑλάκτησεν ὁ Κέρβερος. οὕτω γὰρ ἐντελῆ,
γίγνεται καὶ κύρια τὰ ἀνεγνωσμένα.

*"So much for the decree. But about Teiresias: I found him to
be a little old man, pale, and thin-voiced and blind. He
guessed the object of my journey, but said he couldn't
reveal such secrets. After a little inducement, however, he led me aside and whispered in my ear, 'The
life of a plain citizen is best—make good use of the present time; eschew metaphysical research, and have
nothing to do with philosophers.'*

21. Ταῦτα μὲν δή σοι τὰ ἐν τῇ ἐκκλησίᾳ. ἐγὼ
δὲ, οὗπερ ἀφίγμην ἔνεκα, τῷ Τειρεσίᾳ προσελθὼν 5
ἱκέτευον αὐτὸν τὰ πάντα διηγησάμενος εἰπεῖν πρός με
ποῖόν τινα ἡγεῖται τὸν ἄριστον βίον. ὁ δὲ γελάσας
— ἔστι δὲ τυφλόν τι γερόντιον καὶ ὠχρὸν καὶ λεπτό-
φωνον — ὦ τέκνον, φησί, τὴν μὲν αἰτίαν οἶδά σοι τῆς
ἀπορίας ὅτι παρὰ τῶν σοφῶν ἐγένετο οὐ τὰ αὐτὰ 10
γιγνωσκόντων ἑαυτοῖς· ἀτὰρ οὐ θέμις λέγειν πρὸς σέ·
ἀπείρηται γὰρ ὑπὸ Ῥαδαμάνθυος. μηδαμῶς, ἔφην, ὦ
πατέριον, ἀλλ' εἰπὲ καὶ μὴ περιίδῃς με σοῦ τυφλότε-
ρον περιιόντα ἐν τῷ βίῳ. ὁ δὲ δή με ἀπαγαγὼν καὶ
πολὺ τῶν ἄλλων ἀποσπάσας ἠρέμα προσκύψας πρὸς 15
τὸ οὖς φησιν, ὁ τῶν ἰδιωτῶν ἄριστος βίος, ὥστε τῆς
ἀφροσύνης παυσάμενος τοῦ μετεωρολογεῖν καὶ τέλη
καὶ ἀρχὰς ἐπισκοπεῖν καὶ καταπτύσας τῶν σοφῶν
τούτων συλλογισμῶν καὶ τὰ τοιαῦτα λῆρον ἡγησάμενος τοῦτο μόνον ἐξ ἅπαντος θήρασαι, ὅπως τὸ παρὸν 20
εὖ θέμενος παραδράμῃ γελῶν τὰ πολλὰ καὶ περὶ
μηδὲν ἐσπουδακώς.

ὡς εἰπὼν πάλιν ὦρτο κατ' ἀσφοδελὸν λειμῶνα.

"*Having accomplished my object, I told Mithrobarzanes we had better return. He led me into a very dark tunnel, where a little glimmering of light could be seen through a tiny hole. 'The Temple of Trophonius' he said. I crept through the hole, with some difficulty, and found myself here.*"

22. Ἐγὼ δὲ — καὶ γὰρ ἤδη ὀψὲ ἦν — ἄγε δή, ὦ Μιθροβαρζάνη, φημί, τί διαμέλλομεν καὶ οὐκ ἄπιμεν αὖθις ἐς τὸν βίον ; ὁ δὲ πρὸς ταῦτα, θάρρει, φησίν, ὦ
5 Μένιππε· ταχεῖαν γάρ σοι καὶ ἀπράγμονα ὑποδείξω ἀτραπόν. καὶ δὴ ἀπαγαγών με πρός τι χωρίον τοῦ ἄλλου ζοφερώτερον δείξας τῇ χειρὶ πόρρωθεν ἀμαυρόν τι καὶ λεπτὸν ὥσπερ διὰ κλειθρίας ἐσρέον φῶς, ἐκεῖνο, ἔφη, ἐστὶ τὸ ἱερὸν τὸ Τροφωνίου, κἀκεῖθεν κατίασιν
10 οἱ ἀπὸ Βοιωτίας· ταύτην οὖν ἄνιθι καὶ εὐθὺς ἔσῃ ἐπὶ τῆς Ἑλλάδος. ἡσθεὶς δὲ τοῖς εἰρημένοις ἐγὼ καὶ τὸν μάγον ἀσπασάμενος χαλεπῶς μάλα διὰ τοῦ στομίου ἀνερπύσας οὐκ οἶδ' ὅπως ἐν Λεβαδείᾳ γίγνομαι.

ΤΙΜΩΝ Η ΜΙΣΑΝΘΡΩΠΟΣ.

ΤΙΜΩΝ, ΖΕΥΣ, ΕΡΜΗΣ, ΠΛΟΥΤΟΣ, ΠΕΝΙΑ, ΓΝΑΘΩΝΙΔΗΣ,
ΦΙΛΙΑΔΗΣ, ΔΗΜΕΑΣ, ΘΡΑΣΥΚΛΗΣ.

Timon (*stopping his work, and leaning on his spade*), "*O
Zeus, Thou god of Friendship, Hearths, Oaths, &c.
&c. What* has *become of thy lightning, and thunder
and bolts? Are they all cold? Hast thou not one
spark left with which to scorch rascals? Men are no
longer afraid of thy lightning; it is no better than
a smoky torch. Thou art surely under the influence
of some drug, or half-blind, or deaf.*

1. ΤΙΜ. Ὦ Ζεῦ φίλιε καὶ ξένιε καὶ ἑταιρεῖε καὶ
ἐφέστιε καὶ ἀστεροπητὰ καὶ ὅρκιε καὶ νεφεληγερέτα
καὶ ἐρίγδουπε καὶ εἴ τί σε ἄλλο οἱ ἐμβρόντητοι ποιη-
ταὶ καλοῦσι, καὶ μάλιστα ὅταν ἀπορῶσι πρὸς τὰ
μέτρα· τότε γὰρ αὐτοῖς πολυώνυμος γιγνόμενος ὑπ- 5
ερείδεις τὸ πῖπτον τοῦ μέτρου καὶ ἀναπληροῖς τὸ κεχηνὸς τοῦ ῥυθμοῦ· ποῦ σοι νῦν ἡ ἐρισμάραγος ἀστραπὴ
καὶ ἡ βαρύβρομος βροντὴ καὶ ὁ αἰθαλόεις καὶ ἀργήεις
καὶ σμερδαλέος κεραυνός; ἅπαντα γὰρ ταῦτα λῆρος
ἤδη ἀναπέφηνε καὶ καπνὸς ποιητικὸς ἀτεχνῶς ἔξω 10
τοῦ πατάγου τῶν ὀνομάτων. τὸ δὲ ἀοίδιμόν σου καὶ
ἐκηβόλον ὅπλον καὶ πρόχειρον οὐκ οἶδ᾽ ὅπως τελέως

ἀπέσβη καὶ ψυχρόν ἐστι μηδὲ ὀλίγον σπινθῆρα ὀργῆς
κατὰ τῶν ἀδικούντων διαφυλάττον.

2. Θᾶττον γοῦν τῶν ἐπιορκεῖν τις ἐπιχειρούντων
ἔωλον θρυαλλίδα φοβηθείη ἂν ἢ τὴν τοῦ πανδαμάτο-
5 ρος κεραυνοῦ φλόγα· οὕτω δαλόν τινα ἐπανατείνεσθαι
δοκεῖς αὐτοῖς, ὡς πῦρ μὲν ἢ καπνὸν ἀπ' αὐτοῦ μὴ δεδιέναι, μόνον δὲ τοῦτο οἴεσθαι ἀπολαύσειν τοῦ τραύματος, ὅτι ἀναπλησθήσονται τῆς ἀσβόλου. ὥστε ἤδη
διὰ ταῦτά σοι καὶ ὁ Σαλμωνεὺς ἀντιβροντᾶν ἐτόλμα,
10 οὐ πάντη ἀπίθανος ὤν, πρὸς οὕτω ψυχρὸν τὴν ὀργὴν
Δία θερμουργὸς ἀνὴρ μεγαλαυχούμενος. πῶς γάρ;
ὅπου γε καθάπερ ὑπὸ μανδραγόρα καθεύδεις, ὃς οὔτε
τῶν ἐπιορκούντων ἀκούεις οὔτε τοὺς ἀδικοῦντας ἐπι-
σκοπεῖς, λημᾷς δὲ καὶ ἀμβλυώττεις πρὸς τὰ γιγνό-
15 μενα καὶ τὰ ὦτα ἐκκεκώφησαι καθάπερ οἱ παρηβηκότες.

" When thou wast young and hot-brained, men trembled before
thy arms ; there were most terrible earthquakes and
floods then : now thou art too lazy ; and hast reaped
the fruits of idleness. No man honours thee ; and
soon thy fate will be like thy father's ; thy temples are
robbed, thine own person dishonoured, but thou dost not
even trouble to undo the dogs—Will there never be an
end to all this ?

3. Ἐπεὶ νέος γε ἔτι καὶ ὀξύθυμος ὢν καὶ ἀκμαῖος
τὴν ὀργὴν πολλὰ κατὰ τῶν ἀδίκων καὶ βιαίων ἐποίεις
καὶ οὐδέποτε ἦγες τότε πρὸς αὐτοὺς ἐκεχειρίαν, ἀλλ'
20 ἀεὶ ἐνεργὸς πάντως ὁ κεραυνὸς ἦν καὶ ἡ αἰγὶς ἐπε-
σείετο καὶ ἡ βροντὴ ἐπαταγεῖτο καὶ ἡ ἀστραπὴ συνεχὲς ὥσπερ εἰς ἀκροβολισμὸν προηκοντίζετο· οἱ

σεισμοὶ δὲ κοσκινηδὸν καὶ ἡ χιὼν σωρηδὸν καὶ ἡ χά-
λαζα πετρηδόν· καὶ ἵνα σοι φορτικῶς διαλέγωμαι,
ὑετοί τε ῥαγδαῖοι καὶ βίαιοι, ποταμὸς ἑκάστη σταγών·
ὥστε τηλικαύτη ἐν ἀκαρεῖ χρόνου ναυαγία ἐπὶ τοῦ
Δευκαλίωνος ἐγένετο, ὡς ὑποβρυχίων ἁπάντων κατα- 5
δεδυκότων μόγις ἕν τι κιβώτιον περισωθῆναι προσοκεῖλαν τῷ Λυκωρεῖ ζώπυρόν τι τοῦ ἀνθρωπίνου
σπέρματος διαφυλάττον εἰς ἐπιγονὴν κακίας μείζονος.

4. Τοιγάρτοι ἀκόλουθα τῆς ῥαθυμίας τἀπίχειρα
κομίζῃ παρ᾽ αὐτῶν, οὔτε θύοντός ἔτι σοί τινος οὔτε 10
στεφανοῦντος, εἰ μή τις ἄρα πάρεργον Ὀλυμπίων,
καὶ οὗτος οὐ πάνυ ἀναγκαῖα ποιεῖν δοκῶν, ἀλλ᾽ εἰς
ἔθος τι ἀρχαῖον συντελῶν· καὶ κατ᾽ ὀλίγον Κρόνον
σε, ὦ θεῶν γενναιότατε, ἀποφανοῦσι παρωσάμενοι τῆς
τιμῆς. ἐῶ λέγειν ποσάκις ἤδη σου τὸν νεὼν σεσυλή- 15
κασιν· οἱ δὲ καὶ αὐτῷ σοι τὰς χεῖρας Ὀλυμπίασιν
ἐπιβεβλήκασι, καὶ σὺ ὁ ὑψιβρεμέτης ὤκνησας ἢ ἀναστῆσαι τοὺς κύνας ἢ τοὺς γείτονας ἐπικαλέσασθαι,
ὡς βοηδρομήσαντες αὐτοὺς συλλάβοιεν ἔτι συσκευαζομένους πρὸς τὴν φυγήν· ἀλλ᾽ ὁ γενναῖος καὶ Γιγαν- 20
τολέτωρ καὶ Τιτανοκράτωρ ἐκάθησο τοὺς πλοκάμους
περικειρόμενος ὑπ᾽ αὐτῶν, δεκάπηχυν κεραυνὸν ἔχων
ἐν τῇ δεξιᾷ. ταῦτα τοίνυν, ὦ θαυμάσιε, πηνίκα παύσεται οὕτως ἀμελῶς παρορώμενα; ἢ πότε κολάσῃ τὴν
τοσαύτην ἀδικίαν; πόσοι Φαέθοντες ἢ Δευκαλίωνες 25
ἱκανοὶ πρὸς οὕτως ὑπέραντλον ὕβριν τοῦ βίου;

"Just look at me! How many Athenians have I not exalted,
   and enriched!—aye! poured out my wealth wholesale
   on them, with what result? I am now so poor, they
   will not even look at me. I might be an old moss-

grown stone, they scorn me so! And here I dig—out-cast, and despised—alone with my spade, and clad in an old sheepskin. Well! at least I shall not see 'the ungodly in great power' if I stay here. But, Zeus, Zeus, wake up and blow on thy bolt, and make it blaze—and come and help me!"

5. "Ἵνα γὰρ τὰ κοινὰ ἐάσας τἀμὰ εἴπω, τοσού-τους Ἀθηναίων εἰς ὕψος ἄρας καὶ πλουσίους ἐκ πενεστάτων ἀποφήνας καὶ πᾶσι τοῖς δεομένοις ἐπι-κουρήσας, μᾶλλον δὲ ἀθρόον εἰς εὐεργεσίαν τῶν φίλων
5 ἐκχέας τὸν πλοῦτον, ἐπειδὴ πένης διὰ ταῦτα ἐγενόμην, οὐκέτι οὐδὲ γνωρίζομαι πρὸς αὐτῶν οὐδὲ προσβλέπ-ουσιν οἱ τέως ὑποπτήσσοντες καὶ προσκυνοῦντες κἀκ τοῦ ἐμοῦ νεύματος ἀπηρτημένοι, ἀλλ᾽ ἤν που καὶ ὁδῷ βαδίζων ἐντύχω τινὶ αὐτῶν, ὥσπερ τινὰ στήλην
10 παλαιοῦ νεκροῦ ὑπτίαν ὑπὸ τοῦ χρόνου ἀνατετραμμέ-νην παρέρχονται μηδὲ ἀναγνόντες, οἱ δὲ καὶ πόρρωθεν ἰδόντες ἑτέραν ἐκτρέπονται δυσάντητον καὶ ἀποτρόπ-αιον θέαμα ὄψεσθαι ὑπολαμβάνοντες τὸν οὐ πρὸ πολλοῦ σωτῆρα καὶ εὐεργέτην αὐτῶν γεγενημένον.

15 6. Ὥστε ὑπὸ τῶν κακῶν ἐπὶ ταύτην τὴν ἐσχα-τιὰν τραπόμενος ἐναψάμενος διφθέραν ἐργάζομαι τὴν γῆν ὑπόμισθος ὀβολῶν τεττάρων, τῇ ἐρημίᾳ καὶ τῇ δικέλλῃ προσφιλοσοφῶν. ἐνταῦθα τοῦτο γοῦν μοι δοκῶ κερδανεῖν, μηκέτι ὄψεσθαι πολλοὺς παρὰ τὴν
20 ἀξίαν εὖ πράττοντας· ἀνιαρότατον γὰρ τοῦτό γε. ἤδη ποτὲ οὖν, ὦ Κρόνου καὶ Ῥέας υἱέ, τὸν βαθὺν τοῦτον ὕπνον ἀποσεισάμενος καὶ νήδυμον — ὑπὲρ τὸν Ἐπι-μενίδην γὰρ κεκοίμησαι — καὶ ἀναρριπίσας τὸν κε-ραυνὸν ἢ ἐκ τῆς Αἴτνης ἐναυσάμενος μεγάλην ποιήσας
25 τὴν φλόγα ἐπιδείξαιό τινα χολὴν ἀνδρώδους καὶ νεα-

νικοῦ Διός, εἰ μὴ ἀληθῆ ἐστι τὰ ὑπὸ Κρητῶν περὶ σοῦ
καὶ τῆς ἐκεῖ ταφῆς μυθολογούμενα.

Zeus : " *Hermes, who is that bawling so ? Probably some
philosopher, judging by his language !"* Hermes:
" *What ! father, not know Timon of Athens, the man
who used to treat us so handsomely ?"* " *O how sad !
what a change ! How did it come about ?"*

7. ΖΕΥΣ. Τίς οὗτός ἐστιν, ὦ Ἑρμῆ, ὁ κεκραγὼς
ἐκ τῆς Ἀττικῆς παρὰ τὸν Ὑμηττὸν ἐν τῇ ὑπωρείᾳ
πιναρὸς ὅλος καὶ αὐχμῶν καὶ ὑποδίφθερος; σκάπτει 5
δὲ οἶμαι ἐπικεκυφώς· λάλος ἄνθρωπος καὶ θρασύς.
ἢ που φιλόσοφός ἐστιν· οὐ γὰρ ἂν οὕτως ἀσεβεῖς
τοὺς λόγους διεξῄει καθ᾽ ἡμῶν.

ΕΡΜ. Τί φής, ὦ πάτερ; ἀγνοεῖς Τίμωνα τὸν
Ἐχεκρατίδου τὸν Κολλυτέα; οὗτός ἐστιν ὁ πολλάκις 10
ἡμᾶς καθ᾽ ἱερῶν τελείων ἑστιάσας, ὁ νεόπλουτος, ὁ
τὰς ὅλας ἑκατόμβας, παρ᾽ ᾧ λαμπρῶς εἰώθεμεν ἑορ-
τάζειν τὰ Διάσια.

ΖΕΥΣ. Φεῦ τῆς ἀλλαγῆς· ὁ καλὸς ἐκεῖνος, ὁ
πλούσιος, περὶ ὃν οἱ τοσοῦτοι φίλοι; τί παθών, τοι- 15
οῦτός ἐστιν ; αὐχμηρός, ἄθλιος καὶ σκαπανεὺς καὶ
μισθωτός, ὡς ἔοικεν, οὕτω βαρεῖαν καταφέρων τὴν
δίκελλαν.

" *Well ! to tell you the truth, it was simple-heartedness
which ruined him. He looked upon the greatest of
toadies and ' sharks' as a thorough friend. And now
they have bled him as much as they can, they will not
even look at him ; so he has left the city, and taken to
digging, as a livelihood.*"

8. ΕΡΜ. Οὑτωσὶ μὲν εἰπεῖν, χρηστότης ἐπί-
τριψεν αὐτὸν καὶ φιλανθρωπία καὶ ὁ πρὸς τοὺς δεο-
μένους ἅπαντας οἶκτος, ὡς δὲ ἀληθεῖ λόγῳ, ἄνοια καὶ
εὐήθεια καὶ ἀκρισία περὶ τῶν φίλων, ὃς οὐ συνίει
5 κόραξι καὶ λύκοις χαριζόμενος, ἀλλ' ὑπὸ γυπῶν τοσούτων ὁ κακοδαίμων κειρόμενος τὸ ἧπαρ φίλους εἶναι
αὐτοὺς καὶ ἑταίρους ᾤετο, ὑπ' εὐνοίας τῆς πρὸς αὐτὸν
χαίροντας τῇ βορᾷ· οἱ δὲ τὰ ὀστᾶ γυμνώσαντες ἀκριβῶς καὶ περιτραγόντες, εἰ δέ τις καὶ μυελὸς ἐνῆν,
10 ἐκμυζήσαντες καὶ τοῦτον εὖ μάλα ἐπιμελῶς, ᾤχοντο
αὖον αὐτὸν καὶ τὰς ῥίζας ὑποτετμημένον ἀπολιπόντες,
οὐδὲ γνωρίζοντες ἔτι οὐδὲ προσβλέποντες — πόθεν
γάρ; — ἢ ἐπικουροῦντες ἢ ἐπιδιδόντες ἐν τῷ μέρει.
διὰ ταῦτα δικελλίτης καὶ διφθερίας, ὡς ὁρᾷς, ἀπολι-
15 πὼν ὑπ' αἰσχύνης τὸ ἄστυ μισθοῦ γεωργεῖ μελαγχολῶν τοῖς κακοῖς, ὅτι οἱ πλουτοῦντες παρ' αὐτοῦ μάλα
ὑπεροπτικῶς παρέρχονται οὐδὲ τοὔνομα, εἰ Τίμων
καλοῖτο, εἰδότες.

"*Oh! but this man must not be passed over, or we shall
be as bad as his parasites. The fact is I've been so
occupied with false-swearers, extortioners, and sacrile-
gious rascals, that I've not had time to look at Attica
lately.*

9. ΖΕΥΣ. Καὶ μὴν οὐ παροπτέος ἀνὴρ οὐδὲ
20 ἀμελητέος· εἰκότως γὰρ ἠγανάκτει δυστυχῶν· ἐπεὶ
καὶ ὅμοια ποιήσομεν τοῖς καταράτοις κόλαξιν ἐκείνοις
ἐπιλελησμένοι ἀνδρὸς τοσαῦτα μηρία ταύρων τε καὶ
αἰγῶν πιότατα καύσαντος ἡμῖν ἐπὶ τῶν βωμῶν· ἔτι
γοῦν ἐν ταῖς ῥισὶ τὴν κνῖσαν αὐτῶν ἔχω. πλὴν ὑπ'
25 ἀσχολίας τε καὶ θορύβου πολλοῦ τῶν ἐπιορκούντων

καὶ βιαζομένων καὶ ἁρπαζόντων, ἔτι δε καὶ φόβου τοῦ
παρὰ τῶν ἱεροσυλούντων — πολλοὶ γὰρ οὗτοι καὶ
δυσφύλακτοι καὶ οὐδὲ ἐπ' ὀλίγον καταμύσαι ἡμῖν
ἐφιᾶσι — πολὺν ἤδη χρόνον οὐδὲ ἀπέβλεψα ἐς τὴν
Ἀττικήν, καὶ μάλιστα ἐξ οὗ φιλοσοφία καὶ λόγων 5
ἔριδες ἐπεπόλασαν αὐτοῖς· μαχομένων γὰρ πρὸς ἀλλήλους καὶ κεκραγότων οὐδὲ ἐπακούειν ἔστι τῶν εὐχῶν·
ὥστε ἢ ἐπιβυσάμενον χρὴ τὰ ὦτα καθῆσθαι ἢ ἐπιτρι-
βῆναι πρὸς αὐτῶν, ἀρετήν τινα καὶ ἀσώματα καὶ
λήρους μεγάλῃ τῇ φωνῇ συνειρόντων. διὰ ταῦτά τοι 10
καὶ τοῦτον ἀμεληθῆναι συνέβη πρὸς ἡμῶν οὐ φαῦλον
ὄντα.

"So, Hermes, take Plutus and Thesaurus, and go quickly to
Timon. Meanwhile I will think about punishing
these flatterers; I am sorry to say my two best bolts
are broken; but I think I shall make the scamps pay
sufficient penalty for the present if I make Timon's
wealth an object of the greatest envy."

10. Ὅμως δὲ τὸν Πλοῦτον, ὦ Ἑρμῆ, παραλαβὼν
ἄπιθι παρ' αὐτὸν κατὰ τάχος· ἀγέτω δὲ ὁ Πλοῦτος
καὶ τὸν Θησαυρὸν μεθ' αὑτοῦ καὶ μενέτωσαν ἄμφω 15
παρὰ τῷ Τίμωνι μηδὲ ἀπαλλαττέσθωσαν οὕτω ῥᾳδίως, κἂν ὅτι μάλιστα ὑπὸ χρηστότητος αὖθις ἐκδιώκῃ
αὐτοὺς τῆς οἰκίας. περὶ δὲ τῶν κολάκων ἐκείνων καὶ
τῆς ἀχαριστίας, ἣν ἐπεδείξαντο πρὸς αὐτόν, καὶ αὖθις
μὲν σκέψομαι καὶ δίκην δώσουσιν, ἐπειδὰν τὸν κεραυ- 20
νὸν ἐπισκευάσω· κατεαγμέναι γὰρ αὐτοῦ καὶ ἀπεστο-
μωμέναι εἰσὶ δύο ἀκτῖνες αἱ μέγισται, ὁπότε φιλοτι-
μότερον ἠκόντισα πρώην ἐπὶ τὸν σοφιστὴν Ἀναξαγόραν, ὃς ἔπειθε τοὺς ὁμιλητὰς μηδὲ ὅλως εἶναι [τινας]

ἡμᾶς τοὺς θεούς. ἀλλ᾽ ἐκείνου μὲν διήμαρτον,—ὑπερ-
έσχε γὰρ αὐτοῦ τὴν χεῖρα Περικλῆς—ὁ δὲ κεραυνὸς
ἐς τὸ Ἀνάκειον παρασκήψας ἐκεῖνό τε κατέφλεξε καὶ
αὐτὸς ὀλίγου δεῖν συνετρίβη περὶ τῇ πέτρᾳ. πλὴν
5 ἱκανὴ ἐν τοσούτῳ καὶ αὕτη τιμωρία ἔσται αὐτοῖς, εἰ
ὑπερπλουτοῦντα τὸν Τίμωνα ὁρῶσιν.

Hermes: " *What a fine thing bawling is! Here is
Timon, going to have his poverty changed for great
wealth, all because of his shouting!*" Plut.: "*But I
have no intention of going to him !*" Zeus: "*Not if
I tell you, Plutus ?*"

11. ΕΡΜ. Οἷον ἦν τὸ μέγα κεκραγέναι καὶ
ὀχληρὸν εἶναι καὶ θρασύν. οὐ τοῖς δικαιολογοῦσι
μόνοις, ἀλλὰ καὶ τοῖς εὐχομένοις τοῦτο χρήσιμον·
10 ἰδού γέ τοι αὐτίκα μάλα πλούσιος ἐκ πενεστάτου
καταστήσεται ὁ Τίμων βοήσας καὶ παρρησιασάμενος
ἐν τῇ εὐχῇ καὶ ἐπιστρέψας τὸν Δία· εἰ δὲ σιωπῇ
ἔσκαπτεν ἐπικεκυφώς, ἔτι ἂν ἔσκαπτεν ἀμελούμενος.

ΠΛΟΥΤ. Ἀλλ᾽ ἐγὼ οὐκ ἂν ἀπέλθοιμι, ὦ Ζεῦ,
15 παρ᾽ αὐτόν.

ΖΕΥΣ. Διὰ τί, ὦ ἄριστε Πλοῦτε, καὶ ταῦτα ἐμοῦ
κελεύσαντος;

*Plutus goes on to give his reasons for not wishing to go.
Timon only scatters him wholesale, as soon as he can
get hold of him. Won't Zeus send him to some one
better able to appreciate the gift? Ah! but Timon
will have grown wiser now, replies Zeus ; besides, you
seem very difficult to please. Here you grumble at
being scattered too freely—at other times you make complaint of being shut up under lock and seal, until your*

complexion is quite pale, and your joints stiff; and
those who possess you will neither enjoy you themselves
nor allow others to do so.

12. ΠΛΟΥΤ. Ὅτι νὴ Δία ὕβριζεν εἰς ἐμὲ καὶ
ἐξεφόρει καὶ ἐς πολλὰ κατεμέριζε καὶ ταῦτα πατρῷον
αὐτῷ φίλον ὄντα, καὶ μονονουχὶ δικράνοις με ἐξεώθει
τῆς οἰκίας καθάπερ οἱ τὸ πῦρ ἐκ τῶν χειρῶν ἀπορ-
ριπτοῦντες. αὖθις οὖν ἀπέλθω παρασίτοις καὶ κόλαξι 5
καὶ ἑταίραις παραδοθησόμενος; ἐπ᾽ ἐκείνους, ὦ Ζεῦ,
πέμπε με τοὺς αἰσθησομένους τῆς δωρεᾶς, τοὺς περιέψοντας, οἷς τίμιος ἐγὼ καὶ περιπόθητος· οὗτοι δὲ οἱ
λάροι τῇ πενίᾳ συνέστωσαν, ἣν προτιμῶσιν ἡμῶν, καὶ
διφθέραν παρ᾽ αὐτῆς λαβόντες καὶ δίκελλαν ἀγαπά- 10
τωσαν ἄθλιοι τέτταρας ὀβολοὺς ἀποφέροντες, οἱ δεκα-
ταλάντους δωρεὰς ἀμελητὶ προϊέμενοι.

13. ΖΕΥΣ. Οὐδὲν ἔτι τοιοῦτον ὁ Τίμων ἐργάσεται περὶ σέ· πάνυ γὰρ αὐτὸν ἡ δίκελλα πεπαιδαγώγηκεν, εἰ μὴ παντάπασιν ἀνάλγητός ἐστι τὴν ὀσφύν, 15
ὡς χρῆν σὲ ἀντὶ τῆς πενίας προαιρεῖσθαι. σὺ μέντοι
πάνυ μεμψίμοιρος εἶναί μοι δοκεῖς, ὃς νῦν μὲν τὸν
Τίμωνα αἰτιᾷ, διότι σοι τὰς θύρας ἀναπετάσας ἠφίει
περινοστεῖν ἐλευθέρως οὔτε ἀποκλείων οὔτε ζηλοτυ-
πῶν· ἄλλοτε δὲ τοὐναντίον ἠγανάκτεις κατὰ τῶν 20
πλουσίων κατακεκλεῖσθαι λέγων πρὸς αὐτῶν ὑπὸ
μοχλοῖς καὶ κλεισὶ καὶ σημείων ἐπιβολαῖς, ὡς μηδὲ
παρακῦψαί σοι ἐς τὸ φῶς δυνατὸν εἶναι. ταῦτα γοῦν
ἀπωδύρου πρός με ἀποπνίγεσθαι λέγων ἐν πολλῷ τῷ
σκότῳ· καὶ διὰ τοῦτο ὠχρὸς ἡμῖν ἐφαίνου καὶ φρον- 25
τίδος ἀνάπλεως, συνεσπακὼς τοὺς δακτύλους πρὸς τὸ
ἔθος τῶν λογισμῶν καὶ ἀποδράσεσθαι ἀπειλῶν, εἰ

καιροῦ λάβοιο, παρ' αὐτῶν· καὶ ὅλως, τὸ πρᾶγμα
ὑπέρδεινον ἐδόκει σοι, ἐκ χαλκῷ ἢ σιδηρῷ τῷ θαλάμῳ
καθάπερ τὴν Δανάην παρθενεύεσθαι ὑπ' ἀκριβέσι καὶ
παμπονήροις παιδαγωγοῖς ἀνατρεφόμενον, τῷ Τόκῳ
5 καὶ τῷ Λογισμῷ.

14. Ἄτοπα γοῦν ποιεῖν ἔφασκες αὐτοὺς ἐρῶντας
μὲν εἰς ὑπερβολήν, ἐξὸν δὲ ἀπολαύειν οὐ τολμῶντας,
οὐδὲ ἐπ' ἀδείας χρωμένους τῷ ἔρωτι κυρίους γε ὄντας,
ἀλλὰ φυλάττειν ἐγρηγορότας, ἐς τὸ σημεῖον καὶ τὸν
10 μοχλὸν ἀσκαρδαμυκτὶ βλέποντας, ἱκανὴν ἀπόλαυσιν
οἰομένους οὐ τὸ αὐτοὺς ἀπολαύειν ἔχειν, ἀλλὰ τὸ μη-
δενὶ μεταδιδόναι τῆς ἀπολαύσεως, καθάπερ τὴν ἐν τῇ
φάτνῃ κύνα μήτε αὐτὴν ἐσθίουσαν τῶν κριθῶν μήτε
τῷ ἵππῳ πεινῶντι ἐπιτρέπουσαν. καὶ προσέτι γε καὶ
15 κατεγέλας αὐτῶν φειδομένων καὶ φυλαττόντων καὶ τὸ
καινότατον αὐτοὺς ζηλοτυπούντων, ἀγνοούντων δὲ ὡς
κατάρατος οἰκέτης ἢ οἰκονόμος πεδότριψ ὑπεισιὼν
λαθραίως ἐμπαροινήσει τὸν κακοδαίμονα καὶ ἀνέρα-
στον δεσπότην πρὸς ἀμαυρόν τι καὶ μικρόστομον
20 λυχνίδιον καὶ διψαλέον θρυαλλίδιον ἐπαγρυπνεῖν
ἐάσας τοῖς τόκοις. πῶς οὖν οὐκ ἄδικα ταῦτα, πάλαι
μὲν ἐκεῖνα αἰτιᾶσθαι, νῦν δὲ τῷ Τίμωνι τὰ ἐναντία
ἐπικαλεῖν;

"Well! but there is surely a mean between these two
extremes; there is a wide difference between the extra-
vagant spendthrift, and the stingy miser."

15. ΠΛΟΥΤ. Καὶ μὴν εἴ γε τἀληθὲς ἐξετάζοις,
25 ἄμφω σοι εὔλογα δόξω ποιεῖν· τοῦ τε γὰρ Τίμωνος τὸ
πάνυ τοῦτο ἀνειμένον ἀμελὲς καὶ οὐκ εὐνοϊκὸν ὡς
πρὸς ἐμὲ εἰκότως ἂν δοκοίη, τούς τε αὖ κατάκλειστον

ἐν θύραις καὶ σκότῳ φυλάττοντας, ὅπως αὐτοῖς παχύ-
τερος γενοίμην καὶ πιμελὴς καὶ ὑπέρογκος ἐπιμελου-
μένους, οὔτε προσαπτομένους αὐτοὺς οὔτε ἐς τὸ φῶς
προάγοντας, ὡς μηδὲ ὀφθείην πρός τινος, ἀνοήτους
ἐνόμιζον εἶναι καὶ ὑβριστάς, οὐδὲν ἀδικοῦντά με ὑπὸ 5
τοσούτοις δεσμοῖς κατασήποντας, οὐκ εἰδότας ὡς μετὰ
μικρὸν ἀπίασιν ἄλλῳ τινὶ τῶν εὐδαιμόνων με κατα-
λιπόντες.

*Plutus says his fate is as bad as that of a young maiden
shut up in close confinement by one who professes to
love her deeply.*

16. Οὔτ᾽ οὖν ἐκείνους οὔτε τοὺς πάνυ προχείρους
εἰς ἐμὲ τούτους ἐπαινῶ, ἀλλὰ τούς, ὅπερ ἄριστόν ἐστι, 10
μέτρον ἐπιθήσοντας τῷ πράγματι καὶ μήτε ἀφεξομέ-
νους τὸ παράπαν μήτε προησομένους τὸ ὅλον. σκόπει
γὰρ, ὦ Ζεῦ, πρὸς τοῦ Διός, εἴ τις νόμῳ γήμας γυναῖκα
νέαν καὶ καλὴν ἔπειτα μήτε φυλάττοι μήτε ζηλοτυ-
ποῖ τὸ παράπαν, ἀφιεὶς καὶ βαδίζειν ἔνθα ἂν ἐθέλοι 15
νύκτωρ καὶ μεθ᾽ ἡμέραν, ἆρα ὁ τοιοῦτος ἐρᾶν δόξειεν
ἄν; οὐ σύ γε, ὦ Ζεῦ, τοῦτο φαίης ἂν ἐρασθεὶς πολλάκις.

17. Εἰ δέ τις ἔμπαλιν ἐλευθέραν γυναῖκα ἐς
τὴν οἰκίαν νόμῳ παραλαβών, ὁ δὲ μήτε αὐτὸς προσ- 20
άπτοιτο ἀκμαίας καὶ καλῆς παρθένου μήτε ἄλλῳ
προσβλέπειν ἐπιτρέποι, καὶ ταῦτα ἐρᾶν φάσκων καὶ
δῆλος ὢν ἀπὸ τῆς χρόας καὶ τῆς σαρκὸς ἐκτετηκυίας
καὶ τῶν ὀφθαλμῶν ὑποδεδυκότων, ἔσθ᾽ ὅπως ὁ
τοιοῦτος οὐ παραπαίειν δόξειεν ἄν, καταμαραίνων 25
εὐπρόσωπον οὕτω καὶ ἐπέραστον κόρην καθάπερ
ἱέρειαν τῇ Θεσμοφόρῳ τρέφων διὰ παντὸς τοῦ βίου;

ταῦτα καὶ αὐτὸς ἀγανακτῶ πρὸς ἐνίων μὲν ἀτίμως
λακτιζόμενος καὶ λαφυττόμενος καὶ ἐξαντλούμενος,
ὑπ᾽ ἐνίων δὲ ὥσπερ στιγματίας δραπέτης πεπεδη-
μένος.

"Never mind, Plutus, both get paid out eventually. Anyhow, do go !" "Yes, and be poured out almost before
I'm in—like water from a leaky tub." "Well, good
bye; and, Hermes, don't forget to remind the Cyclops
about my bolt."

5   18. ΖΕΥΣ. Τί οὖν ἀγανακτεῖς κατ᾽ αὐτῶν; διδόασι γὰρ ἄμφω καλὴν τὴν δίκην, οἱ μὲν ὥσπερ ὁ
Τάνταλος ἄποτοι καὶ ἄγευστοι καὶ ξηροὶ τὸ στόμα,
ἐπικεχηνότες μόνον τῷ χρυσίῳ, οἱ δὲ καθάπερ ὁ
Φινεὺς ἀπὸ τῆς φάρυγγος τὴν τροφὴν ὑπὸ τῶν Ἁρ-
10 πυιῶν ἀφαιρούμενοι. ἀλλ᾽ ἄπιθι ἤδη σωφρονεστέρῳ
παρὰ πολὺ τῷ Τίμωνι ἐντευξόμενος.

ΠΛΟΥΤ. Ἐκεῖνος γάρ ποτε παύσεται ὥσπερ ἐκ
κοφίνου τετρυπημένου, πρὶν ὅλως εἰσρυῆναί με, κατὰ
σπουδὴν ἐξαντλῶν, φθάσαι βουλόμενος τὴν ἐπιρροήν,
15 μὴ ὑπέραντλος ἐσπεσὼν ἐπικλύσω αὐτόν; ὥστε ἐς
τὸν τῶν Δαναΐδων πίθον ὑδροφορήσειν μοι δοκῶ καὶ
μάτην ἐπαντλήσειν, τοῦ κύτους μὴ στέγοντος, ἀλλὰ
πρὶν εἰσρυῆναι, σχεδὸν ἐκχυθησομένου τοῦ ἐπιρρέον-
τος· οὕτως εὐρύτερον τὸ πρὸς τὴν ἔκχυσιν κεχηνὸς
20 τοῦ πίθου καὶ ἀκώλυτος ἡ ἔξοδος.

19. ΖΕΥΣ. Οὐκοῦν εἰ μὴ ἐμφράξεται τὸ κεχηνὸς τοῦτο καὶ ἐς τὸ ἅπαξ ἀναπεπταμένον, ἐκχυθέντος
ἐν βραχεῖ σου ῥᾳδίως εὑρήσει τὴν διφθέραν αὖθις καὶ
τὴν δίκελλαν ἐν τῇ τρυγὶ τοῦ πίθου. ἀλλ᾽ ἄπιτε ἤδη
25 καὶ πλουτίζετε αὐτόν· σὺ δὲ μέμνησο, ὦ Ἑρμῆ, ἐπα-

νιὼν πρὸς ἡμᾶς ἄγειν τοὺς Κύκλωπας ἐκ τῆς Αἴτνης,
ὅπως τὸν κεραυνὸν ἀκονήσαντες ἐπισκευάσωσιν· ὡς
ἤδη γε τεθηγμένου αὐτοῦ δεησόμεθα.

Hermes and Plutus converse as they go. *Hermes finds*
Plutus is lame. "*It is my general complaint, when I*
am going to any one's house. *When I am leaving, I*
run swifter than a bird." "*And yet I've known men*
who were exceedingly poor become quite wealthy in
a single day."

20. ΕΡΜ. Προΐωμεν, ὦ Πλοῦτε. τί τοῦτο;
ὑποσκάζεις; ἐλελήθεις με, ὦ γεννάδα, οὐ τυφλὸς μό- 5
νον, ἀλλὰ καὶ χωλὸς ὤν.

ΠΛΟΥΤ. Οὐκ ἀεὶ τοῦτο, ὦ Ἑρμῆ, ἀλλ᾽ ὁπόταν
μὲν ἀπίω παρά τινα πεμφθεὶς ὑπὸ τοῦ Διός, οὐκ οἶδ᾽
ὅπως βραδύς εἰμι καὶ χωλὸς ἀμφοτέροις, ὡς μόλις
τελεῖν ἐπὶ τὸ τέρμα, προγηράσαντος ἐνίοτε τοῦ περι- 10
μένοντος, ὁπόταν δὲ ἀπαλλάττεσθαι δέῃ, πτηνὸν ὄψει,
πολὺ τῶν ὀνείρων ὠκύτερον· ἅμα γοῦν ἔπεσεν ἡ
ὕσπληγξ, κἀγὼ ἤδη ἀνακηρύττομαι νενικηκώς, ὑπερ-
πηδήσας τὸ στάδιον οὐδὲ ἰδόντων ἐνίοτε τῶν θεατῶν.

ΕΡΜ. Οὐκ ἀληθῆ ταῦτα φής· ἐγὼ δέ τοι πολ- 15
λοὺς ἂν εἰπεῖν ἔχοιμί σοι χθὲς μὲν οὐδὲ ὀβολόν, ὥστε
πρίασθαι βρόχον, ἐσχηκότας, ἄφνω δὲ τήμερον πλουσίους καὶ πολυτελεῖς ἐπὶ λευκοῦ ζεύγους ἐξελαύνοντας, οἷς οὐδὲ κἂν ὄνος ὑπῆρξε πώποτε· καὶ ὅμως
πορφυροῖ καὶ χρυσόχειρες περιέρχονται οὐδ᾽ αὐτοὶ 20
πιστεύοντες, οἶμαι, ὅτι μὴ ὄναρ πλουτοῦσιν.

"*That's another matter; I don't go on my own feet then:*
others send me. *A little tablet does it, and you should*

see how all those around open their mouths when the
seal is broken and the tablet opened.

21. ΠΛΟΥΤ. Ἑτεροῖον τοῦτ' ἐστίν, ὦ Ἑρμῆ,
καὶ οὐχὶ τοῖς ἐμαυτοῦ ποσὶ βαδίζω τότε, οὐδὲ ὁ Ζεύς,
ἀλλ' ὁ Πλούτων ἀποστέλλει με παρ' αὐτοὺς ἅτε
πλουτοδότης καὶ μεγαλόδωρος καὶ αὐτὸς ὤν· δηλοῖ
5 γοῦν καὶ τῷ ὀνόματι. ἐπειδὰν τοίνυν μετοικισθῆναι
δέῃ με παρ' ἑτέρου πρὸς ἕτερον, ἐς δέλτον ἐμβαλόντες
με καὶ κατασημηνάμενοι ἐπιμελῶς φορηδὸν ἀράμενοι
μετακομίζουσι· καὶ ὁ μὲν νεκρὸς ἐν σκοτεινῷ που τῆς
οἰκίας πρόκειται ὑπὲρ τὰ γόνατα παλαιᾷ τῇ ὀθόνῃ
10 σκεπόμενος, περιμάχητος ταῖς γαλαῖς, ἐμὲ δὲ οἱ ἐπελ-
πίσαντες ἐν τῇ ἀγορᾷ περιμένουσι κεχηνότες ὥσπερ
τὴν χελιδόνα προσπετομένην τετριγότες οἱ νεοττοί.
22. Ἐπειδὰν δὲ τὸ σημεῖον ἀφαιρεθῇ καὶ τὸ λίνον
ἐντμηθῇ καὶ ἡ δέλτος ἀνοιχθῇ καὶ ἀνακηρυχθῇ μου ὁ
15 καινὸς δεσπότης ἤτοι συγγενής τις ἢ κόλαξ ἢ κατα-
πύγων οἰκέτης, ἐκεῖνος μέν, ὅστις ἂν ᾖ ποτε, ἁρπασά-
μενός με αὐτῇ δέλτῳ θεῖ φέρων ἀντὶ τοῦ τέως Πυρρίου
ἢ Δρόμωνος ἢ Τιβίου Μεγακλῆς ἢ Μεγάβυζος ἢ
Πρώταρχος μετονομασθείς, τοὺς μάτην κεχηνότας
20 ἐκείνους εἰς ἀλλήλους ἀποβλέποντας καταλιπὼν
ἀληθὲς ἄγοντας τὸ πένθος, οἷος αὐτοὺς ὁ θύννος ἐκ
μυχοῦ τῆς σαγήνης διέφυγεν οὐκ ὀλίγον τὸ δέλεαρ
καταπιών.

"*The man lucky enough to catch me, though he may before*
have known the feel of chains, and made acquaintance
with the treadmill, becomes overbrimming with pride
and insult, while he is of course surrounded with the
most abject flattery."

23. Ὁ δὲ ἐμπεσὼν ἀθρόος εἰς ἐμὲ ἀπειρόκαλος
καὶ παχύδερμος ἄνθρωπος, ἔτι τὴν πέδην πεφρικὼς
καὶ εἰ παριὼν μαστίξειέ τις, ὄρθιον ἐφιστὰς τὸ οὖς
καὶ τὸν μυλῶνα ὥσπερ τὸ Ἀνάκτορον προσκυνῶν
οὐκέτι φορητός ἐστι τοῖς ἐντυγχάνουσιν, ἀλλὰ τούς 5
τε ἐλευθέρους ὑβρίζει καὶ τοὺς ὁμοδούλους μαστιγοῖ
ἀποπειρώμενος εἰ καὶ αὐτῷ τὰ τοιαῦτα ἔξεστιν, ἄχρι
ἂν ἢ ἐς πορνίδιόν τι ἐμπεσὼν ἢ ἱπποτροφίας ἐπιθυ-
μήσας ἢ κόλαξι παραδοὺς ἑαυτὸν ὀμνύουσιν ἢ μὴν
εὐμορφότερον μὲν Νιρέως εἶναι αὐτόν, εὐγενέστερον δὲ 10
τοῦ Κέκροπος ἢ Κόδρου, συνετώτερον δὲ τοῦ Ὀδυσσέως, πλουσιώτερον δὲ συνάμα Κροίσων ἑκκαίδεκα,
ἐν ἀκαρεῖ τοῦ χρόνου ἄθλιος ἐκχέῃ τὰ κατ' ὀλίγον ἐκ
πολλῶν ἐπιορκιῶν καὶ ἁρπαγῶν καὶ πανουργιῶν
συνειλεγμένα.   15

"And how do you distinguish men, if you are blind?" "I
   don't distinguish men; I wait about till some one carries me off."

24. ΕΡΜ. Αὐτά που σχεδὸν φῂς τὰ γιγνόμενα·
ὁπόταν δ' οὖν αὐτόπους βαδίζῃς, πῶς οὕτω τυφλὸς ὢν
εὑρίσκεις τὴν ὁδόν; ἢ πῶς διαγιγνώσκεις ἐφ' οὓς ἄν σε
ὁ Ζεὺς ἀποστείλῃ κρίνας εἶναι τοῦ πλουτεῖν ἀξίους;

ΠΛΟΥΤ. Οἴει γὰρ εὑρίσκειν με οἵτινές εἰσι; μὰ 20
τὸν Δία οὐ πάνυ· οὐ γὰρ ἂν Ἀριστείδην καταλιπὼν
Ἱππονίκῳ καὶ Καλλίᾳ προσῄειν καὶ πολλοῖς ἄλλοις
Ἀθηναίων οὐδὲ ὀβολοῦ ἀξίοις.

ΕΡΜ. Πλὴν ἀλλὰ τί πράττεις καταπεμφθείς;

ΠΛΟΥΤ. Ἄνω καὶ κάτω πλανῶμαι περινοστῶν, 25
ἄχρι ἂν λάθω τινὶ ἐμπεσών· ὁ δέ, ὅστις ἂν πρῶτός
μοι περιτύχῃ, ἀπαγαγὼν [παρ' αὐτὸν] ἔχει, σὲ τὸν

Ἑρμῆν ἐπὶ τῷ παραλόγῳ τοῦ κέρδους προσ-
κυνῶ.

" *Then Zeus makes a great mistake in sending you?*" " *Yes,
he does. The evil are many more than the good; so
that I generally fall into* their *hands.*" " *And how do
you get away from them ?*" " *I become swift and keen-
sighted for the nonce.*"

25. ΕΡΜ. Οὐκοῦν ἐξηπάτηται ὁ Ζεὺς οἰόμενός
σε κατὰ τὸ αὐτῷ δοκοῦν πλουτίζειν ὅσους ἂν οἴηται
5 τοῦ πλουτεῖν ἀξίους;

ΠΛΟΥΤ. Καὶ μάλα δικαίως, ὦγαθέ, ὅς γε τυφλὸν
ὄντα εἰδὼς ἔπεμπεν ἀναζητήσοντα δυσεύρετον οὕτω
χρῆμα καὶ πρὸ πολλοῦ ἐκλελοιπὸς ἐκ τοῦ βίου, ὅπερ
οὐδ᾽ ὁ Λυγκεὺς ἂν ἐξεύροι ῥᾳδίως, ἀμαυρὸν οὕτω καὶ
10 μικρὸν ὄν. τοιγαροῦν ἅτε τῶν μὲν ἀγαθῶν ὀλίγων
ὄντων, πονηρῶν δὲ πλείστων ἐν ταῖς πόλεσι τὸ πᾶν
ἐπεχόντων, ῥᾷον ἐς τοὺς τοιούτους ἐμπίπτω περιιὼν
καὶ σαγηνεύομαι πρὸς αὐτῶν.

ΕΡΜ. Εἶτα πῶς, ἐπειδὰν καταλίπῃς αὐτούς, ῥᾳ-
15 δίως φεύγεις οὐκ εἰδὼς τὴν ὁδόν;

ΠΛΟΥΤ. Ὀξυδερκὴς τότε πως καὶ ἀρτίπους
γίγνομαι πρὸς μόνον τὸν καιρὸν τῆς φυγῆς.

" *Is it not strange (excuse my remark) that, being lame and
blind and sickly-looking as you are, you should have
so many admirers?   They seem ready to do anything
for your sake.*"

26. ΕΡΜ. Ἔτι δή μοι καὶ τοῦτο ἀπόκριναι,
πῶς τυφλὸς ὤν, εἰρήσεται γάρ, καὶ προσέτι ὠχρὸς
20 καὶ βαρὺς ἐκ τοῖν σκελοῖν τοσούτους ἐραστὰς ἔχεις,

ὥστε πάντας ἀποβλέπειν ἐς σέ, καὶ τυχόντας μὲν εὐ-
δαιμονεῖν οἴεσθαι, εἰ δὲ ἀποτύχοιεν, οὐκ ἀνέχεσθαι
ζῶντας; οἶδα γοῦν τινας οὐκ ὀλίγους αὐτῶν οὕτω σου
δυσέρωτας ὄντας, ὥστε καὶ ἐς βαθυκήτεα πόντον φέροντες ἔρριψαν αὑτοὺς καὶ πετρῶν κατ' ἠλιβάτων 5
ὑπερορᾶσθαι νομίζοντες ὑπὸ σοῦ, ὅτιπερ οὐδὲ τὴν
ἀρχὴν ἑώρας αὐτούς. πλὴν ἀλλὰ καὶ σὺ ἂν εὖ οἶδα
ὅτι ὁμολογήσειας, εἴ τι συνίης σαυτοῦ, κορυβαντιᾶν
αὐτοὺς ἐρωμένῳ τοιούτῳ ἐπιμεμηνότας.

" *They never see me as I really am; they are blind and
foolish; I wear a mask, so that they never see my real
self underneath.*"

27. ΠΛΟΥΤ. Οἴει γὰρ τοιοῦτον οἷός εἰμι ὁρᾶ- 10
σθαι αὐτοῖς, χωλὸν ἢ τυφλὸν ἢ ὅσα ἄλλα μοι πρόσ-
εστιν;

ΕΡΜ. Ἀλλὰ πῶς, ὦ Πλοῦτε, εἰ μὴ τυφλοὶ καὶ
αὐτοὶ πάντες εἰσίν;

ΠΛΟΥΤ. Οὐ τυφλοί, ὦ ἄριστε, ἀλλ' ἡ ἄγνοια 15
καὶ ἡ ἀπάτη, αἵπερ νῦν κατέχουσι τὰ πάντα, ἐπισκιά-
ζουσιν αὐτούς· ἔτι δὲ καὶ αὐτός, ὡς μὴ παντάπασιν
ἄμορφος εἴην, προσωπεῖόν τι περιθέμενος ἐρασμιώ-
τατον, διάχρυσον καὶ λιθοκόλλητον, καὶ ποικίλα ἐν-
δὺς ἐντυγχάνω αὐτοῖς· οἱ δὲ αὐτοπρόσωπον οἰόμενοι 20
ὁρᾶν τὸ κάλλος ἐρῶσι καὶ ἀπόλλυνται μὴ τυγχάνον-
τες. ὡς εἴ γέ τις αὐτοῖς ὅλον ἀπογυμνώσας ἐπέδειξέ
με, δῆλον ὡς κατεγίνωσκον ἂν αὑτῶν ἀμβλυώττοντες
τὰ τηλικαῦτα καὶ ἐρῶντες ἀνεράστων καὶ ἀμόρφων
πραγμάτων. 25

" *But when men really have you in possession are they still
ignorant of your characteristics ?*" " *Yes, Hermes, be-*

*cause Pride, Ignorance, Insult, and such like, always
follow closely behind me into whatsoever house I may
enter."*

28. ΕΡΜ. Τί οὖν ὅτι καὶ ἐν αὑτῷ ἤδη τῷ πλουτεῖν γενόμενοι καὶ τὸ προσωπεῖον αὐτοὶ περιθέμενοι
ἔτι ἐξαπατῶνται, καὶ ἤν τις ἀφαιρῆται αὐτούς, θᾶττον ἂν τὴν κεφαλὴν ἢ τὸ προσωπεῖον πρόοιντο; οὐ
5 γὰρ δὴ καὶ τότε ἀγνοεῖν εἰκὸς αὐτοὺς ὡς ἐπίχριστος ἡ
εὐμορφία ἐστίν, ἔνδοθεν τὰ πάντα ὁρῶντας.

ΠΛΟΥΤ. Οὐκ ὀλίγα, ὦ Ἑρμῆ, καὶ πρὸς τοῦτό
μοι συναγωνίζεται.

ΕΡΜ. Τὰ ποῖα;

10 ΠΛΟΥΤ. Ἐπειδάν τις ἐντυχὼν τὸ πρῶτον ἀναπετάσας τὴν θύραν ἐσδέχηταί με, συμπαρεισέρχεται
μετ᾿ ἐμοῦ λαθὼν ὁ τῦφος καὶ ἡ ἄνοια καὶ ἡ μεγαλαυ-
χία καὶ μαλακία καὶ ὕβρις καὶ ἀπάτη καὶ ἄλλ᾿ ἄττα
μυρία· ὑπὸ δὴ τούτων ἀπάντων καταληφθεὶς τὴν
15 ψυχὴν θαυμάζει τε τὰ οὐ θαυμαστὰ καὶ ὀρέγεται τῶν
φευκτῶν κἀμὲ τὸν πάντων ἐκείνων πατέρα τῶν εἰσε-
ληλυθότων κακῶν τέθηπε δορυφορούμενον ὑπ᾿ αὐτῶν,
καὶ πάντα πρότερον πάθοι ἂν ἢ ἐμὲ προέσθαι ὑπο-
μείνειεν ἄν.

*" And how slippery you are too, while Poverty sticks like
bird-lime. But, oh ! dear, we've forgotten Thesaurus."
" Never mind, I left him safe at home. But what is
that noise ?"*

20 29. ΕΡΜ. Ὡς δὲ λεῖος εἶ, ὦ Πλοῦτε, καὶ ὀλισθηρὸς καὶ δυσκάτοχος καὶ διαφευκτικός, οὐδεμίαν
ἀντιλαβὴν παρεχόμενος βεβαίαν, ἀλλ᾿ ὥσπερ αἱ
ἐγχέλεις ἢ οἱ ὄφεις διὰ τῶν δακτύλων δραπετεύεις

οὐκ οἶδ' ὅπως· ἡ Πενία δ' ἔμπαλιν ἰξώδης τε καὶ
εὐλαβὴς καὶ μυρία τὰ ἄγκιστρα ἐκπεφυκότα ἐξ ἅπαντος τοῦ σώματος ἔχουσα, ὡς πλησιάσαντας εὐθὺς
ἔχεσθαι καὶ μὴ ἔχειν ῥᾳδίως ἀπολυθῆναι. ἀλλὰ με-
ταξὺ φλυαροῦντας ἡμᾶς πρᾶγμα ἤδη οὐ μικρὸν διέ- 5
λαθε.

ΠΛΟΥΤ. Τὸ ποῖον;

ΕΡΜ. "Οτι τὸν Θησαυρὸν οὐκ ἐπηγαγόμεθα,
οὗπερ ἔδει μάλιστα.

30. ΠΛΟΥΤ. Θάρρει τούτου γε ἕνεκα· ἐν τῇ γῇ 10
αὐτὸν ἀεὶ καταλιπὼν ἀνέρχομαι παρ' ὑμᾶς ἐπισκήψας ἔνδον μένειν ἐπικλεισάμενον τὴν θύραν, ἀνοίγειν
δὲ μηδενί, ἢν μὴ ἐμοῦ ἀκούσῃ βοήσαντος.

ΕΡΜ. Οὐκοῦν ἐπιβαίνωμεν ἤδη τῆς Ἀττικῆς·
καί μοι ἕπου ἐχόμενος τῆς χλαμύδος, ἄχρι ἂν πρὸς 15
τὴν ἐσχατιὰν ἀφίκωμαι.

ΠΛΟΥΤ. Εὖ ποιεῖς, ὦ Ἑρμῆ, χειραγωγῶν· ἐπεὶ
ἤν γε ἀπολίπῃς με, Ὑπερβόλῳ τάχα ἢ Κλέωνι ἐμπε-
σοῦμαι περινοστῶν. ἀλλὰ τίς ὁ ψόφος οὗτός ἐστι
καθάπερ σιδήρου πρὸς λίθον ;   20

"*It is Timon digging; and he has Poverty with all her
bodyguard around him.*"—"*Then let us run away by
the shortest cut.*" "*No, Zeus has sent us.*"

31. ΕΡΜ. Ὁ Τίμων οὑτοσὶ σκάπτει πλησίον
ὀρεινὸν καὶ ὑπόλιθον γήδιον. παπαῖ, καὶ ἡ Πενία
πάρεστι καὶ ὁ Πόνος ἐκεῖνος, ἡ Καρτερία τε καὶ ἡ
Σοφία καὶ ἡ Ἀνδρεία καὶ ὁ τοιοῦτος ὄχλος τῶν ὑπὸ
τῷ Λιμῷ ταττομένων ἁπάντων, πολὺ ἀμείνους τῶν 25
σῶν δορυφόρων.

ΠΛΟΥΤ. Τί οὖν οὐκ ἀπαλλαττόμεθα, ὦ Ἑρμῆ,

τὴν ταχίστην; οὐ γὰρ ἄν τι ἡμεῖς δράσαιμεν ἀξιόλο-
γον πρὸς ἄνδρα ὑπὸ τηλικούτου στρατοπέδου περιε-
σχημένον.

ΕΡΜ. Ἄλλως ἔδοξε τῷ Διΐ· μὴ ἀποδειλιῶμεν
5 οὖν.

*Poverty naturally grumbles a great deal at finding herself
ousted, and Plutus once more re-instated in Timon's
favour. But she will go, and take her companions
with her; and Timon will find out very soon what a
friend he has lost.*

32. ΠΕΝ. Ποῖ τοῦτον ἀπάγεις, ὦ Ἀργειφόντα,
χειραγωγῶν;

ΕΡΜ. Ἐπὶ τουτονὶ τὸν Τίμωνα ἐπέμφθημεν ὑπὸ
τοῦ Διός.

10 ΠΕΝ. Νῦν ὁ Πλοῦτος ἐπὶ Τίμωνα, ὁπότε αὐτὸν
ἐγὼ κακῶς ἔχοντα ὑπὸ τῆς Τρυφῆς παραλαβοῦσα,
τουτοισὶ παραδοῦσα, τῇ Σοφίᾳ καὶ τῷ Πόνῳ, γενναῖον
ἄνδρα καὶ πολλοῦ ἄξιον ἀπέδειξα; οὕτως ἄρα εὐκαταφρόνητος ὑμῖν ἡ Πενία δοκῶ καὶ εὐαδίκητος ὥσθ'
15 ὃ μόνον κτῆμα εἶχον ἀφαιρεῖσθαί με, ἀκριβῶς πρὸς
ἀρετὴν ἐξειργασμένον, ἵν' αὖθις ὁ Πλοῦτος παραλαβὼν αὐτὸν Ὕβρει καὶ Τύφῳ ἐγχειρίσας ὅμοιον τῷ
πάλαι, μαλθακὸν καὶ ἀγεννῆ καὶ ἀνόητον ἀποφήνας
ἀποδῷ πάλιν ἐμοὶ ῥάκος ἤδη γεγενημένον;
20 ΕΡΜ. Ἔδοξε ταῦτα, ὦ Πενία, τῷ Διΐ.

33. ΠΕΝ. Ἀπέρχομαι· καὶ ὑμεῖς δὲ, ὦ Πόνε
καὶ Σοφία καὶ οἱ λοιποί, ἀκολουθεῖτέ μοι. οὗτος δὲ
τάχα εἴσεται οἵαν με οὖσαν ἀπολείψει, ἀγαθὴν συνερ-
γὸν καὶ διδάσκαλον τῶν ἀρίστων, ᾗ συνὼν ὑγιεινὸς
25 μὲν τὸ σῶμα, ἐρρωμένος δὲ τὴν γνώμην διετέλεσεν,

ἀνδρὸς βίον ζῶν καὶ πρὸς αὐτὸν ἀποβλέπων, τὰ δὲ
περιττὰ καὶ πολλὰ ταῦτα, ὥσπερ ἐστίν, ἀλλότρια
ὑπολαμβάνων.

ΕΡΜ. Ἀπέρχονται· ἡμεῖς δὲ προσίωμεν αὐτῷ.

Timon :—"*Go away, go away, you scoundrels! Don't come
near me, or I will pelt you with sods and stones.*"
*Hermes explains who his visitors are; but Timon
says, gods or men, he will have none of them.*

34. ΤΙΜ. Τίνες ἐστέ, ὦ κατάρατοι; ἢ τί βουλό- 5
μενοι δεῦρο ἥκετε ἄνδρα ἐργάτην καὶ μισθοφόρον ἐνο-
χλήσοντες; ἀλλ' οὐ χαίροντες ἄπιτε μιαροὶ πάντες
ὄντες· ἐγὼ γὰρ ὑμᾶς αὐτίκα μάλα βάλλων ταῖς βώλοις καὶ τοῖς λίθοις συντρίψω.

ΕΡΜ. Μηδαμῶς, ὦ Τίμων, μὴ βάλῃς· οὐ γὰρ 10
ἀνθρώπους ὄντας βαλεῖς, ἀλλ' ἐγὼ μὲν Ἑρμῆς εἰμι,
οὑτοσὶ δὲ ὁ Πλοῦτος· ἔπεμψε δὲ ὁ Ζεὺς ἐπακούσας
τῶν εὐχῶν. ὥστε ἀγαθῇ τύχῃ δέχου τὸν ὄλβον ἀπο-
στὰς τῶν πόνων.

ΤΙΜ. Καὶ ὑμεῖς οἰμώξεσθε ἤδη καίτοι θεοὶ ὄντες, 15
ὥς φατε· πάντας γὰρ ἅμα καὶ θεοὺς καὶ ἀνθρώπους
μισῶ, τουτονὶ δὲ τὸν τυφλόν, ὅστις ἂν ᾖ, καὶ ἐπιτρί-
ψειν μοι δοκῶ τῇ δικέλλῃ.

ΠΛΟΥΤ. Ἀπίωμεν, ὦ Ἑρμῆ, πρὸς τοῦ Διός·
μελαγχολᾶν γὰρ ὁ ἄνθρωπός μοι οὐ μετρίως δοκεῖ, 20
μή τι κακὸν ἀπέλθω προσλαβών.

"*Come, come, Timon, don't be foolish. Make the most of
your good fortune.—Because you hate men, you need
not hate gods.*"

35. ΕΡΜ. Μηδὲν σκαιόν, ὦ Τίμων, ἀλλὰ τὸ
πάνυ τοῦτο ἄγριον καὶ τραχὺ καταβαλὼν προτείνας

42   ΛΟΥΚΙΑΝΟΥ   [35—36

τὼ χεῖρε λάμβανε τὴν ἀγαθὴν τύχην καὶ πλούτει
πάλιν καὶ ἴσθι Ἀθηναίων τὰ πρῶτα καὶ ὑπερόρα τῶν
ἀχαρίστων ἐκείνων μόνος αὐτὸς εὐδαιμονῶν.

TIM.   Οὐδὲν ὑμῶν δέομαι· μὴ ἐνοχλεῖτέ μοι·
5 ἱκανὸς ἐμοὶ πλοῦτος ἡ δίκελλα· τὰ δ' ἄλλα εὐδαιμο-
νέστατός εἰμι, μηδενός μοι πλησιάζοντος.

EPM.   Οὕτως, ὦ τᾶν, ἀπανθρώπως;
τόνδε φέρω Διὶ μῦθον ἀπηνέα τε κρατερόν τε;
καὶ μὴν εἰκὸς ἦν μισάνθρωπον μὲν εἶναί σε τοσαῦτα
10 ὑπ' αὐτῶν δεινὰ πεπονθότα, μισόθεον δὲ μηδαμῶς,
οὕτως ἐπιμελουμένων σου τῶν θεῶν.

"Do you think I'm going to have P. back, when he was the
cause of all my misery—while Poverty taught me how
to support myself, and to live in peace and contentment?

36. TIM.   Ἀλλὰ σοὶ μέν, ὦ Ἑρμῆ, καὶ τῷ Διὶ
πλείστη χάρις τῆς ἐπιμελείας, τουτονὶ δὲ τὸν Πλοῦτον οὐκ ἂν λάβοιμι.
15 EPM.   Τί δή;
TIM.   Ὅτι καὶ πάλαι μυρίων κακῶν μοι αἴτιος
οὗτος κατέστη κόλαξί τε παραδοὺς καὶ ἐπιβούλους
ἐπαγαγὼν καὶ μῖσος ἐπεγείρας καὶ ἡδυπαθείᾳ διαφθεί-
ρας καὶ ἐπίφθονον ἀποφήνας, τέλος δὲ ἄφνω καταλι-
20 πὼν οὕτως ἀπίστως καὶ προδοτικῶς· ἡ βελτίστη δὲ
Πενία πόνοις με τοῖς ἀνδρικωτάτοις καταγυμνάσασα
καὶ μετ' ἀληθείας καὶ παρρησίας προσομιλοῦσα τά
τε ἀναγκαῖα κάμνοντι παρεῖχε καὶ τῶν πολλῶν ἐκείνων καταφρονεῖν ἐπαίδευεν ἐξ αὐτοῦ ἐμοῦ τὰς ἐλπί-
25 δας ἀπαρτήσασά μοι τοῦ βίου καὶ δείξασα ὅστις ἦν ὁ
πλοῦτος ὁ ἐμός, ὃν οὔτε κόλαξ θωπεύων οὔτε συκο-

φάντης φοβῶν, οὐ δῆμος παροξυνθείς, οὐκ ἐκκλη-
σιαστὴς ψηφοφορήσας, οὐ τύραννος ἐπιβουλεύσας
ἀφελέσθαι δύναιτ᾽ ἄν.

"So now I can get along very well with my spade.—Run
　　away back, Hermes, and take P. with you."

37. Ἐρρωμένος τοιγαροῦν ὑπὸ τῶν πόνων τουτονὶ
τὸν ἀγρὸν φιλοπόνως ἐργαζόμενος, οὐδὲν ὁρῶν τῶν 5
ἐν ἄστει κακῶν, ἱκανὰ καὶ διαρκῆ ἔχω τὰ ἄλφιτα
παρὰ τῆς δικέλλης. ὥστε παλίνδρομος ἄπιθι, ὦ
Ἑρμῆ, τὸν Πλοῦτον ἀπάγων τῷ Διί· ἐμοὶ δὲ τοῦτο
ἱκανὸν ἦν, πάντας ἀνθρώπους ἡβηδὸν οἰμώζειν ποιῆ-
σαι.　　　　　　　　　　　　　　　　　　　10

ΕΡΜ. Μηδαμῶς, ὠγαθέ· οὐ γὰρ πάντες εἰσὶν
ἐπιτήδειοι πρὸς οἰμωγήν. ἀλλ᾽ ἔα τὰ ὀργίλα ταῦτα
καὶ μειρακιώδη καὶ τὸν Πλοῦτον παράλαβε. οὗτοι
ἀπόβλητά ἐστι τὰ δῶρα τὰ παρὰ τοῦ Διός.

ΠΛΟΤΤ. Βούλει, ὦ Τίμων, δικαιολογήσωμαι 15
πρὸς σέ; ἢ χαλεπανεῖς μοι λέγοντι;

ΤΙΜ. Λέγε, μὴ μακρὰ μέντοι, μηδὲ μετὰ προοι-
μίων, ὥσπερ οἱ ἐπίτριπτοι ῥήτορες· ἀνέξομαι γάρ σε
ὀλίγα λέγοντα διὰ τὸν Ἑρμῆν τουτονί.

Plutus now speaks up, and reasons with T., pointing out
　　that if either side has good cause for grumbling, it is
　　he, and not T. He had been the means of all T.'s
　　honour and titles—and in return had only been
　　bundled out of doors, and given over to cheats and
　　rascals; it is with no willing consent that he has been
　　sent back again.

38. ΠΛΟΤΤ. Ἐχρῆν μὲν ἴσως καὶ μακρὰ εἰπεῖν, 20

οὕτω πολλὰ ὑπὸ σοῦ κατηγορηθέντα· ὅμως δὲ ὅρα εἰ
τί σε, ὡς φής, ἠδίκηκα, ὃς τῶν μὲν ἡδίστων ἀπάντων
αἴτιός σοι κατέστην, τιμῆς καὶ προεδρίας καὶ στεφάνων καὶ τῆς ἄλλης τρυφῆς, περίβλεπτός τε καὶ ἀοί-
5 διμος δι' ἐμὲ ἦσθα καὶ περισπούδαστος· εἰ δέ τι
χαλεπὸν ἐκ τῶν κολάκων πέπονθας, ἀναίτιος ἐγώ σοι·
μᾶλλον δὲ αὐτὸς ἠδίκημαι τοῦτο ὑπὸ σοῦ, διότι με
οὕτως ἀτίμως ὑπέβαλες ἀνδράσι καταράτοις ἐπαι-
νοῦσι καὶ καταγοητεύουσι καὶ πάντα τρόπον ἐπιβου-
10 λεύουσί μοι· καὶ τό γε τελευταῖον ἔφησθα ὡς προδέ-
δωκά σε, τοὐναντίον δὲ αὐτὸς ἐγκαλέσαιμί σοι πάντα
τρόπον ἀπελαθεὶς ὑπὸ σοῦ καὶ ἐπὶ κεφαλὴν ἐξωσθεὶς
τῆς οἰκίας. τοιγαροῦν ἀντὶ μαλακῆς χλανίδος ταύτην
τὴν διφθέραν ἡ τιμιωτάτη σοι Πενία περιτέθεικεν.
15 ὥστε μάρτυς ὁ Ἑρμῆς οὑτοσὶ πῶς ἱκέτευον τὸν Δία
μηκέθ' ἥκειν παρὰ σὲ οὕτω δυσμενῶς μοι προσενηνεγμένον.

*Timon at last gives way, since no one can go against the
gods. Hermes says good bye, and Plutus summons
Thesaurus to come forth to the sound of Timon's
spade.*

39. ΕΡΜ. Ἀλλὰ νῦν ὁρᾷς, ὦ Πλοῦτε, οἷος ἤδη
γεγένηται; ὥστε θαρρῶν συνδιάτριβε αὐτῷ· καὶ σὺ
20 μὲν σκάπτε ὡς ἔχεις· σὺ δὲ τὸν Θησαυρὸν ὑπάγαγε
τῇ δικέλλῃ· ὑπακούσεται γὰρ ἐμβοήσαντί σοι.
ΤΙΜ. Πειστέον, ὦ Ἑρμῆ, καὶ αὖθις πλουτητέον.
τί γὰρ ἂν καὶ πάθοι τις, ὁπότε οἱ θεοὶ βιάζοιντο;
πλὴν ὅρα γε εἰς οἷά με πράγματα ἐμβάλλεις τὸν κακο-
25 δαίμονα, ὃς ἄχρι νῦν εὐδαιμονέστατα διάγων χρυσὸν

ἄφνω τοσοῦτον λήψομαι οὐδὲν ἀδικήσας καὶ τοσαύτας
φροντίδας ἀναδέξομαι.

40. ΕΡΜ. Ὑπόστηθι, ὦ Τίμων, δι' ἐμέ, καὶ εἰ
χαλεπὸν τοῦτο καὶ οὐκ οἰστόν ἐστιν, ὅπως οἱ κόλακες
ἐκεῖνοι διαρραγῶσιν ὑπὸ τοῦ φθόνου· ἐγὼ δὲ ὑπὲρ τὴν 5
Αἴτνην ἐς τὸν οὐρανὸν ἀναπτήσομαι.

ΠΛΟΥΤ. Ὁ μὲν ἀπελήλυθεν, ὡς δοκεῖ· τεκμαί-
ρομαι γὰρ τῇ εἰρεσίᾳ τῶν πτερῶν· σὺ δὲ αὐτοῦ περί-
μενε· ἀναπέμψω γάρ σοι τὸν Θησαυρὸν ἀπελθών·
μᾶλλον δὲ παῖε. σέ φημι, Θησαυρὲ χρυσοῦ, ὑπάκου- 10
σον Τίμωνι τουτῳὶ καὶ παράσχες σεαυτὸν ἀνελέσθαι.
σκάπτε, ὦ Τίμων, βαθείας καταφέρων. ἐγὼ δὲ ὑμῖν
ὑπεκστήσομαι.

*Timon discovers vast treasures.—Such wealth seems more
like a dream. But, having gold in such quantities
that even Cræsus or Midas might well envy him, he
determines to live a life of solitude—and proposes to
himself, and passes, a law, forbidding himself to mix
with the rest of mankind.*

41. ΤΙΜ. Ἄγε, ὦ δίκελλα, νῦν μοι ἐπίρρωσον
σεαυτὴν καὶ μὴ κάμῃς ἐκ τοῦ βάθους τὸν Θησαυρὸν 15
ἐς τοὐμφανὲς προκαλουμένη. ὦ Ζεῦ τεράστιε καὶ
φίλοι Κορύβαντες καὶ Ἑρμῆ κερδῷε, πόθεν χρυσίον
τοσοῦτον; ἦ που ὄναρ ταῦτά ἐστι; δέδια γοῦν μὴ
ἄνθρακας εὕρω ἀνεγρόμενος· ἀλλὰ μὴν χρυσίον ἐστὶν
ἐπίσημον, ὑπέρυθρον, βαρὺ καὶ τὴν πρόσοψιν ὑπερή- 20
διστον.

Ὦ χρυσέ, δεξίωμα κάλλιστον βροτοῖς·
αἰθόμενον γὰρ πῦρ ἅτε διαπρέπεις καὶ νύκτωρ καὶ
μεθ' ἡμέραν. ἐλθέ, ὦ φίλτατε καὶ ἐρασμιώτατε. νῦν

πείθομαί γε καὶ Δία ποτὲ γενέσθαι χρυσόν· τίς γὰρ
οὐκ ἂν παρθένος ἀναπεπταμένοις τοῖς κόλποις ὑπεδέξατο οὕτω καλὸν ἐραστὴν διὰ τοῦ τέγους καταρρέ-
οντα;

5 42. Ὦ Μίδα καὶ Κροῖσε καὶ τὰ ἐν Δελφοῖς ἀνα-
θήματα ὡς οὐδὲν ἄρα ἦτε ὡς πρὸς Τίμωνα καὶ τὸν
Τίμωνος πλοῦτον, ᾧ γε οὐδὲ ὁ βασιλεὺς ὁ Περσῶν
ἴσος. ὦ δίκελλα καὶ φιλτάτη διφθέρα, ὑμᾶς μὲν τῷ
Πανὶ τούτῳ ἀναθεῖναι καλόν· αὐτὸς δὲ ἤδη πᾶσαν
10 πριάμενος τὴν ἐσχατιάν, πυργίον οἰκοδομησάμενος
ὑπὲρ τοῦ θησαυροῦ, μόνῳ ἐμοὶ ἱκανὸν ἐνδιαιτᾶσθαι,
τὸν αὐτὸν καὶ τάφον ἀποθανὼν ἕξειν μοι δοκῶ. δεδόχθω δὲ ταῦτα καὶ νενομοθετήσθω πρὸς τὸν ἐπίλοιπον
βίον, ἀμιξία πρὸς ἅπαντας καὶ ἀγνωσία καὶ ὑπερο-
15 ψία· φίλος δὲ ἢ ξένος ἢ ἑταῖρος ἢ Ἐλέου βωμὸς
ὕθλος πολύς· καὶ τὸ οἰκτεῖραι δακρύοντα ἢ ἐπικου-
ρῆσαι δεομένῳ παρανομία καὶ κατάλυσις τῶν ἐθῶν·
μονήρης δὲ ἡ δίαιτα καθάπερ τοῖς λύκοις, καὶ φίλος
εἷς Τίμων.

"May the day be cursed whereon I see, or speak with, any
    man.—I will have no more to do with demes and
    tribes.—I, Timon, stand alone, in my wealth—scorn-
    ing all else. Alone I live, and alone will I die!
    Henceforth my name shall be The Misanthrope. I
    will hold out no hand of succour to any man—not
    even if he be drowning. Thus will I requite man-
    kind. I, Timon, put this to the assembly, and pass
    it!

20 43. Οἱ δὲ ἄλλοι πάντες ἐχθροὶ καὶ ἐπίβουλοι·
καὶ τὸ προσομιλῆσαί τινι αὐτῶν μίασμα· καὶ ἤν τινα

ἴδω μόνον, ἀποφρὰς ἡ ἡμέρα· καὶ ὅλως ἀνδριάντων
λιθίνων ἢ χαλκῶν μηδὲν ἡμῖν διαφερέτωσαν· καὶ
μήτε κήρυκα δεχώμεθα παρ' αὐτῶν μήτε σπονδὰς
σπενδώμεθα· ἡ ἐρημία δὲ ὄρος ἔστω πρὸς αὐτούς.
φυλέται δὲ καὶ φράτορες καὶ δημόται καὶ ἡ πατρὶς 5
αὐτὴ ψυχρὰ καὶ ἀνωφελῆ ὀνόματα καὶ ἀνοήτων ἀν-
δρῶν φιλοτιμήματα. πλουτείτω δὲ Τίμων μόνος καὶ
ὑπεροράτω ἁπάντων καὶ τρυφάτω μόνος καθ' ἑαυτόν,
κολακείας καὶ ἐπαίνων φορτικῶν ἀπηλλαγμένος· καὶ
θεοῖς θυέτω καὶ εὐωχείσθω μόνος ἑαυτῷ γείτων καὶ 10
ὅμορος, ἑκαστάτω τῶν ἄλλων. καὶ ἅπαξ ἑαυτὸν δεξιώσασθαι δεδόχθω, ἢν δέῃ ἀποθανεῖν, καὶ ἑαυτῷ
στέφανον ἐπενεγκεῖν.

44. Καὶ ὄνομα μὲν ἔστω ὁ Μισάνθρωπος ἥδιστον,
τοῦ τρόπου δὲ γνωρίσματα δυσκολία καὶ τραχύτης 15
καὶ σκαιότης καὶ ὀργὴ καὶ ἀπανθρωπία· εἰ δέ τινα
ἴδοιμι ἐν πυρὶ διαφθειρόμενον καὶ κατασβεννύναι
ἱκετεύοντα, πίττῃ καὶ ἐλαίῳ κατασβεννύναι· καὶ ἤν
τινα τοῦ χειμῶνος ὁ ποταμὸς παραφέρῃ, ὁ δὲ τὰς
χεῖρας ὀρέγων ἀντιλαβέσθαι δέηται, ὠθεῖν καὶ τοῦτον 20
ἐπὶ κεφαλὴν βαπτίζοντα, ὡς μηδὲ ἀνακύψαι δυνηθείη·
οὕτω γὰρ ἂν τὴν ἴσην ἀπολάβοιεν. εἰσηγήσατο τὸν
νόμον Τίμων Ἐχεκρατίδου Κολλυτεύς, ἐπεψήφισεν
τῇ ἐκκλησίᾳ Τίμων ὁ αὐτός. εἶεν, ταῦτα ἡμῖν δεδόχθω καὶ ἀνδρικῶς ἐμμένωμεν αὐτοῖς. 25

"*All men shall know my exceeding great wealth. They
will hang themselves from envy. See! already they
come running to me. I will put aside my own law
this once, and go and converse with them.*"

45. Πλὴν ἀλλὰ περὶ πολλοῦ ἂν ἐποιησάμην

ἅπασι γνώριμά πως ταῦτα γενέσθαι, διότι ὑπερπλου-
τῷ· ἀγχόνη γὰρ ἂν τὸ πρᾶγμα γένοιτο αὐτοῖς. καίτοι
τί τοῦτο; φεῦ τοῦ τάχους. πανταχόθεν συνθέουσι
κεκονιμένοι καὶ πνευστιῶντες, οὐκ οἶδα ὅθεν ὀσφραι-
5 νόμενοι τοῦ χρυσίου. πότερον οὖν ἐπὶ τὸν πάγον
τοῦτον ἀναβὰς ἀπελαύνω αὐτοὺς τοῖς λίθοις ἐξ ὑπερδεξίων ἀκροβολιζόμενος, ἢ τό γε τοσοῦτον παρανομή-
σωμεν εἰσάπαξ αὐτοῖς ὁμιλήσαντες, ὡς πλέον ἀνιῷντο
ὑπερορώμενοι; τοῦτο οἶμαι καὶ ἄμεινον. ὥστε δεχώ-
10 μεθα ἤδη αὐτοὺς ὑποστάντες. φέρ᾽ ἴδω, τίς ὁ πρῶτος
αὐτῶν οὗτός ἐστι; Γναθωνίδης ὁ κόλαξ, ὁ πρῴην
ἔρανον αἰτήσαντί μοι ὀρέξας τὸν βρόχον, πίθους ὅλους
παρ᾽ ἐμοὶ πολλάκις ἐμημεκώς. ἀλλ᾽ εὖ γε ἐποίησεν
ἀφικόμενος· οἰμώξεται γὰρ πρὸ τῶν ἄλλων.

*Gnathonides is the first to arrive; he addresses Timon in
the most flattering terms, but only gets blows for his
pains, which causes him to hurry away vowing vengeance.*

15 46. ΓΝΑΘ. Οὐκ ἐγὼ ἔλεγον ὡς οὐκ ἀμελήσουσι
Τίμωνος ἀγαθοῦ ἀνδρὸς οἱ θεοί; χαῖρε Τίμων εὐμορ-
φότατε καὶ ἥδιστε καὶ συμποτικώτατε.

ΤΙΜ. Νηδὶ καὶ σύ γε, ὦ Γναθωνίδη, γυπῶν ἁπάντων βορώτατε καὶ ἀνθρώπων ἐπιτριπτότατε.

20 ΓΝΑΘ. Ἀεὶ φιλοσκώμμων σύ γε· ἀλλὰ ποῦ τὸ
συμπόσιον; ὡς καινόν τί σοι ᾆσμα τῶν νεοδιδάκτων
διθυράμβων ἥκω κομίζων.

ΤΙΜ. Καὶ μὴν ἐλεγεῖά γε ᾄσῃ μάλα περιπαθῶς
ὑπὸ ταύτῃ τῇ δικέλλῃ.

25 ΓΝΑΘ. Τί τοῦτο; παίεις, ὦ Τίμων; μαρτύρομαι·

ᾦ Ἡράκλεις, ἰοὺ ἰού, προσκαλοῦμαί σε τραύματος εἰς
Ἄρειον πάγον.

ΤΙΜ. Καὶ μὴν ἄν γε μικρὸν ἔτι βραδύνῃς, φόνου
τάχα προσκεκλήσομαι.

ΓΝΑΘ. Μηδαμῶς· ἀλλὰ σύ γε πάντως τὸ τραῦμα 5
ἴασαι μικρὸν ἐπιπάσας τοῦ χρυσίου· δεινῶς γὰρ
ἴσχαιμόν ἐστι τὸ φάρμακον.

ΤΙΜ. Ἔτι γὰρ μένεις;

ΓΝΑΘ. Ἄπειμι· σὺ δὲ οὐ χαιρήσεις οὕτω σκαιὸς
ἐκ χρηστοῦ γενόμενος.   10

*Philiades is the next, whose professed friendship for Timon
totally disappeared with his wealth. He has a good
deal to say for himself, but fares no better than the
last man.*

47. ΤΙΜ. Τίς οὗτός ἐστιν ὁ προσιών, ὁ ἀναφαλαντίας; Φιλιάδης, κολάκων ἁπάντων ὁ βδελυρώτατος. οὗτος δὲ ἀγρὸν ὅλον παρ' ἐμοῦ λαβὼν καὶ τῇ
θυγατρὶ προῖκα δύο τάλαντα, μισθὸν τοῦ ἐπαίνου,
ὁπότε ᾄσαντά με πάντων σιωπώντων μόνος ὑπερεπή- 15
νεσεν ἐπομοσάμενος ᾠδικώτερον εἶναι τῶν κύκνων,
ἐπειδὴ νοσοῦντα πρῴην εἶδέ με καὶ προσῆλθον ἐπι-
κουρίας δεόμενος, πληγὰς ὁ γενναῖος προσενέτεινεν.

48. ΦΙΛ. Ὦ τῆς ἀναισχυντίας. νῦν Τίμωνα
γνωρίζετε; νῦν Γναθωνίδης φίλος καὶ συμπότης; τοι- 20
γαροῦν δίκαια πέπονθεν οὗτος ἀχάριστος ὤν. ἡμεῖς
δὲ οἱ πάλαι συνήθεις καὶ συνέφηβοι καὶ δημόται
ὅμως μετριάζομεν, ὡς μὴ ἐπιπηδᾶν δοκῶμεν. χαῖρε,
ὦ δέσποτα, καὶ ὅπως τοὺς μιαροὺς τούτους κόλακας
φυλάξῃ, τοὺς ἐπὶ τῆς τραπέζης μόνον, τὰ ἄλλα δὲ 25
κοράκων οὐδὲν διαφέροντας. οὐκέτι πιστευτέα τῶν

νῦν οὐδενί· πάντες ἀχάριστοι καὶ πονηροί. ἐγὼ δὲ
τάλαντόν σοι κομίζων, ὡς ἔχοις πρὸς τὰ κατεπείγοντα
χρῆσθαι, καθ᾽ ὁδὸν ἤδη πλησίον ἤκουσα ὡς πλουτοίης
ὑπερμεγέθη τινὰ πλοῦτον. ἤκω τοιγαροῦν ταῦτά σε
5 νουθετήσων· καίτοι σύ γε οὕτω σοφὸς ὢν οὐδὲν ἴσως
δεήσῃ τῶν παρ᾽ ἐμοῦ λόγων, ὃς καὶ τῷ Νέστορι τὸ
δέον παραινέσειας ἄν.
ΤΙΜ. Ἔσται ταῦτα, ὦ Φιλιάδη. πλὴν ἀλλὰ
πρόσιθι· καὶ σὲ φιλοφρονήσομαι τῇ δικέλλῃ.
10 ΦΙΛ. Ἄνθρωποι, κατέαγα τοῦ κρανίου ὑπὸ τοῦ
ἀχαρίστου, διότι τὰ συμφέροντα ἐνουθέτουν αὐτόν.

*Demeas is the third, another example of the grossest in-
gratitude. He professes to be the bearer of good tidings
for Timon ; viz. that the "assemblies" have passed a
resolution that inasmuch as Timon had won the
contest at the Olympian games (it is useless for Timon
to declare that he had never been to Olympia even as a
spectator) and had vanquished the Peloponnesians,*

49. ΤΙΜ. Ἰδοὺ τρίτος οὗτος ὁ ῥήτωρ Δημέας
προσέρχεται ψήφισμα ἔχων ἐν τῇ δεξιᾷ καὶ συγγενὴς ἡμέτερος εἶναι λέγων. οὗτος ἑκκαίδεκα παρ᾽ ἐμοῦ
15 τάλαντα μιᾶς ἡμέρας ἐκτίσας τῇ πόλει—κατεδεδίκαστο γὰρ καὶ ἐδέδετο οὐκ ἀποδιδούς, κἀγὼ ἐλεήσας
ἐλυσάμην αὐτόν—ἐπειδὴ πρῴην ἔλαχε τῇ Ἐρεχθηῖδι
φυλῇ διανέμειν τὸ θεωρικὸν κἀγὼ προσῆλθον αἰτῶν
τὸ γιγνόμενον, οὐκ ἔφη γνωρίζειν πολίτην ὄντα με.
20 50. ΔΗΜ. Χαῖρε, ὦ Τίμων, τὸ μέγα ὄφελος τοῦ
γένους, τὸ ἔρεισμα τῶν Ἀθηνῶν, τὸ πρόβλημα τῆς
Ἑλλάδος· καὶ μὴν πάλαι σε ὁ δῆμος συνειλεγμένος
καὶ αἱ βουλαὶ ἀμφότεραι περιμένουσι. πρότερον δὲ

ἄκουσον τὸ ψήφισμα, ὃ ὑπὲρ σοῦ γέγραφα· " ἐπειδὴ
Τίμων ὁ Ἐχεκρατίδου Κολλυτεύς, ἀνὴρ οὐ μόνον
καλὸς κἀγαθός, ἀλλὰ καὶ σοφὸς ὡς οὐκ ἄλλος ἐν τῇ
Ἑλλάδι, παρὰ πάντα χρόνον διατελεῖ τὰ ἄριστα
πράττων τῇ πόλει, νενίκηκε δὲ πὺξ καὶ πάλην καὶ 5
δρόμον ἐν Ὀλυμπίᾳ μιᾶς ἡμέρας καὶ τελείῳ ἅρματι
καὶ συνωρίδι πωλικῇ —"
    ΤΙΜ. Ἀλλ' οὐδὲ ἐθεώρησα ἐγὼ πώποτε εἰς
Ὀλυμπίαν.
    ΔΗΜ. Τί οὖν; θεωρήσεις ὕστερον· τὰ τοιαῦτα 10
δὲ πολλὰ προσκεῖσθαι ἄμεινον. " καὶ ἠρίστευσε δὲ
ὑπὲρ τῆς πόλεως πέρυσι πρὸς Ἀχαρναῖς καὶ κατέ-
κοψε Πελοποννησίων δύο μόρας —"

    and had otherwise performed the highest services for the
    state, it was their intention to present him with a
    golden crown at the coming "Dionysian festival."
    Demeas himself was the first to propose this.

    51. ΤΙΜ. Πῶς; διὰ γὰρ τὸ μὴ ἔχειν ὅπλα οὐδὲ
προὐγράφην ἐν τῷ καταλόγῳ.   15
    ΔΗΜ. Μέτρια τὰ περὶ σαυτοῦ λέγεις, ἡμεῖς δὲ
ἀχάριστοι ἂν εἴημεν ἀμνημονοῦντες. " ἔτι δὲ καὶ ψηφίσματα γράφων καὶ συμβουλεύων καὶ στρατηγῶν
οὐ μικρὰ ὠφέλησε τὴν πόλιν· ἐπὶ τούτοις ἅπασι
δεδόχθω τῇ βουλῇ καὶ τῷ δήμῳ καὶ τῇ Ἡλιαίᾳ κατὰ 20
φυλὰς καὶ τοῖς δήμοις ἰδίᾳ καὶ κοινῇ πᾶσι χρυσοῦν
ἀναστῆσαι τὸν Τίμωνα παρὰ τὴν Ἀθηνᾶν ἐν τῇ ἀκροπόλει, κεραυνὸν ἐν τῇ δεξιᾷ ἔχοντα καὶ ἀκτῖνας ἑπτὰ
περὶ τῇ κεφαλῇ, καὶ στεφανῶσαι αὐτὸν χρυσοῖς στεφάνοις καὶ ἀνακηρυχθῆναι τοὺς στεφάνους τήμερον 25
Διονυσίοις τραγῳδοῖς καινοῖς—ἀχθῆναι γὰρ δι' αὐτὸν

δεῖ τήμερον τὰ Διονύσια.—εἶπε τὴν γνώμην Δημέας
ὁ ῥήτωρ, συγγενὴς αὐτοῦ ἀγχιστεὺς καὶ μαθητὴς
ὤν· καὶ γὰρ ῥήτωρ ἄριστος ὁ Τίμων καὶ τὰ ἄλλα
πάντα ὁπόσα ἂν ἐθέλῃ."

*Moreover D. intends to name his future son after Timon,
and......but he is stopped short in his harangue by a
good blow with the spade and he too goes off to seek
requital in the law courts.*

5   52. Τουτὶ μὲν οὖν σοι τὸ ψήφισμα. ἐγὼ δὲ καὶ
τὸν υἱὸν ἐβουλόμην ἀγαγεῖν παρὰ σέ, ὃν ἐπὶ τῷ σῷ
ὀνόματι Τίμωνα ὠνόμακα.

TIM. Πῶς, ὦ Δημέα, ὃς οὐδὲ γεγάμηκας, ὅσα γε
καὶ ἡμᾶς εἰδέναι;

10   ΔΗΜ. Ἀλλὰ γαμῶ, ἢν διδῷ θεός, ἐς νέωτα καὶ
παιδοποιήσομαι καὶ τὸ γεννηθησόμενον—ἄρρεν γὰρ
ἔσται—Τίμωνα ἤδη καλῶ.

TIM. Οὐκ οἶδα εἰ γαμεῖς ἔτι, ὦ οὗτος, τηλικαύ-
την παρ' ἐμοῦ πληγὴν λαμβάνων.

15   ΔΗΜ. Οἴμοι, τί τοῦτο; τυραννίδι, Τίμων, ἐπιχειρεῖς καὶ τύπτεις τοὺς ἐλευθέρους οὐ καθαρῶς ἐλεύ-
θερος οἰδ' ἀστὸς ὤν; ἀλλὰ δώσεις ἐν τάχει τὴν δίκην
τά τε ἄλλα καὶ ὅτι τὴν ἀκρόπολιν ἐνέπρησας.

*Nay, more! he will denounce Timon as an incendiary, and
a pillager of the Treasury. But he only gets a second
and a third blow for his trouble.*

53. TIM. Ἀλλ' οὐκ ἐμπέπρησται, ὦ μιαρέ, ἡ
20 ἀκρόπολις· ὥστε δῆλος εἶ συκοφαντῶν.

ΔΗΜ. Ἀλλὰ καὶ πλουτεῖς τὸν ὀπισθόδομον διο-
ρίξας.

ΤΙΜ. Οὐ διώρυκται οὐδὲ οὗτος ὥστε ἀπίθανά σου καὶ ταῦτα.

ΔΗΜ. Διορυχθήσεται μὲν ὕστερον· ἤδη δὲ σὺ πάντα τὰ ἐν αὐτῷ ἔχεις.

ΤΙΜ. Οὐκοῦν καὶ ἄλλην λάμβανε.   5

ΔΗΜ. Οἴμοι τὸ μετάφρενον.

ΤΙΜ. Μὴ κέκραχθι· κατοίσω γάρ σοι καὶ τρίτην· ἐπεὶ καὶ γελοῖα πάμπαν ἂν πάθοιμι δύο μὲν Λακεδαιμονίων μόρας κατακόψας ἄνοπλος, ἐν δὲ μιαρὸν ἀνθρώπιον μὴ ἐπιτρίψας· μάτην γὰρ ἂν εἴην καὶ 10 νενικηκὼς Ὀλύμπια πὺξ καὶ πάλην.

The next to come is the philosopher Thrasycles.—His garb, face, gait, and demeanour all mark him out as a typical philosopher: his mode of eating is on a par with everything else. He is excessively selfish and greedy, given to intemperance, if nothing worse; and none can beat him in the art of lying, cupidity, flattery, perjury, and shamelessness.

54. Ἀλλὰ τί τοῦτο; οὐ Θρασυκλῆς ὁ φιλόσοφος οὗτός ἐστιν; οὐ μὲν οὖν ἄλλος· ἐκπετάσας γοῦν τὸν πώγωνα καὶ τὰς ὀφρῦς ἀνατείνας καὶ βρενθυόμενός τι πρὸς αὑτὸν ἔρχεται, τιτανῶδες βλέπων, ἀνασεσοβη- 15 μένος τὴν ἐπὶ τῷ μετώπῳ κόμην, Αὐτοβορέας τις ἢ Τρίτων, οἵους ὁ Ζεῦξις ἔγραψεν. οὗτος ὁ τὸ σχῆμα εὐσταλὴς καὶ κόσμιος τὸ βάδισμα καὶ σωφρονικὸς τὴν ἀναβολὴν ἕωθεν μυρία ὅσα περὶ ἀρετῆς διεξιὼν καὶ τῶν ἡδονῇ χαιρόντων κατηγορῶν καὶ τὸ ὀλιγαρκὲς 20 ἐπαινῶν, ἐπειδὴ λουσάμενος ἀφίκοιτο ἐπὶ τὸ δεῖπνον καὶ ὁ παῖς μεγάλην τὴν κύλικα ὀρέξειεν αὐτῷ—τῷ ζωροτέρῳ δὲ χαίρει μάλιστα—καθάπερ τὸ Λήθης

ὕδωρ ἐκπιὼν ἐναντιώτατα ἐπιδείκνυται τοῖς ἑωθινοῖς
ἐκείνοις λόγοις προαρπάζων ὥσπερ ἰκτῖνος τὰ ὄψα
καὶ τὸν πλησίον παραγκωνιζόμενος, καρύκης τὸ γένειον ἀνάπλεως, κυνηδὸν ἐμφορούμενος, ἐπικεκυφώς,
5 καθάπερ ἐν ταῖς λοπάσι τὴν ἀρετὴν εὑρήσειν προσδο-
κῶν, ἀκριβῶς τὰ τρύβλια τῷ λιχανῷ ἀποσμήχων, ὡς
μηδὲ ὀλίγον τοῦ μυττωτοῦ καταλίποι.

55. Μεμψίμοιρος ἀεί, κἂν τὸν πλακοῦντα ὅλον ἢ
τὸν σῦν μόνος τῶν ἄλλων λάβῃ, [ἢ] ὅ τι περ λιχνείας
10 καὶ ἀπληστίας ὄφελος, μέθυσος καὶ πάροινος, οὐκ
ἄχρι ᾠδῆς καὶ ὀρχηστύος μόνον, ἀλλὰ καὶ λοιδορίας
καὶ ὀργῆς προσέτι. καὶ λόγοι πολλοὶ ἐπὶ τῇ κύλικι,
τότε δὴ καὶ μάλιστα, περὶ σωφροσύνης καὶ κοσμιότη-
τος· καὶ ταῦτά φησιν ἤδη ὑπὸ τοῦ ἀκράτου πονήρως
15 ἔχων καὶ ὑποτραυλίζων γελοίως· εἶτα ἔμετος ἐπὶ τού-
τοις· καὶ τὸ τελευταῖον ἀράμενοί τινες ἐκφέρουσιν
αὐτὸν ἐκ τοῦ συμποσίου τῆς αὐλητρίδος ἀμφοτέραις
ἐπειλημμένον. πλὴν ἀλλὰ καὶ νήφων οὐδενὶ τῶν
πρωτείων παραχωρήσειεν ἂν ψεύσματος ἕνεκα ἢ θρα-
20 σύτητος ἢ φιλαργυρίας· ἀλλὰ καὶ κολάκων ἐστὶ τὰ
πρῶτα καὶ ἐπιορκεῖ προχειρότατα, καὶ ἡ γοητεία
προηγεῖται καὶ ἡ ἀναισχυντία παρομαρτεῖ, καὶ ὅλως
πάνσοφόν τι χρῆμα καὶ πανταχόθεν ἀκριβὲς καὶ ποι-
κίλως ἐντελές. οἰμώξεται τοιγαροῦν οὐκ ἐς μακρὰν
25 χρηστὸς ὤν. τί τοῦτο; παπαῖ, χρόνιος ἡμῖν Θρασυκλῆς.

*He tells Timon much about his own abstemiousness, and
simple habits of living, and his utter disregard of
wealth. It would be well if T. would throw all his
gold into the sea—but not so far out but what Thras.
can walk in and pick it up.*

56. ΘΡΑΣ. Οὐ κατὰ ταὐτά, ὦ Τίμων, τοῖς πολλοῖς τούτοις ἀφῖγμαι, ὥσπερ οἱ τὸν πλοῦτόν σου τεθη-
πότες ἀργυρίου καὶ χρυσίου καὶ δείπνων πολυτελῶν
ἐλπίδι συνδεδραμήκασι πολλὴν τὴν κολακείαν ἐπι-
δειξόμενοι πρὸς ἄνδρα οἷον σὲ ἁπλοϊκὸν καὶ τῶν 5
ὄντων κοινωνικόν· οἶσθα γὰρ ὡς μᾶζα μὲν ἐμοὶ δεῖπνον ἱκανόν, ὄψον δὲ ἥδιστον θύμον ἢ κάρδαμον ἢ εἴ
ποτε τρυφῴην, ὀλίγον τῶν ἁλῶν· ποτὸν δὲ ἡ ἐννεά-
κρουνος· ὁ δὲ τρίβων οὗτος ἧς βούλει πορφυρίδος
ἀμείνων. τὸ χρυσίον μὲν γὰρ οὐδὲν τιμιώτερον τῶν 10
ἐν τοῖς αἰγιαλοῖς ψηφίδων μοι δοκεῖ. σὴν δὲ αὐτοῦ
χάριν ἐστάλην, ὡς μὴ διαφθείρῃ σε τὸ κάκιστον τοῦτο
καὶ ἐπιβουλότατον κτῆμα ὁ πλοῦτος, ὁ πολλοῖς πολλάκις αἴτιος ἀνηκέστων συμφορῶν γεγενημένος· εἰ
γάρ μοι πείθοιο, μάλιστα μὲν ὅλον ἐς τὴν θάλατταν 15
ἐμβαλεῖς αὐτόν, οὐδὲν ἀναγκαῖον ἀνδρὶ ἀγαθῷ ὄντι καὶ
τὸν φιλοσοφίας πλοῦτον ὁρᾶν δυναμένῳ· μὴ μέντοι
ἐς βάθος, ὦγαθέ, ἀλλ' ὅσον ἐς βουβῶνας ἐπεμβὰς
ὀλίγον πρὸ τῆς κυματωγῆς, ἐμοῦ ὁρῶντος μόνου·

*Or better still—let T. dispose of his wealth to those in need;
all philosophers to have triple shares. Thrasycles will
be contented if he gets only 20 gallons or so of gold:
a philosopher's needs do not go beyond a wallet-full.
He fares however no better than the others—and finds
himself getting full measure not of gold, but of blows!*

57. Εἰ δὲ μὴ τοῦτο βούλει, σὺ δὲ ἄλλον τρόπον 20
ἀμείνω κατὰ τάχος ἐκφόρησον αὐτὸν ἐκ τῆς οἰκίας
μηδ' ὀβολὸν σαυτῷ ἀνείς, διαδιδοὺς ἅπασι τοῖς δεομένοις, ᾧ μὲν πέντε δραχμάς, ᾧ δὲ μνᾶν, ᾧ δὲ ἡμιτάλαν-
τον· εἰ δέ τις φιλόσοφος εἴη, διμοιρίαν ἢ τριμοιρίαν

φέρεσθαι δίκαιος· ἐμοὶ δέ—καίτοι οὐκ ἐμαυτοῦ χάριν
αἰτῶ, ἀλλ' ὅπως μεταδῶ τῶν ἑταίρων τοῖς δεομένοις—
ἱκανὸν εἰ ταυτηνὶ τὴν πήραν ἐκπλήσας παράσχοις
οὐδὲ ὅλους δύο μεδίμνους χωροῦσαν Αἰγινητικούς.
5 ὀλιγαρκῇ δὲ καὶ μέτριον χρὴ εἶναι τὸν φιλοσοφοῦντα
καὶ μηδὲν ὑπὲρ τὴν πήραν φρονεῖν.

ΤΙΜ. Ἐπαινῶ ταῦτά σου, ὦ Θρασύκλεις· πρὸ
γοῦν τῆς πήρας, εἰ δοκεῖ, φέρε σοι τὴν κεφαλὴν ἐμ-
πλήσω κονδύλων ἐπιμετρήσας τῇ δικέλλῃ.

10   ΘΡΑΣ. Ὦ δημοκρατία καὶ νόμοι, παιόμεθα ὑπὸ
τοῦ καταράτου ἐν ἐλευθέρᾳ τῇ πόλει.

ΤΙΜ. Τί ἀγανακτεῖς, ὦγαθέ; μῶν παρακέκρουσμαί σε; καὶ μὴν ἐπεμβαλῶ χοίνικας ὑπὲρ τὸ μέτρον
τέτταρας.

*Many more now come up. Timon is wearied with using
his spade so freely, and changes his mode of reception.
We take leave of him standing on a rock, and keeping
off all intruders and beggars by pelting them with
stones.*

15   58. Ἀλλὰ τί τοῦτο; πολλοὶ συνέρχονται· Βλεψίας ἐκεῖνος καὶ Λάχης καὶ Γνίφων καὶ ὅλως τὸ σύν-
ταγμα τῶν οἰμωξομένων. ὥστε τί οὐκ ἐπὶ τὴν πέτραν
ταύτην ἀνελθὼν τὴν μὲν δίκελλαν ὀλίγον ἀναπαύω
πάλαι πεπονηκυῖαν, αὐτὸς δὲ ὅτι πλείστους λίθους
20 συμφορήσας ἐπιχαλαζῶ πόρρωθεν αὐτοῖς;

ΒΛΕΨ. Μὴ βάλλε, ὦ Τίμων· ἄπιμεν γάρ.

ΤΙΜ. Ἀλλ' οὐκ ἀναιμωτί γε ὑμεῖς οὐδὲ ἄνευ
τραυμάτων.

NOTES.

MENIPPUS.

p. 1. § 1. Enter Menippus, on his return from a visit to the shades, where he has been to consult Teiresias (like Odysseus in the 11th Book of the *Odyssey*) as to what is the "best life." He naturally recalls to mind the words which Euripides puts into the mouth of Heracles (*Her. Fur.* 523) on returning from the lower world:—
"All hail! thou hall, and thou porch of my home, how gladly I see thee, coming again to the light!"

4 κύων. A word commonly employed of Menippus, cf. *Inf. Dial.* 1. 1, ἤν που ἴδῃς Μένιππον τὸν κύνα: Id. 2. 7, οὐ φέρομεν Μένιππον τουτονὶ τὸν κύνα παροικοῦντα: and Id. 27. 7, where Men. himself says to Cerberus, ὦ Κέρβερε (συγγενὴς γάρ εἰμί σοι, κύων καὶ αὐτὸς ὤν). The idea is in special reference to the snarling dog-like nature of a Cynic (κυνικός). See Introduction, Section on Men. the philosopher.

μὲν οὖν or μενοῦν is sometimes a stronger form of οὖν = "so then," but in answer to questions it generally implies a concession of more than was asked, cf. the Latin *immo vero*. Thus Plat. *Gorg.* 466, ἐγὼ οὐ φημί; φημὶ μὲν οὖν ἔγωγε. "Do I deny it? Nay indeed, I assert it." So here, "Is this the dog Menippus?" "Why, surely it can be none other."

5 παραβλέπω, "I am mistaken:" cf. next note; not used elsewhere by L.

Μένιππος ὅλος. The MSS. have ὅλους Μενίππους, and no stop at παραβλέπω, "unless I am quite mistaken in Menippuses:" but παραβ. does not take an accus. in sense of "being mistaken." The emendation given above was first made by Graevius, and is adopted by Dindorf and editors generally. If *Inf. Dial.* 16. 1 is anything to go by, it is a certain emendation.

When they are placed in columns one may see the close parallelism between the two passages.

Inf. Dial. 16. 1.	*Menippus* 1.
Οὐχ Ἡρακλῆς οὗτός ἐστιν; οὐ μὲν οὖν ἄλλος, μὰ τὸν Ἡρα-κλέα· τὸ τόξον, τὸ ῥόπαλον, ἡ λεοντῆ, τὸ μέγεθος, ὅλος Ἡρα-κλῆς ἐστιν.	Οὐ Μένιππος οὗτός ἐστιν ὁ κύων; οὐ μὲν οὖν ἄλλος, εἰ μὴ ἐγὼ παραβλέπω· Μένιππος ὅλος. ......πῖλος, καὶ λύρα, καὶ λεοντῆ.

Trans. "Surely, it's none other, unless my eyes deceive me; its M. all over!"

6 βούλεται, "mean;" so in *Tyr.* § 3, τί βουλόμενος ἀπεδίδρασκε; "what did he mean by running away?" and § 9, τί βουλόμενος ταῦτα ἔπραξε; "what did he do this for?"

σχῆμα differs from μορφή as *habitus* (the thing worn or external appearance) differs from *figura* (the bodily shape). Here we have "the strangeness of his *garb*," but τὰς μορφὰς ἀλλοκότους in *Conc. Deor.* § 4 = "monstrous in *shape*," where it is used of the Satyrs. Thus in § 76 σχῆμα is used throughout, μορφή not once. So again in *Pisc.* § 35 the diadem, tiara, sceptre, &c. are called σχῆμα βασιλικὸν, cf. *de Saltat.* 29 τὸ τοῦ ὀρχηστοῦ σχῆμα.

πῖλος, λύρα, λεοντῆ. Odysseus is represented with the *cap*, Orpheus with the *lyre*, Heracles with the *lion's skin;* in § 8 Menippus explains why he is wearing this strange garb. In the dialogue "on history," § 10, we have Omphale belabouring Heracles with a slipper, and τὴν λεοντῆν αὐτοῦ περιβεβλημένην καὶ τὸ ξύλον ἔχουσαν, "as though she were Heracles herself," cf. *adv. ind.* § 23, *Vit. auc.* § 8.

8 ἡμῖν, *not* dat. of motion to, but of person concerned, cf. ἀσμένοις ἡμῖν ἀφῖγμαι, and Aesch. *Prom.* 23, ἀσμένῳ δέ σοι...νὺξ ἀποκρύψει φάος.

10 Ἥκω, κ.τ.λ. The opening lines of Eur. *Hecuba*, spoken by the ghost of Polydorus. "I am come from the house of the dead and the gates of darkness where, &c."

12 Ἡράκλεις, a common form of affirmation. More commonly ὦ, μά, or νὴ is prefixed.

ἐλελήθει ἀποθανών, lit. "he had escaped notice dying," i.e.
"died without our knowing it." Cf. note *Timon* § 20, ἐλελήθεις με
οὐ τυφλός, κ.τ.λ. See also § 4 this dialogue. Cf. Hor. *Ep.* I. 17. 10
for something similar : "qui *natus moriensque fefellit*"="lived and
died *unnoticed*."

13   **ἐξ ὑπαρχῆς**=*de novo* "anew." So, in *Tyran.* 24, πῶς καθαρὸς
ἐξ ὑπαρχῆς ἀναπέφηνας ;

14   **Οὔκ, ἀλλ' ἔτ',** also from Euripides.   ἔτ' ἔμπνουν, cf. Thuc. I.
134, "still breathing."   Cf. *Phalaris* 12, ἐγὼ δὲ ἔτι ἔμπνουν καὶ
ζῶντα τὸν ἄνδρα ἐξαιρεθῆναι κελεύσας.

p. 2. 3 **Νεότης μ',** from Eur. *Androm.* of which only a few
fragments are extant (Dind. 138). σθένος is read there instead of
θράσος.

5   **οὑτωσί πως ἁπλῶς,** "just simply."   οὕτω not uncommonly has
the force of "merely," cf. *Il.* II. 120 for μὰψ οὕτως. So Plat.
Gorg. 506 D, οὕτως εἰκῆ.   In Plat. *Laws* 633 C, ἁπλῶς οὕτως occurs
again. Cf. also Luc. *Pisc.* § 4, οὕτω ῥαδίως, and *Harm.* 2, οὑτωσί
πως "just anyhow." The usage of *sic* in Latin is parallel, as Hor.
Od. II. 11. 14, " jacentes sic temere."

6   **καταβάς,** quite literally, "coming down from your iambics," for
he had been "talking on stilts." Cf. § 16, l. 22.

7   **ἄλλως γάρ,** "for otherwise," i.e. if you hadn't some good cause
for going.

9   **Ὦ φιλότης,** κ.τ.λ. From Hom. *Odys.* XI. 163 ; only Homer has
μῆτερ ἐμὴ as the first two words.

10   **χρησόμενον,** future participle, expressing "purpose,"=" to consult."   For Teiresias see note § 6.
        Inf. Dial. 28 is between Teiresias and Odysseus. So in *de
Astrolog.* § 24 Lucian says : "so Odysseus, when weary of wandering,
being anxious to hear accurately of his own matters, came to Hades,
not for the purpose of seeing the dead and the joyless region, but
from desire to consult Teiresias."

11   **Οὗτος, ἀλλ' ἢ παραπαίεις ;** So Dindorf for ἀλλ' ἢ and no inter-
rogation given in the MSS. "What, can it be that you have taken
leave of your senses?" This is a frequent use of οὗτος=Lat. *heus tu!*
"Hallo! you there."
        For π α ρ α π α ι ε ι ν, "to be out of one's senses," cf. *Inf. D.* 27. 9,
παραπαίεις ὦ γέρον. *Harm.* 3, ἢ τίνα γὰρ ἂν πρὸ σοῦ ἑλόμενος οὐχὶ
παραπαίειν ἂν εἰκότως νομισθείην ; v. *Timon* 17, and *P. V.* 1077, τί

γὰρ ἐλλείπει μὴ παραπαίειν ; The word literally means "to strike aside," or "to slip aside "—of the plough from the furrow. Cf. Lat. *delirare*, e g. Hor. *Ep*. 1. 2. 14.

οὐ γὰρ ἂν οὕτως "otherwise you would not," &c. So in *Timon* § 7.

12   ἐρραψῴδεις. The imperfect denotes *continuous* action, "you wouldn't *keep on quoting* poetry in this way." The word is often used by Lucian in this sense; technically a ῥαψῳδός was a man who got his living by going about from place to place reciting Homer's poems. The last lines which Menippus quoted being from Homer would suggest the use of this word to Philonides.

14   οὐκ οἶδ' ὅπως. The phrase occurs again in § 19, and at the very end of this dialogue, also twice in the *Timon*, §§ 1, 20. It seems best to take it parenthetically "somehow or other." It is used in much the same way by Plutarch, e.g. *Themist.* XXIV. 3, εἶτ' οὐκ οἶδ' ὅπως ἐπιλαθόμενος...φησίν. Lucian is very fond of it.

20   § 2. τοκογλυφοῦσιν (so τοκογλύφοι § 11) "split interest," "calculate minute fractions," i.e. "practise usury." This metaphor is of "*dotting down*," as ὀβολοστατοῦσιν is usury by "*weighing*" every obol. Cf. Aristoph. *Nub.* 1155, κλάετ' ὡβολοστάται. Becker, *Char.* 71, quoting this passage from the *Menippus* says "from their weighing the coin thus the 'trapezitae' were contemptuously called ὀβολοστάται." Cf. *Symp.* 36, δανείζετε καὶ τοκογλυφεῖτε καὶ ἐπὶ μισθῷ παιδεύετε.

22   οἷα ἔναγχος κεκύρωται, "what law has just now been ratified."

οἷα...τὰ ψηφίσματα. Notice this is not οἷα ψηφίσματα but οἷα τὰ ψηφ. "how fearful are the decrees, which they have passed." Lucian is *very* fond of this use of the predicate; see a little lower down in this section, χαλεπὸν...τοὐπίταγμα and cf. p. 9, l. 1 ; p. 17, l. 13; *Timon* § 7, ἀσεβεῖς τοὺς λόγους.

24   μὰ τὸν Κέρβερον. A very natural oath, considering he had only just come up from the lower world, and was himself a κύων, cousin to Cerberus as he jocularly says elsewhere.

p. 3.   3   οὐ θέμις...Μηδαμῶς, for a similar turn of phrase cf. note on § 21. Μηδαμῶς, "Don't by any means."

4   τὰ ἀπόρρητα ἐξαγορεύειν : ἀπόρρητα = *tacenda* = things which should not be mentioned. The word is especially applied to the secrets of the Eleusinian mysteries, cf. our Freemasonry. See note

on μεμνημένον below. Cf. *Pisc.* § 33, οὐκοῦν ἦν τινα καὶ τῶν μεμνημένων ἰδὼν ἐξαγορεύοντα τοῖν θεοῖν τἀπόρρητα.

5   γράψηται γραφὴν ἀσεβείας. The technical phrase for "bringing an indictment" is γράφεσθαι γραφὴν or δίκην. The charge is put in the genitive as here; ἐπί "before the tribunal" is also the legal word.

9   τά τ' ἄλλα καὶ πρὸς μεμυημένον, "and what is more to one who has been initiated." Cf. Arist. *Ran.* 456, ὅσοι μεμνήμεθα, and *Pisc.* quoted just above. The reference is to the mysteries of Eleusis, which had a share of Lucian's satire like every other form of religious worship in Greece.

10   Χαλεπόν...τούπίταγμα. Cf. § 2 just above.

11   πλὴν ἀλλά, another very common expression of Lucian's, see § 7. *Timon* §§ 24, 26, 45, 48, 55. It simply = πλήν.

13   ὥσπερ τὴν Δανάην, "keep guard over their gold shut up, as over a Danaë." The story of Danaë is well known. She was daughter of Acrisius, king of Argos. In fear of an oracle which declared her son should put him to death, Acrisius had her confined in a brazen tower. The story, told with true poetical power, may be found in Kingsley's *Heroes* or Morris's *Earthly Paradise.* Her fate was a very common subject of allusion in ancient poetry. She is mentioned again in *Timon* §§ 13, 41. Νῦν πείθομαί γε καὶ Δία ποτὲ γενέσθαι χρυσόν is a tacit allusion to her. Cf. also Hor. *Od.* III. 16. 1, "Inclusam Danaën turris aenea | Robustaeque fores... munierant," &c.

15   ὠγαθέ, "my good sir." The expression occurs again in *Timon* §§ 25, 37, and elsewhere frequently. It implies a gentle remonstrance.

21   § 3. τί γὰρ ἂν πάθοι, κ.τ.λ., quite a favourite turn of sentence, cf. *Timon* § 39, τί γὰρ ἂν καὶ πάθοι τις, ὁπότε οἱ θεοὶ βιάζοιντο; "what can a man do, when the gods compel?" and note there.

22   βιάζοιτο. This optat. is due to the previous πάθοι. It is not an uncommon thing for one optative to succeed another through attraction, cf. below, p. 44, l. 23. So *Ajax* 1218, γενοίμαν ἵνα...προσείποιμεν (Jebb's note), and Aesch. *Eum.* 288, ἔλθοι...ὅπως γένοιτο.

    καὶ δή, "so there." One can't resist a bosom-friend, "so here goes," to use a slang term.

p. 4. 1   ὅθεν ὡρμήθην πρός, "what prompted me to make the descent."

    ἐγὼ γάρ, κ.τ.λ. The order in translation is ἐγὼ γάρ, ἄχρι μὲν

ἐν παισὶν ἦν, ἀκούων Ὁμήρου καὶ Ἡσ. διηγουμένων πολέμους, καὶ στάσεις
οὐ μόνον...ἡγούμην πάντα ταῦτα, &c.

7 **οὐ παρέργως.** παρέργως, or ἐν παρέργῳ, is a good classical
term = Lat. *obiter*, "by the way." Here it means "by no means
as a secondary consideration" i.e. "very zealously." Cf. *Epis. to
Nigr.*, ὅπως τε νῦν ἔχω καὶ ὅτι μὴ παρέργως εἴλημμαι πρὸς τῶν
σῶν λόγων..."how I now am, and that I am 'taken' with your
arguments *in no slight degree*." So *Apol.* 15, οὐκ ἐν παρέργῳ
θέμενος. Cf. *Tim.* § 4, πάρεργον.

8 **εἰς ἄνδρας τελεῖν,** "to arrive at the full stage of manhood," "to
take a place among men." So in Soph. *Oed. Tyr.* 222, νῦν δ'
ὕστερος γὰρ ἀστὸς εἰς ἀστοὺς τελῶ, "I become a full citizen,"
Plat. *Menexenus* 21, ἐπειδὰν εἰς ἀνδρὸς τέλος ἴωσιν.

πάλιν αὖ. The double adverb is not at all uncommon, αὖθις
πάλιν, πάλιν αὖθις, αὖ πάλιν, even αὖθις αὖ πάλιν, and αὖ πάλιν
αὖθις, are all used classically. Here it = "on the contrary." αὖ
πάλιν occurs in the next section.

11 **ὅ τι χρησαίμην ἐμαυτῷ,** "in what way I should make use of
myself," i.e. "what I was to do with myself." χρῆσθαι ἑαυτῷ
ἀφειδῶς πρός τι, Plut. *Alex.* § 45; and so in next section, as he
does not know what to do with himself he goes to the philosophers
δεηθῆναι αὐτῶν χρῆσθαί μοι ὅ τι βούλοιντο.

13 **εἰ μὴ ὡς περὶ καλῶν τούτων ἐγίγνωσκον.** The meaning is plain,
but the construction mixed; = εἰ μὴ ἐγίγνωσκον περὶ τούτων ὡς ὄντων
καλῶν; "unless they judged of these actions as being honourable,"
i.e. "if they had not regarded them as honourable."

14 **οὔτ' ἂν τοὺς νομοθέτας.** The τοὺς is "generic," i.e. it denotes
the *class*, "lawgivers" generally, e.g. Solon and Lycurgus, "nor
would lawgivers have laid down rules contrary to these, had they not
deemed them expedient."

This passage is only one among scores in which L. spends his
humour upon satirizing philosophy, or rather, not philosophy herself
so much as that tribe of professed philosophers, rhetoricians and
dialecticians, who abounded in his day. Not being able to solve a
difficulty, he naturally applies to those who made such solutions
their daily profession (παρὰ τοὺς καλουμένους φιλοσόφους), only to
find that he had "jumped out of the frying-pan into the fire."

In *Dial. Inf.* 20. 4 in answer to Socrates' question, "Well, what's
doing at Athens?" Menippus says: "Many of the young men say

they are philosophers; and if one is to judge by their swagger
and their general 'cut' there are many consummate philosophers!"
v. Introd. Section on "L.'s attitude toward philosophy."

17   § **4.** διηπόρουν, "*utterly* at a loss," διά in composition frequently denotes *thoroughness*, e. g. διαπράττειν =*conficere*, διαπονεῖν
=*elaborare*.

18   ἐγχειρίσαι τε ἐμαυτόν, "to place myself in their hands," so in
Tim. § 32 ὁ Πλοῦτος…"Ὕβρει καὶ Τύφῳ ἐγχειρίσας, "having given him
over to insult," &c., *Icarom.* 5 τούτοις ἐγχειρίσας ἐμαυτόν.

22   ἐλελήθειν δ' ἐμαυτόν…βιαζόμενος, "but without knowing it, I
had forced myself;" see note on ἐλελήθει, § 1.

      εἰς αὐτὸ…τὸ πῦρ, "right into the fire."

      φασί = ὥς φασι as often in Lucian; cf. *de merc. cond.* § 1, τί
πρῶτον, ἢ τί ὕστατον, φασί, καταλέξω. *Apolog.* § 9, κᾆτα εὑρίσκωμαι
ἥλῳ, φασίν, ἐκκρούων τὸν ἧλον.

24   ηὕρισκον ἐπισκοπῶν, "on examination I found," cf. p. 5, l. 18.

25   χρυσὸν…τὸν τῶν ἰδιωτῶν βίον, "that the life of an ordinary
man is the golden one." This was the general cry of ancient
philosophy; cf. the following from among several passages: Arist.
Pol. IV. 11, ὁ μέσος βίος βέλτιστος; Plat. *Rep.* X. § 14, τὸν μέσον, κ.τ.λ.
"One should ever choose the moderate life, and flee excess on either
hand…for so does a man become the more blessed." Hor. *Od.* II.
10. 5, "Auream quisquis mediocritatem | Diligit," and Aesch. *Supp.*
244. So in Prov. xxx. 8, "Give me neither poverty nor riches."
Cf. *Tim.* 16.

26   τῶν ἰδιωτῶν. ἰδιώτης is used in innumerable passages by Lucian
=the unprofessional man, opposed to φιλόσοφος, e.g. *Fugit.* § 3,
εἰ μήτε τοὺς ἰδιώτας μήτε τοὺς φιλοσόφους αἰτιᾷ, and § 21, where the
usual wallet, cloak, &c. of the philosopher are mentioned, and he
adds: οἱ ἰδιῶται δὲ ταῦτα ὁρῶντες καταπτύουσιν ἤδη φιλοσοφίας.

      ὁ μὲν…ὁ δέ τις—ἄλλος…ὁ δέ τις. In philosophic writers the
indefinite τις was often added to the *article*, in order to individualize
a general term, especially in opposite clauses as here. See L. and S.
(τις, A. 11. c).

      ἀμέλει ὁ μὲν αὐτῶν, κ.τ.λ. Here and in the following lines are
given four chief schools of philosophy, with their "summum bonum,"
or highest perfection of happiness.

      (*a*) The Epicurean, founder Epicurus (B.C. 341—270), taught
in his gardens (κῆποι). Chief good, *pleasure*.

(*b*) The Cynics, founder Antisthenes, first half of 4th cent. B.C. (Diogenes, the most famous), taught abstinence from marriage, repudiation of all civil claims, like mendicant friars. Received their name from their churlish manners; endured hard fare, begged their bread, rebuked luxury, and posed as models of virtue. Chief good, *wisdom.*

(*c*) Stoic, founder Zeno (320—260, B.C. circ.), taught in porch (στοά). Chief good finally stood with them as *life in accordance with nature.*

(*d*) Peripatetic, really founded by Aristotle (B.C. 384—322), though his successors Theophrastus and Strato departed widely from his teaching, taught in "Lyceum" *while walking* (περιπατῶν), hence their name. Chief good, *happiness.*

The well-known lines of Pope (*Essay on Man* 4) are very apposite:—

> "Ask of the learned the way? The learned are blind :
> This bids to serve, and that to shun, mankind;
> Some place their bliss in action, some in ease,
> Those call it pleasure, and contentment these;
> Some sunk to beasts find pleasure end in pain,
> Some swelled to gods, confess e'en virtue vain;
> Or indolent, to each extreme they fall,
> To trust in ev'rything, or doubt of all.
> Who thus define it, say they more or less
> Than this, that happiness is happiness?"

Varro (B. C. 50) reckoned 288 different opinions held on the point.

31 **συνεχὲς.** The neuter adjective used as an adverb, as is commonly the case. Cf. *Timon* § 3, and § 9 in this book παμμέγεθες ἀνακραγών, and εἰκότα = εἰκότως *Timon* § 9. So in Lat., e.g. Verg. *Aen.* VI. 288, *horrendum stridens.*

ἐπιρραψῳδῶν, cf. note on § 1.

τὰ πάνδημα ἐκεῖνα ἔπη, "those well-known lines of Hesiod." The lines referred to are in *Works and Days* (287—290),

> τῆς ἀρετῆς ἱδρῶτα θεοὶ προπάροιθεν ἔθηκαν
> ἀθάνατοι· μακρὸς δὲ καὶ ὄρθιος οἶμος ἐπ' αὐτὴν
> καὶ τρηχὺς τὸ πρῶτον, ἐπὴν δ' εἰς ἄκρον ἵκηται
> ῥηιδίη δ' ἔπειτα πέλει, χαλεπή περ ἐοῦσα.

p. 5. 2 τὴν ἀνάβασιν. There is a sarcastic hit at this "steep ascent" in the *V. Hist.* II. § 18, where the Stoics are absent from the philosophers in the Isles of the Blessed, as not yet having got up "the straight ascent" (ἔτι γὰρ ἐλέγοντο ἀναβαίνειν τὸν τῆς ἀρετῆς ὄρθιον λόφον).

3   **ἀδιάφορον.** Things "indifferent" were with the Stoics everything between the "summum bonum" and "summum malum."

6   **ὃς γε** is subject of ἐναντίων ἀκούων, "sick of hearing." This, the reading of a few MSS., is almost certain; most have ἤκουον ἐναντίων.

ἰδέαι, the Platonic "ideas," or "originals," of which existing things are only patterns.

7   **ἀσώματα,** "incorporeal things," *Tim.* § 9, cf. *V. H.* II. § 12, Jerram's note.

ἀτόμους, κενά, of Epicurus. Democritus originated the theory that varied atoms combined to form all existing things. And so Democritus says in *Sale of Philosophers' Lives,* § 13, κενὰ δὲ τὰ πάντα, καὶ ἀτόμων φορή.

8   **ὁσημέραι,** contracted from ὅσαι ἡμέραι (εἰσίν): cf. quoti-die, quotannis; "daily."

11   **ὥστε...ἀντιλέγειν ἔχειν,** "so that one could not contradict even," &c....**καὶ ταῦτα εἰδότα σαφῶς,** "and *that too,* though one knew perfectly well." καὶ ταῦτα is used not uncommonly by the best writers in this way, i.e. as a particle, quite irrespective of construction, and very frequently by Lucian, cf. *Tim.* § 11, καὶ ταῦτα ἐμοῦ κελεύσαντος. *Gallus* § 10, καὶ ταῦτα φιλόσοφον ἄνδρα. Cf. § 14, καὶ ταῦτα, πῶς οἴει, βαρεῖς ὄντες. *Navig.* § 19, καὶ ταῦτα εἰσηγητὴς αὐτὸς γενόμενος. § 46, καὶ ταῦτα φιλοσοφίαν ἐπαινοῦντες. Cf. too Cic. *Phil.* II. 27, "Totos dies potabatur, *atque id* locis pluribus."

14   **ἀτεχνῶς οὖν ἔπασχον, κ.τ.λ.,** "I was, therefore, in the same condition as those nodding puppets, now bobbing forward, now back again;" for this use of πάσχω cf. *Char.* 22, παγγέλοι' ἂν ἔπασχες, "you would have been in the same ridiculous condition;" *de dips.* § 9, ὅμοιόν τι καὶ αὐτὸς παθεῖν πρὸς ὑμᾶς οἷον ἐκεῖνοι πάσχουσι πρὸς τὸ ποτὸν οἱ δηχθέντες ὑπὸ τῆς διψάδος, "I was in much the same condition toward you, as those who are bitten by the thirst-snake feel toward drink."

15   For **νυστάζουσι,** cf. *de mer. cond.* § 29, οὐ μόνον τἀληθῆ ὁρῶντες ἀλλ' ἀεί τι καὶ προσεπιμετροῦντες, ὡς μὴ νυστάζειν δοκοῖεν.

ἐπινεύων, nodding 'yes.' **ἀνανεύων,** shaking the head for 'no.'

In *adv. indoc.* § 5 the distinction is clearly seen. "If you think
good, answer me; or rather, since this is impossible for you,"
ἐπίνευσον γοῦν ἢ ἀνάνευσον πρὸς τὰ ἐρωτώμενα..."answer my
questions with a nod or shake"...εὖ γε ἀνένευσας, "You are right,
in saying no." For the general sentiment, cf. Hor. *Sat.* II. 7. 82,
"Duceris ut nervis alienis mobile lignum."

17   § 5. Πολλῷ...ἀλογώτερον, MSS. ἀτοπώτερον which is probable;
just above it was πάντων δεινῶν ἀτοπώτατον, and now it is
πολλῷ ἐκείνων ἀτοπώτερον. ἐκεῖνο, of what follows, as Cicero
often uses *illud.*

19   γοῦν, "at any rate." ἀπρίξ, "tooth and nail."

21   τόκων. Aristotle, for one, condemned *usury*, on the principle
that *money*, being naturally *barren*, if it beget offspring (τόκος,
τίκτω, I bear) acts *contrary to nature* (*Polit.* I. 10. 5). Shakespeare's
"breed of barren metal" is well known. Bacon calls interest, "the
bastard use of money."

ἐπὶ μισθῷ παιδεύοντας. The sophists and rhetoricians demanded
often a most exorbitant fee, making no reduction for a poorer pupil.
Aristippus and Isocrates charged 1000 drachmae (£40). Socrates
most strongly condemned this money-taking. He himself taught
gratis to all comers, and is said to have lived on £20 a year.

23   αὐτῆς ταύτης χάριν, "for the sake of this very thing" (i.e. δόξα).

26   προσηρτημένους. Lucian is fond of this verb with its different
compounds: "clinging to it alone." Cf. *Tim.* §§ 5, 36.

p. 6. 1 § 6. Σφαλείς, "being disappointed of my hope." σφάλλω
usually takes the *genitive* in this sense. Cf. Thuc. IV. 85, σφάλλεσθαι
τῆς δόξης. *pro laps.* 1, ἀπεσφάλην τοῦ καλῶς ἔχοντος. Cf. Plato
Phaed. § 47, where Socrates says ἀπὸ δὴ θαυμαστῆς, ὦ ἑταῖρε, ἐλπίδος
ᾠχόμην φερόμενος.

2   ἠρέμα παραμυθούμενος ἐμαυτόν, ὅτι, κ.τ.λ. Paraphrased, the
passage means, "I consoled myself with the thought that I was not the
only foolish and ignorant one; I had many to keep me company, aye,
wise men too (so people called them), and men famed for their sense."

3   ἐπὶ συνέσει διαβεβοημένων, "celebrated *for* prudence." So in
Somnium § 13 we have τὸ ἐπὶ συνέσει εὐδαιμονίζεσθαι. An Athenian
especially prided himself on his σύνεσις.

7   Ζωροάστρου. Zoroaster was said to have been the founder of the
Median or Magian religion, i.e. a religion of fire-worship. No Greek
writer mentions him before the time of Plato.

8 ἐπῳδαῖς τε καὶ τελεταῖς. The former refers to *incantations*, or charms, sung over some one to heal or harm. The latter is *initiation* into some mystic rites. The witches of *Macbeth* are instances of the first; the ceremony of initiating into the Eleusinian mysteries gives an example of the second.

11 ἄριστον οὖν, κ.τ.λ. "I deemed it best therefore, having effected my descent through one of these, to go to Teiresias," &c.

12 Τειρεσίαν τὸν Βοιώτιον. The old blind prophet of Thebes, who had extraordinary powers of divination conferred upon him. He was held in great honour by the ancients. Circe thus describes him to Odysseus. Cf. *Odys.* x. 493 :

> μάντηος ἀλαοῦ, τοῦ τε φρένες ἔμπεδοί εἰσι·
> τῷ καὶ τεθνηῶτι νόον πόρε Περσεφόνεια
> οἴῳ πεπνῦσθαι.

Cf. also note § 1; in *de Astrol.* § 11 he calls him ἄνδρα Βοιώτιον, τοῦ δὴ κλέος μαντοσύνης πέρι πολλὸν ἀείρεται.

13 ἅτε. One of L.'s most favourite words. Cf. in this dialogue § 8, ἅτε συνηθέστερον : § 11, ἅτε ἀεὶ συνοῦσαι, and *Timon* § 21, ἅτε πλουτοδότης: § 25, ἅτε τῶν μὲν ἀγαθῶν : § 41, &c. = "as," "as being," "inasmuch as;" the omission of the participle is particularly Lucianic.

14 ὃν ἄν...φρονῶν. ὅν is a relative, "the life which," not interrogative like τίς before, "which is the best life and the one which a man would be wise in choosing." Notice that the participle often in Greek carries the main idea, and becomes in English the finite verb.

15 καὶ δή. Cf. note §§ 3, 22. They help to cut short the previous conversation (something like the Tacitean *ceterum* after a digression), cf. the three places in this dialogue : § 3, "I can't refuse you, *so* I'll begin by telling you," &c. *Here*, "So up I jumped." § 22, "And so, true to his word, he led me off."

ὡς εἶχον τάχους. For similar phrases, cf. πῶς ἔχεις δόξης, ἱκανῶς ἐπιστήμης ἕξει, ὡς ποδῶν εἶχον, &c., e.g. Herod. VIII. 107, ὡς τάχεος εἶχε ἕκαστος. Lit. "according to what (measure) of speed I had," "as quickly as I could."

16 εὐθὺ Βαβυλῶνος. In Xen. *Cyr.* v. 2. 37 we have εὐθὺ ἐπὶ Βαβυλῶνος, but εὐθὺ is commonly used as a *prepos. gov. the genitive* itself. Aristophanes is fond of it: cf. among several passages, *Pax* 68, εὐθὺ τοῦ Διός. So Eur. *Hipp.* 1197, τὴν εὐθὺς Ἄργους κἀπι-

δαυρίας ὁδόν, "the road leading direct to Argos and Epidaurus."
Cf. *Hermot*. § 46, μαθὼν ὡς μόνη ἄγει εὐθὺ τῆς εὐδαιμονίας.

18   γένειον δὲ μάλα σεμνὸν κc.θειμένῳ. A beard was esteemed "a
sign of manliness and power," a necessary concomitant of a philosopher, "a dignified ornament of maturity and old age." Beck. *Char.*
457. Cf. *Tim*. § 54, ἐκπετάσας τὸν πώγωνα; see the passage from
Dial. Inf. x. 7 quoted there. Missionaries from the Beloochees
relate that the natives despise all white men who have no beard and
no wife.

19   **Μιθροβαρζάνης,** who conducts Menippus to the lower world, as
Vergil did Dante, and the Sybil Vergil, and shews him the way back
again (see end of dialogue), is quite an imaginary person. The name
is formed, no doubt, on the analogy of Ariobarzanes, and other
historic names, from Mithras the sun-god of the Magi, mentioned
by Lucian in *Jup. Trag*. 8 with Attis, Anubis, and Mên, and in
Conc. Deor. 9 with Attis, Sabazius and Corybas, as ὁ Μίθρης
ἐκεῖνος, ὁ Μῆδος, ὁ τὸν κάνδυν καὶ τὴν τιάραν, οὐδὲ ἑλληνίζων τῇ φωνῇ·
ὥστε οὐδ', ἢν προπίῃ τις, ξυνίησι, "that Mithras, the Median, with
the robe and diadem, who can't even speak Greek, and won't
understand you, if you drink his health." Cf. also Xen. *Cyr*. VII.
5. 53, and Mithropaustes, Plut. *Them*. 29. 3.

21   καθηγήσασθαι...τῆς ὁδοῦ. The genitive is here a partitive one,
cf. Xen. *Anab*. I. 3. 1, ἰέναι τοῦ πρόσω, Thuc. IV. 47, ἐπιταχύνειν
(τινὰς) τῆς ὁδοῦ, "to hasten them on their way."

p. 7.   2 § **7.** ἅμα τῇ σελήνῃ, "at full moon."

6   ἐπίτροχόν τι καὶ ἀσαφὲς, "some indistinct gabble."
πλὴν, "save that."

7   δ' οὖν. "Well! and after the incantation," used to emphasize
or else to pick up the thread after some digression, v. p. 8, l. 12;
and p. 11, l. 6; 9. 24, &c. Cf. Arist. *Ach*. 186, οἱ δ' οὖν βοώντων,
"Then *let* them shout." Eur. *Herc. F*. 213, εἰ δ' οὖν θέλεις, "but if
you *do* wish."

8   ἐπῳδήν, cf. note, § 6.
τρὶς ἄν...ἀποπτύσας. "Having spat in my face three times."
The number three seems specially devoted to superstitions and mystic
rites, cf. *Philops*. 35, μιᾷ δέ ποτε ἡμέρα λαθὼν ἐπήκουσα τῆς ἐπῳδῆς
—ἦν δὲ τρισύλλαβος. Hor. *Od*. I. 28. 35, "Licebit *injecto ter pul-
vere* curras." Verg. *Aen*. VI. 229, "Idem *ter* socios pura circumtulit
unda." Cf. Theoc. quoted below.

The usage of "spitting in the face" is clearly explained by Becker, *Char.* p. 132. He there says it was (1) To appease the vengeance of the gods for having cherished over-sanguine expectations, (2) a preventive against the evil eye, or some bad malady, cf. Pliny, *N. H.* XXVIII. 4. 7, "Veniam quoque a deis spei alicujus audacioris petimus *in sinum spuentes*." So Theoc. VI. 39, ὡς μὴ βασκανθῶ δέ, τρὶς εἰς ἐμὸν ἔπτυσα κόλπον. Becker also quotes Lucian *Navig.* 15, ὑπερμ'ξῷs γε, ὦ 'Αδείμαντε, καὶ ἐς τὸν κόλπον οὐ πτύεις. Theoph. *Char.* 16, on the "superstitious" man: "And if he sees a madman, or an epileptic person, he shudders *ana spits into his own bosom.*" Plaut. *Capt.* III. 4. 18, "Et illic isti, qui sputatur, morbus interdum venit."

The ἄν goes, not with ἀποπτύσας, as it seems to do, but with the finite verb ἐπανήειν, and has a frequentative sense; cf. § 12, προσιὼν ἄν, and see Heitland's note on *Somnium* § 2, and *Pisc.* § 11 ; so in Macrob. 7, οὕτω γὰρ ἂν ἀπιδὼν καὶ σὺ...ἐλπίσειας γῆρας ὑγιεινόν.

9   ἐπανήειν. MSS. ἐπανήει. The first person (Dindorf, &c.) makes better sense, as Menippus much more than his guide would be likely to have to avoid looking at anyone lest the spell should be broken. The chief difficulty, however, is that ἀποπτύσας becomes a nom. absolute.

10   τὰ ἀκρόδρυα. In Theoc. XV. 112 we find the word broken into its two parts : ὅσα δρύες ἄκρα φέροντι. The word therefore means literally all the eatable produce of δρύες, or forest trees (acorns, walnuts, &c.), as opposed to fruit trees (Snow).

11   μελίκρατον, a mixture of wine and honey. Heitland, in his note on *Char.* § 22, where the word occurs again, refers to Hom. *Odys.* X. 519, πρῶτα μελικρήτῳ μετέπειτα δὲ ἡδέϊ οἴνῳ τὸ τρίτον αὖθ' ὕδατι, a quotation especially apposite to the present passage, as Odysseus used these three, when descending to Hades, like Menippus here. Cf. also *Philops.* 21, εἴ τις ἐναγίσειεν αὐτῷ ἢ μελίκρατον ἐπισπείσειεν.

Χοάσπου. The water of the Choaspes, one of the tributaries of the Tigris, was so pure, that the kings of Persia always drank of it. Cf. Milt. *Par. Reg.* III. 289, "The drink of none but kings," and Tib. IV. 140, "Regia lympha Choaspes."

12   προδιαίτησις, "preliminary mode of living," "preparatory diet."

13   περὶ μέσας νύκτας, "about the middle watch of the night"; νὺξ in the plural is used of the night *watches*, which with the Greeks were three. Cf. Hom. *Od.* XII. 312 τρίχα νυκτὸς ἔην.

14   **ἀπέμαξε—περιήγνισε—καταμαγεύσας,** "wipe down," "thoroughly purify," "cast spells over me." Cf. a similar ceremonial in *Philops.* § 12, ἐς τὸν ἀγρὸν γὰρ ἐλθὼν ἕωθεν, ἐπειπὼν ἱερατικά τινα ἐκ βίβλου παλαιᾶς ὀνόματα ἑπτά, θείῳ καὶ δᾳδὶ καθαγνίσας τὸν τόπον περιελθὼν ἐς τρίς, ἐξήλασεν ὅσα ἦν ἑρπετὰ ἐντὸς τῶν ὅρων.

15   **σκίλλῃ,** the "squill," an onion-shaped plant, used in medicines. Cf. *Alex.* § 47, καθαῖρον ὡς ἀληθῶς τὰς γνώμας οὐχὶ δᾳδὶ καὶ σκίλλῃ καὶ τοιαύταις φλυαρίαις, ἀλλὰ λόγῳ ὀρθῷ, κ.τ.λ.

16   **ὑποτονθορύσας.** The simple verb is used at the very opening to the *Deor. Conc.*, Μηκέτι τονθορύζετε, ὦ θεοί, "mutter that same old incantation" which he had uttered for 29 days previously. For the mumbled prayers, cf. Juv. VI. 539, "Illius lacrimae *meditataque murmura* praestant."

The force of the word is well seen in the *Symposium* (§ 12), where the Cynic Alcidamas comes to the banquet uninvited, and all the philosophers ἄλλοι ἄλλα πρὸς τὸν καιρὸν εὔστοχα καὶ χαρίεντα ὑποτονθορύζοντες· ἐς μέντοι τὸ φανερὸν οὐδεὶς ἐτόλμα λέγειν. "They each *muttered low* (ὑπὸ) some suitable quotation, but not out loud" for fear of Alcidamas. Cf. also *bis accus.* § 4, καὶ ἐς τὸ φανερὸν μὲν οὐ τολμῶσι λέγειν ὑποτονθορύζουσι δὲ συγκεκυφότες.

18   **ὡς εἶχον,** "just as I *was*." ἔχειν with adv. = εἶναι. **ἀναποδίζοντα,** "walking backwards."

19   **τὸ λοιπὸν,** adverbially, "for the future," "*forthwith.*" ἔχειν ἀμφὶ = "to busy oneself about." Cf. *bis accus.* § 12, ὥστε ὑμεῖς μὲν ἀμφὶ τὰς δίκας ἔχετε...ἐγὼ δὲ συρίξομαί τι μέλος. Pan is speaking to Zeus, Hermes and Dikê.

22   § **8. πίλῳ—λεοντῇ—λύρᾳ.** See note on § 1 for the use of these words. *Heracles* went down to bring up Cerberus; *Odysseus* to consult Teiresias as to his future; *Orpheus* to bring back his wife.

p. 8.   3   **Ὡς δὴ τί τοῦτο;** elliptical = ὡς δὴ τί γένοιτο, τοῦτο ἔλεξεν; "for what reason did he say this?"

6   **Καὶ μὴν,** "yet surely." It occurs in *Tim.* § 15 and § 46 (twice), and § 9 = "Well!" Cf. the use of it in two consecutive lines in Soph. *Oed. Tyr.* 1004, 5.

8   **εἰς Ἅδου.** In such expressions the δόμον is easily understood. This elliptical use is chiefly employed with proper names, e.g. ἐς Πριάμοιο, ἐς Διονύσου, &c., cf. Latin *ad Castoris, templum* being understood. So we talk of going "to S. Paul's."

10   **καὶ ἀκωλύτως**, "and should get across without any hindrance, as being more accustomed (ὄντα supplied, cf. note p. 6, l. 13), commended in true tragic style by my garb."

12   **§ 9. ὑπέφαινεν.** ὑπό, like Lat. *sub*, in composition denotes what is *gradual*. The word is of course properly transitive, but is frequently used intransitively as here in reference to day-break, &c.; cf. Xen. *Anab.* III. 2. 1, ἐπεὶ δὲ ἡμέρα σχεδὸν ὑπέφαινε, and ἕως ὑπέφαινεν (IV. 3. 9). This is the morning of the 30th day from the "new moon" of § 7 (beginning). For **δ' οὖν** cf. p. 7, l. 7.

13   **ἐγιγνόμεθα περὶ**=εἴχομεν ἀμφί, end of § 7.

14   **αὐτῷ.** The dative of the agent is commonly used after the perf. and plup. passive, e.g. p. 11, l. 2; less frequently with other tenses, cf. Thuc. III. 64, τίνες ἂν ὑμῶν δικαιότερον πᾶσι τοῖς Ἕλλησι μισοῖντο; it is used after 1st aor. p. 12, l. 3.

    μελίκρατον, cf. note § 7.

18   **βαίνομεν, κ.τ.λ.** Hom. *Odys.* XI. 5, which whole passage Lucian had in his mind, as is clear from the following columns:

Homer.	*Lucian.*
XI. 1.	
ἐπὶ νῆα κατήλθομεν ἠδὲ θάλασσαν.	κατελθόντες ἐπὶ τὸν ποταμὸν —παρεσκεύαστο σκάφος.
XI. 4.	
ἐν δὲ τὰ μῆλα λαβόντες ἐβήσαμεν.	ἐμβαλόμενοι οὖν ἅπαντα τὰ παρεσκευασμένα. [Cf. μῆλα (note), below.]
XI. 4, 5.	
ἂν δὲ καὶ αὐτοὶ βαίνομεν, κ.τ.λ.	οὕτω δὴ καὶ αὐτοὶ βαίνομεν, κ.τ.λ.

(Cf. also *Odys.* X. 517 quoted below.)

  The κατά is separated from χέοντες by tmesis = καταχέοντες.

19   **ὑπεφερόμεθα,** "be borne down stream"; cf. *defero*, often employed by Caesar of vessels storm-tossed and driven by the wind.

20   **ἐς τὸ ἕλος.** Yonge well refers to the passage in Pliny, "Euphraten dexteriore alveo...distrahi in partes" (*N. H.* v. 26).

21   **ἀφανίζεται,** "loses itself."

24   **βόθρον τε ὠρυξάμεθα.** So in *Charon* 22, Charon asks Hermes why at the tombs βόθρον τινὰ ὀρύξαντες καίουσί τε ταυτὶ τὰ πολυτελῆ δεῖπνα and pour μελίκρατον, to which Hermes replies that the be-

reaved imagine the dead can drink the μελίκρατον out of the
trench. In *Philops.* 14 βόθρον τε ὀρυξάμενος is part of the preliminaries for calling up the dead. In Hom. *Odys.* x. 517 and XI. 25,
which I have said in the last note Luc. had in his mind, part of the
ceremony is βόθρον ὀρύξαι ὅσον τε πυγούσιον ἔνθα καὶ ἔνθα "to dig
a trench a foot and a half each way."

τὰ μῆλα. No "sheep" have been mentioned before, but it is
clear from *Odys.* XI. quoted above that they were included in the
things put into the boat.

25 ἐν τοσούτῳ, "meanwhile."

p. 9. 1 ἠρεμ. τῇ φωνῇ. For L.'s frequent use of the predicate in
this way cf. note, p. 2, l. 22.

2 παμμέγεθες δὲ ἀνακραγὼν. For the adverbial use cf. συνεχές,
note § 4. We have a similar phrase in *Char.* § 20, ἀναβοήσας παμμέγεθες, and *de Luc.* § 19, παμμέγεθες ἀνακαγχάσαι. The word
παμμεγέθης is used by classical writers, but by no one more frequently than Lucian. It is merely an intensified form of μέγας.

δαίμονας...ἐπεβοᾶτο, "he invoked all the deities (of the nether
world) in a body."

3 Ποινὰς καὶ 'Ερινύας, the evil geniuses and furies. The latter
are three in number. Cf. Dante, *Inf.* c. IX.:

> " He, knowing well the miserable hags
> Who tend the queen of endless woe, thus spake:
> 'Mark thou each dire *Erinnys.* To the left
> This is *Megaera;* on the right hand, she
> Who wails, *Allecto;* and *Tisiphone*
> I' th' midst.'"

4 νυχίαν 'Εκάτην, Persephone. In heaven she is the *Moon;* on
earth *Diana.*

ἐπαινὴν Περσεφόνειαν. The combination used by Homer,
Odys. x. 564, XI. 47, &c. The epithet ἐπαινὴ is only found in the
feminine, and always of Persephone in relation to Hades. Its derivation and meaning are doubtful, but the interpretation of it by the
Schol. as = αἰνή, "dread," is most probably right.

6 πολυσύλλαβα. Cf. Hor. *Ars Poet.* 97, " Projicit ampullas et
sesquipedalia verba " (words a foot and a half long). Of course the
various deities of the Chaldaeans would be a *sine quâ non* with a
Babylonian.

8   § **10.** τοὔδαφος = τὸ ἔδαφος.

9   **Κερβέρου.** See Dante's fine description (*Inf.* VI.),

> "Cerberus, cruel monster, fierce and strange,
> Through his wide threefold throat, barks as a dog.
> Over the multitude immersed beneath,
> His eyes glare crimson, black his unctuous beard,
> His belly large, and clawed the hands, with which
> He tears the spirits, flays them, and their limbs
> Piecemeal disparts."

Cf. also Verg. *Aen.* VI. 417, Hor. *Od.* III. 11. 17.

10 **ὑπερκατηφὲς,** "very gloomy."

11 **Ἔδδεισεν,** cf. *Il.* XX. 61, whence L. gets his idea.

> ἔδδεισεν δ᾽ ὑπένερθεν ἄναξ ἐνέρων ᾽Αϊδωνεύς.
> δείσας δ᾽ ἐκ θρόνου ἆλτο, καὶ ἴαχε, μή οἱ ὕπερθεν
> γαῖαν ἀναρρήξειε Ποσειδάων ἐνοσίχθων,
> οἰκία δὲ θνητοῖσι καὶ ἀθανάτοισι φανήῃ
> σμερδαλέ᾽ εὐρώεντα, τά τε στυγέουσι θεοί περ.

13 **Πυριφλεγέθων.** Lucian seems particularly fond of this special river, probably as being the most terrible in sound; cf. *Inf. Dial.* 30. 1, ἐς τὸν Πυριφλ. ἐμβεβλήσθω, and *Tyran. ad fin.*, ἆρ᾽ ἐς τὸν Πυριφ. ἐστιν ἐμβλητέος: so also *Char.* § 13, *de Luctu* § 3, *Philops.* 24, &c.

For the four rivers of hell cf. Hom. *Od.* X. 512,

> ἔνθα μὲν εἰς ᾽Αχέροντα, Πυριφλεγέθων τε ῥέουσι
> Κώκυτός θ᾽ ὅς δὴ Στυγὸς ὕδατός ἐστιν ἀπορρώξ.

So Milton, *P. L.* II. 577,

> "Abhorred *Styx*, the flood of deadly hate;
> Sad *Acheron* of sorrow, black and deep;
> *Cocytus*, named of lamentation loud
> Heard on the rueful stream. Fierce *Phlegethon*
> Whose waves of torrent fire inflame with rage."

15 **μικροῦ δεῖν,** "all but," lit. "to want a little," just as δυοῖν δέοντα ἕκατον = 100 − 2 = 98. This, with ὀλίγου δεῖν, is a very common phrase; cf. *Asin.* 38, ὀλίγου ἐδέησαν ἀποκτεῖναι; *Hermot.* 71, ὀλίγου δέουσι τὴν ῥῖνα τοῦ παιδὸς ἀποτραγεῖν. The infinitives ὀλίγου δεῖν, μικροῦ δεῖν, πολλοῦ δεῖν, ἐμοὶ δοκεῖν (just below, and also § 17), οὑτωσὶ μὲν εἰπεῖν (*Timon* § 8), are all similar constructions.

16   **παρεκίνησε.** The word is here used intransitively = *permotus est,*
a not uncommon usage, though it is more generally used actively,
= *permovit.* Hence in *Cal.* 50 we have the passive παρακεκινημένον.
For the intransitive, however, cf. *On History,* § 1, ἄπαντες γὰρ ἐς
τραγῳδίαν παρεκίνουν.

17   **κρούσαντος τὴν λύραν.** Menippus follows the example of
Orpheus, and calms the monster with musical strains. But in
Verg. (*Aen.* VI.) the Sybil quiets him by giving him a soporiferous
cake, and Vergil when he conducts Dante (*Inf.* Canto VI. 24) throws
a handful of earth into his maw.

19   **μικροῦ,** see just above : "had the greatest difficulty in getting
across."

21   **τραυματίαι.** This is the chief word in the sentence; so make
it the verb (ἐπέπλεον being only subsidiary, = "all who sailed were
wounded"). τραυματίας is a substantive, cf. *Tyran.* 6, τοὺς
τραυματίας ἐπὶ τούτοις, ὦ Ἑρμῆ, παράγαγε; so *Inf. D.,* 4. 2 ;
Nigr. 37; *V. H.* 2. 38. The wounds in arms and legs, &c. are
probably due to Charon's bad temper, cf. Dante, *Inf.* III. 101:

> "Charon, demoniac form,
> With eyes of burning coal, collects them all,
> Beckoning, and each, that lingers, with his oar
> Strikes."

Solanus thinks this "recent war" points to the year 163 A.D. as
the date of the dialogue, viz. the stormy time immediately after the
death of Antoninus.

24   For **δ' οὖν** cf. 7. 7.
ὁ **βέλτιστος Χάρων,** whom Vergil (*Aen.* VI. 298) describes thus :

> "Portitor has horrendus aquas et flumina servat
> Terribili squalore Charon, cui plurima mento
> Canities inculta jacet; stant lumina flamma."

In *Inf. Dial.* XXII. there is an amusing scene between these
two, where Menippus refuses to pay any passage-money, and jumps
out of the boat as soon as it puts into shore and runs off, calling out
that Charon shall have his money "as soon as you can catch me."
The passage-money was one obol, which was put into a dead
person's mouth before burial. A full account of the ceremonial of
burying is given in Lucian's *de Luctu;* as regards the obol he
says, § 10, ἐπειδάν τις ἀποθάνῃ τῶν οἰκείων, πρῶτα μὲν φέροντες

ὀβολὸν ἐς τὸ στόμα κατέθηκαν αὐτῷ μισθὸν τῷ πορθμεῖ ναυτι-
λίας γενησόμενον.

οἰηθείς με τὸν Ἡρακ. The old ferryman seems to have had a
special dread of Heracles, cf. *Aen.* VI. 392, "Nec vero *Alciden* me
sum laetatus euntem | Accepisse lacu." So he dared not oppose
this pseudo-Heracles again.

p. 10. 1 **ἀποβᾶσι.** Understand ἡμῖν. "Showed us the path when
we landed."

4   **§ 11. ἐχόμενος αὐτοῦ.** The partitive genitive is common after
verbs of this class, chiefly in the middle voice, as λαμβάνομαι,
ἅπτομαι, &c., implying "touching," or "cleaving to;" cf. next
section, *ἐκείνων ἥπτετο.*

6   **ἀσφοδέλῳ,** cf. § 21, very nearly the end of the dialogue, and
de Luc. § 7, and *Char.* § 22. In Hom. *Od.* XI. 539 and 573 we
have *κατ' ἀσφοδελὸν λειμῶνα*; cf. also Theoc. VII. 68, Calverley's
version:

> "They shall roast me beans,
> And elbow-deep in thyme and *asphodel*
> And quaintly-curling parsley shall be piled
> My bed of rushes."

7   **τετριγυῖαι...αἱ σκιαί.** The word τρίζω is evidently an *ono-
matopoeic* word. In *Tim.* 21 we have it of the twittering of
swallows. Here it refers to the cries of the bodiless spirits; so in
Hor. *Sat.* I. 8. 41 we have "Umbrae.. resonarent triste et acutum."
Cf. *Aen.* XII. *ad fin.*; and Shak.'s "squeak and gibber."

8   **τὸ τοῦ Μίνω:** cf. *Aen.* VI. 432: "Quaesitor Minos urnam movet;
ille silentum | Consiliumque vocat vitasque et crimina discit."

10   **παρειστήκεσαν.** Remember that the pluperf. of ἵστημι has an
imperfect signification; cf. καθειστήκειν, § 3.

ἀλάστορες, "avenging spirits," much the same as the Ποιναί:
§ 9, note.

13   **τελῶναι.** The "publicans" or "tax-gatherers" have become well-
known from Biblical usage. In *Char.* § 2 Oeacus, who generally
is ranked with Minos and Rhadamanthus as a supreme judge in
the nether world, is mentioned as the τελώνης, to collect the
passage money. In *Tyrannus* § 4 he performs the same kind of
office. Atropos, one of the three Moirae, enters the spirits on the
pass-sheet, and Hermes has to make account for every spirit so
entered.

κόλακες. Becker (*Char.* p. 92, note) divides the "*parasites*" of Greek and Roman society into three classes. (1) The γελωτο-ποιοί "the professional wit," something after the fashion of a king's "fool." (2) The κόλακες, "the toadies," who were always flattering their patrons. (3) θεραπευτικοί the "cavalier servente," who did various little services, enough to warrant a place at table. The Gnatho of Terence, and Artotrogus in Plautus' *Miles Gloriosus* are instances. They were all men οὕς οὔτε πῦρ οὔτε σίδηρος οὔτε χαλκὸς εἴργει μὴ φοιτᾶν ἐπὶ δεῖπνον (Plutarch).

14　συκοφάνται, a much more detestable class than the flatterers. They were the very bane of Greek as of Roman society under the Empire; men whose whole and sole occupation was to spy out any one doing anything likely to prove disastrous to him in a law-court, and who then extorted money from him or threatened to report him. The rich and influential were, therefore, naturally the most exposed to these wretches, and many a one was compelled to purchase silence at a great price; groundless though the charge might be, the verdict was almost always a foregone conclusion.

15　τοκογλύφοι. Cf. note § 2.

16　ὠχροί, προγάστορες, ποδαγροί, "sallow, pot-bellied, and gouty." The first is the usual epithet applied by Lucian to philosophers; to Zeus in *Jup. Trag.* § 1 twice, as being careworn. So ὑπωχρον in *Fugit.* 27, also in *Tyr.* 17 to a miser, and in *Tim.* 14 to Plutus through confinement. In the last epithet no doubt L. speaks feelingly, if tradition is to be relied on. He is said to have been troubled much with the gout in his later years. He makes Gout the principal character in two of his extant works; v. Introd. Section on "Timon the Misanthrope." προγάστωρ is a somewhat favourite epithet. In *Philops.* 24 it is applied to Socrates; cf. also *de merc. cond.* 42, *Philops.* 18, *Bacc.* 2 (of Silenus).

17　κλοιός. This instrument of punishment for slaves is not identical with the ξύλον. The latter was more like our "stocks," feet, hands and neck being in five different holes. But the κλοιός did not keep the *feet* confined at all, and not always, or necessarily, the *hands*. So that it would then become a mere "dog-collar," a heavy wooden burden, which would prevent a man standing or walking, and force him to keep in a bent position; it seems to have been much the same as κύφων § 14, which gets its name from κύπτω.

σκύλακα. Hemst. first restored this word for the corrupt κόραια of previous editors. Lit. it is a young dog, then the collar it wore, and so an instrument of punishment. Cf. Plaut. *Curc.* v. 3. 13, "Delicatum te hodie faciam cum catello ut accubes, | Ferreo ego dico."

διτάλαντον. The weight of these instruments speaks for itself, something over a hundredweight.

ἐπικείμενος, commonly employed as the passive, sometimes (as here) is the middle of ἐπιτίθημι, so again in § 15, ἄχθος ἐπικείμενος. Cf. Eur. *Supp.* 717, κἀπικείμεναι κάρα κυνέας, "having their heads covered with helmets," and Hor. *Sat.* I. 6. 74, "Laevo *suspensi loculos tabulamque* lacerto." So here "having placed upon them."

24 ἀποτελουμένας, "formed."

p. 11. 2 τὰ πεπραγμένα ἡμῖν. Notice the dative of the agent, and cf. note on p. 8, l. 14. So also in Latin.

6 **§ 12.** It is not unlikely that the well-known myth of Er, at the end of Plato's *Republic*, was in the mind of Lucian, when he wrote this scene of the trial of the spirits in the world below

'Ο δ' οὖν Μίνως, cf. note on last section, and for δ' οὖν, p. 7, l. 7. With ἐπιμελῶς ἐξετάζων, κ.τ.λ. cf. Dante *Inf.* c. v.,

> "There Minos stands
> Grinning with ghastly feature; he of all
> Who enter *strict examining the crimes*
> Gives sentence, and *dismisses them beneath.*"

7 ὑφέξοντα. Fut. participle to express *purpose.*

9 ἐκείνων ἥπτετο. For the genitive cf. the note at beginning of last section; for this use of ἅπτομαι, "to lay hands upon," in violence, cf. Aesch. *Agam.* 1608, καὶ τοῦδε τἀνδρὸς ἡψάμην θυραῖος ὤν. Translate, "and he was particularly hard upon those who had been inflated with pride through their riches or position," &c.

10 προσκυνεῖσθαι περιμενόντων: so in *Nigr.* 21, οἱ δὲ σεμνότεροι καὶ προσκυνεῖσθαι περιμένοντες. The whole passage there is very similar to this, v. l. 20, below; cf. note on ll. 20—23 just below.

13 θνητῶν ἀγαθῶν, "because they had not remembered that both *they themselves* were mortal and the goods they possessed were mortal too." They, like Dives in the parable, "had in their life-time received their good things."

15 κάτω νενευκότες, "with heads bent down," through shame-facedness. In *Somn.* § 13 we have the same expression κάτω

νενευκὼς ἐς τὸ ἔργον, but that refers to grovelling over some
mechanical work.

16   ἀναπεμπαζόμενοι (ἀνὰ—πέντε) "to count up on five fingers,"
"reckon." It is worth while comparing a very similar passage at
the end of the *Tyrannus:*—χαλεπὴν οὕτως ὑφέξει τὴν δίκην
μεμνημένος οἷος ἦν καὶ ὅσον ἐδύνατο ἐν τοῖς ἄνω, καὶ ἀναπεμ-
παζόμενος τὴν τρυφήν.

19   προσιὼν ἄν...ὑπεμίμνησκον. For the position of ἄν, and its
frequentative use, cf. note on § 7, "going up to him gently, I
would remind him." παρὰ with the acc. of *time* is post-Homeric,
and not very frequent; v. Plat. *Legg.* 733 A, παρὰ τὸν βίον ἅπαντα,
and cf. παρὰ δεῖπνον, παρὰ τὴν κύλικα.

20   ἐφύσα, not to be confounded with ἔφυσα, 1 aor. of φύω. This
word comes from φυσάω.

πολλοὶ μὲν ἔωθεν, cf. a similar passage in *Nigr.* §§ 21, 22, οἱ δὲ
σεμνότεροι καὶ προσκυνεῖσθαι περιμένοντες...δεῖ προσελθόντα καὶ ὑποκύψαντα...τὸ στῆθος ἢ τὴν δεξιὰν καταφιλεῖν...νυκτὸς μὲν ἐξανιστάμενοι
μέσης, περιθέοντες δὲ ἐν κύκλῳ τὴν πόλιν καὶ πρὸς τῶν οἰκετῶν ἀποκλειόμενοι. And Luc. goes on to say how the reward of all this
devotion is τὸ φορτικὸν ἐκεῖνο δεῖπνον, κ.τ.λ.

21   πυλὼν, the vestibule of the house, where the clients of a great
man assembled. In addition to other duties, the client had to
accompany his patron when he went out, an office to which Luc. is
here alluding. Such a man was called an "anteambulo." Martial
who belongs to the century before Luc. spends a good deal of satire
upon such people. Cf. II. 18, where we clearly see the abuse of such
a system. This wealthy man has Martial as an "anteambulo," and
yet performs the same functions to a wealthier patron himself.

"Sum comes ipse tuus timidique anteambulo regis,
    Tu comes alterius; jam sumus ergo pares."

Cf. *Somn.* § 9, εὐτελὴς τὴν πρόοδον, "making a shabby show,
when you go out."

23   μόγις ἀνατείλας. As may well be imagined, the patron did not
put himself out, however many clients might be waiting to salute
him, as Juvenal says *Sat.* x. 161, "the client may sit at the door
until it may please his Bithynian majesty to get up." The customary
mode of salutation was to kiss the patron's breast, right hand, or
knee. Cf. *Alex.* 55, προὔτεινέ μοι κῦσαι τὴν δεξιὰν, ὥσπερ εἰώθει

τοῖς πολλοῖς. So *Nigrinus* 21, δεῖ προσελθόντα καὶ ὑποκύψαντα, ...τὸ στῆθος ἢ τὴν δεξιὰν καταφιλεῖν.

ἂν ἀνατείλας...ᾤετο, cf. note on προσιὼν ἂν just above.

24 εὐδαίμονας, κ.τ.λ. The order is ᾤετο ἂν ἀποφαίνειν τοὺς προσει-πόντας εὐδαίμονας καὶ μακαρίους, κ.τ.λ. In fact snobs were much the same then as now, thinking it a great condescension to offer you two fingers to shake.

p. 12. 4 § 13. Dionysius the younger, tyrant of Syracuse 367 B.C., expelled Dion his brother-in-law from his kingdom for treason (360 B.C.); who, in revenge, collected an army and expelled Dionysius (356 B.C.). But three years later he was murdered by one of his own friends. Dionysius, like his father, the elder tyrant, affected litera-ture, and welcomed men of learning (Plato among others) at his court. It is for this that he is here acquitted.

The structure of the whole section is grammatically rather confused. Σικελιώτην Διονύσιον is accusative after παρέλυσε some lines down. Ἀρίστιππος is subject of the whole sentence, παρελθὼν and λέγων (lower down) agreeing with it. In agreement with Διονύσιον we have κατηγορηθέντα, καταμαρτυρηθέντα, and παραδο-θέντα. Lucian alludes to D. in several places.

6 τῆς σκιᾶς, his own shadow, which followed him in life; see § 11, end.

7 Ἀρίστιππος ὁ Κυρηναῖος, founder of the Cyrenaic school (early half of 4th cent. B.C.). He placed "the highest good" in pleasure; he was famous for his apothegms and witticisms. We find him honoured, as here, in *The Sale of Philos. Lives* § 12, τὸν Κυρηναῖον τὸν ἐν τῇ πορφυρίδι, τὸν ἐστεφανωμένον. So in *Dem. vita* Demonax, being asked which of the philosophers he liked most, said πάντες μὲν θαυμαστοί, ἐγὼ δὲ Σωκράτην μὲν σέβω, θαυμάζω δὲ Διογένην καὶ φιλῶ Ἀρίστιππον. Cf. *V. H.* II. 18.

9 μικροῦ δεῖν: see note on § 10.

τῇ Χιμαίρᾳ, a monster so fabulous, as now to be a term denoting what has no foundation. So in *Philops.* 2 Lucian classes Pegasuses, Chimaeras, Gorgons and Cyclopes as πάνυ ἀλλόκοτα καὶ τεράστια μυθίδια. It was supposed to have infested Lycia, being the offspring of Typhon and Echidna (Cerberus had the same parents); it was like a lion in front, a goat in the middle, and a dragon be-hind, afterwards slain by Bellerophon on his winged horse Pegasus.

It seems to have been a monster of special fearfulness, and an-

swered well as a "bogey" to frighten with; cf. *Inf. Dial.* 30. 1, ὁ
δὲ ἱερόσυλος ὑπὸ τῆς Χιμαίρας διασπασθήτω, v. Verg. *Aen.* VI. 288,
and Hor. *Od.* I. 27. 23.

11   τῶν πεπαιδευμένων, "men of learning."

πρός, "in the matter of."

With this section, cf. a passage very similar in *Ver. Hist.* II. 29,
καὶ μαστίγων ψόφος ἠκούετο καὶ οἰμωγὴ ἀνθρώπων πολλῶν, ...
καὶ κνίσσα δὲ πονηρά...ὥσπερ ἀπ' ἀνθρώπων ὀπτωμένων. Cf. also
Phalaris § 8, ὅλως δὲ τίνα οἴεσθε οὕτως ἄγριον ἢ ἀνήμερον ἄνθρωπον
εἶναι ὡς ἥδεσθαι μαστιγοῦντα καὶ οἰμωγῶν ἀκούοντα καὶ
σφαττομένους ὁρῶντα.

Cf. Verg. *Aen.* VI. 557, "Hinc exaudiri gemitus, et saeva sonare |
Verbera." So in Milton, *P. L.* VIII. 242,

> "But long, ere our approaching, heard within
> Noise, other than the sound of dance or song,
> Torment and loud lament."

17   § **14.** κίφωνες, probably identical with the κλοιός (see § 11, and
Beck. *Char.* 370).

στρέβλαι...τροχοί. The "rack" and the "wheel" were punishments not allowed to masters, but only inflicted by the public exe-
cutioner (δήμιος).

18   ἐδάρδαπτε, a word found both in *Iliad* (e.g. II. 479) and *Odys.*
(XIV. 92, XVI. 315); it is a stronger form of δάπτω, = "tear to pieces."

19   βασιλεῖς...σατράπαι. These words occur together again in § 17,
so too in *Nig.* § 20, we have τὸν δὲ σατράπην (προϊόντα) ἐκ
πένητος ἢ βασιλέα, and in *Inf. Dial.* 27. 9, ἦπου βασιλεὺς ἦσθα;
οὐδαμῶς...ἀλλὰ σατράπης; They are somewhat similar to *reges*
and *tetrarchae* in Latin, cf. Hor. *Sat.* I. 3. 12, and Sall. *Cat.* 20
(Long's note).

20   πένητες...πτωχοί. Cf. *Timon* § 5, note. The former are *poor*,
the latter *beggars*. It is πένης that is continually opposed to πλούσιος: cf. *Nigr.* § 1, ἀντὶ δὲ πένητος ὡς ἀληθῶς πλούσιον. *Jupp.*
confut. § 8, καὶ ἐκ πλουσιωτάτων.πενέστατοι ἐν ἀκαρεῖ γίγνεσθε.

23   ἐνεκαλύπτοντο, κ.τ.λ. "they covered their faces, and turned their
heads away; and if they did look, it was truly a servile and
cringing look:" with δουλοπρεπὲς understand προσέβλεπον.

25   καὶ ταῦτα, cf. note, § 4.

πῶς οἴει; parenthetic; "and that too, having been in this life,
how important and overweening *think you?*"

p. 13. 3 **Ἰξίονα, Σίσυφον, Τάνταλον.** These three poor wretches are in scores of passages classed together as typical of the general misery of the wicked in Tartarus.

Tantalus (v. *Timon* § 18; cf. "tantalize") stood up to his neck in water, which receded when he tried to drink it, while apples hung over his head, ready to spring back when he tried to pluck the fruit. Thus he endured the endless agony of hunger and thirst.

Sisyphus rolled a stone up a hill, which, as soon as it neared the summit, fell to the bottom again. His punishment was an endless life of fruitless toil.

Ixion revolved continually on a wheel, bound arms and legs to the spokes, cf. Verg. *Georg.* III. 38.

5 **Τιτυὸν,** a son of Earth, who covered nine acres of ground in Tartarus, and had vultures eternally feeding on his heart (cf. *Odys.* XI. 576).

Ἡράκλεις ὅσος, "My word! what a monster!" Cf. *Aen.* VI. 596,

> "Nec non et Tityon, Terrae omniparentis alumnum,
> Cernere erat, *per tota novem cui jugera corpus*
> Porrigitur."

10 **§ 15. κατὰ ἔθνη.** With the *acc.* κατά has a distributive sense, and corresponds to the Latin adverbs in *-atim*, e.g. κατ' ὀλίγον (*Tim.* § 4)=*paulatim*=little by little; καθ' ἕνα=*singulatim*=one by one; κατ' ὄνομα=*nominatim*=name by name.

διαιτωμένους, cf. *Tim.* 42, μόνῳ ἐμοὶ ἱκανὸν ἐνδιαιτᾶσθαι.

11 **εὐρωτιῶντας,** der. from εὐρώς (*Bis acc.* 3), "mould." The verb also occurs in *Jup. Trag.* 15. The adjec. εὐρώεις occurs as a general epithet of the nether world in Homer, e.g. οἰκία εὐρώεντα, *Il.* XX.65; εὐρώεντα κέλευθα, *Od.* XXIV. 10. L. doubtless had *Odys.* x. 512 in his mind, where it says αὐτὸς δ' εἰς Ἀΐδεω ἰέναι δόμον εὐρώεντα, for he is at once reminded of ἀμενηνός "ὥς φησιν Ὅμηρος" occurring a few lines later (521), πολλὰ δὲ γουνοῦσθαι νεκύων ἀμενηνὰ κάρηνα. The line is parodied in *Char.* § 22 also, and cf. *Inf. Dial.* 20. 2, ἀμενηνὰ ὡς ἀληθῶς κάρηνα="unsubstantial," "fleeting." ἀμενηνός is apparently from α priv. and μένος="strength-less."

12 **νεαλεῖς** opposed to παλαιούς, as "fresh" to "stale."

13 **συνεστηκότας** opposed to εὐρωτιῶντας, as "firm" to "gone soft."

τοὺς Αἰγυπτίους αὐτῶν, "those of them who were Egyptians."
Some MSS. have τοὺς Αἰγυπτίων αὐτούς which is hardly Greek.
Hemst. wished to read ἀλύτους for αὐτούς.

Αἰγυπτίους…τῆς ταριχείας: so in *de Luctu* § 20 we have "the
Greek cremated, the *Persian* buried, the *Indian* besmeared with
alabaster, the *Scythian* devours, ὁ δὲ Αἰγύπτιος ταριχεύει,"
"pickles," "embalms." "The word refers in strictness only to that
part of the embalming process, which consisted in laying the body
to soak in a bath of λίτρον or νίτρον (hydrocarbonate of soda, acc. to
Blakesley)." Heitland *in loc.* Cf. Herod. II. 86—88.

16   τῶν ὀστῶν γεγυμνωμένων. So too in the *Inf. Dial.* 18. 1,
        "*Menip.* Where are all the beautiful men and women, Hermes?
        Shew me.
        Herm. I have no time, Menippus, only look there on the right,
            where are Hyacinthus, Narcissus, Nireus, &c.
        Menip. I see only bones and skulls, devoid of flesh, for the most
            part indistinguishable."
    See Bacon's allusion to this passage, quoted in the Introd.,
Section on "Menippus, the Dialogue."

21   φοβερόν τι…δεδορκότων. For the form of sentence cf. note (last
section) on μάλα δουλοπρεπές.

p. 14. 2 Θερσίτην…Νιρέως. The former the most ugly, the latter
the most beautiful man (except Achilles) at Troy; cf. for the former
Hom. *Il.* II. 216; for the latter, *Timon* § 23, note. *Inf. Dial.*
25. 2 is very similar, where Menip. is talking to Nireus: τὸ δὲ
κρανίον ταύτῃ μόνον ἄρα διακρίνοιτο ἀπὸ τοῦ Θερσίτου κρανίου, ὅτι
εὔθρυπτον τὸ σόν. So in *pro Imagin.* § 20 L. says the κόλαξ has
no hesitation in declaring Nestor the youngest of those who served
under Troy, or τὸν Θερσίτην εὐμορφότερον ἀποφῆναι τοῦ Ἀχιλλέως.

τὸν Ἶρον. The beggar Irus used to wait upon the suitors of
Penelope in the house of Odysseus. The latter, when returning
from his wanderings, disguised as a beggar also, picked a quarrel
with Irus, broke his jaw and turned him out of the palace. So
Adeimantus says in *Navig.* 24, of those whom he is paying out
for their former slights, οἱ δὲ νῦν πλούσιοι πρὸς ἐμὲ Ἶροι δηλαδὴ
ἅπαντες, and in *Char.* 22 Lucian makes Charon parody lines from
Homer and say, ἐν δὲ ἰῇ τιμῇ Ἶρος κρείων τ' Ἀγαμέμνων. | Θερσίτῃ
δ' ἴσος Θέτιδος παῖς ἠϋκόμοιο. The older editions insert μεταίτην
("beggar"), probably a gloss.

3   τοῦ Φαιάκ. βασιλέως. Alcinous, whose gardens bloomed continually, and who treated Odysseus so hospitably in his wanderings;
and before whom Odysseus recounts his descent to Hades, which
L. parodies here.

Πυρρίας. Nothing to do with the Pyrrhias in *Tim.* § 22, mentioned as a common name for a Greek slave.

5   ὅμοια τὰ ὀστᾶ ἦν, κ.τ.λ. So in *Inf. Dial.* 25. 2 of Nireus and
Thersites, τὰ μὲν ὀστᾶ ὅμοια...ἰσοτιμία γὰρ ἐν ᾅδου καὶ
ὅμοιοι ἅπαντες.

6   ἀνεπίγραφα, lit. "without any inscription" on them, i.e. "without anything to distinguish." So in *Tyran.* 25 Rhadamanthus says,
εὖγε, ὦ Μίκυλλε, καθαρὸς ἀκριβῶς καὶ ἀνεπίγραφος (σκυτοτόμος εἶ)
=*nulla nota inscriptus*, "known by no mark."

§ 16. The fickleness of fortune is illustrated by the following
epigram of Lucian:—

   ἀγρὸς Ἀχαιμενίδου γενόμην ποτέ, νῦν δὲ Μενίππου·
      καὶ πάλιν ἐξ ἑτέρου βήσομαι εἰς ἕτερον.
   καὶ γὰρ ἐκεῖνος ἔχειν μέ ποτ' ᾤετο, καὶ πάλιν οὗτος
      οἴεται· εἰμὶ δ' ὅλως οὐδενός, ἀλλὰ Τύχης.

9   χορηγεῖν δὲ, technically "to serve as choregus," whose duty it
was to find choruses, actors, and chorus masters, at his own expense;
here merely = "to marshal."

10   ἡ Τύχη. So Dem. says (*Olyn.* II. 22), "For Fortune is a great
influence (ῥοπή), nay, rather, she is everything in all the concerns of
men." So another epigram of Luc. says:—

   ἂν πταίσῃς, οὐδείς ἔτι σοι φίλος, ἀλλ' ἅμα πάντα
      ἐχθρά, τύχης τε ῥοπαῖς συμμεταβαλλόμενα.

13   τιάραν ἐπιθεῖσα. Cf. Hor. *Od.* I. 34. 14, "hinc apicem rapax
Fortuna cum stridore acuto Sustulit, hic posuisse gaudet," "placing
the tiara on his head." Perhaps the ἐπί has the force of "placing
upright," which is allowed only to the great king. Plut. *Them.*
XXIX. 3, and Xen. *Anab.* II. 5. 23.

δορυφόρους παραδοῦσα. To get a body-guard was one of the
first steps with one aiming at despotism. Cf. *Tyran.* 26, ἐπεὶ δὲ τοὺς
θρασυτάτους προσεταιρισάμενος καὶ δορυφόρους συναγαγὼν ἐπαναστὰς τῇ
πόλει τύραννος κατέστη.

14   τὴν κεφαλὴν στέψασα τῷ διαδήματι. Cf. *Piscator* § 35, which
bears out the probability of the force of ἐπί mentioned in the last

note, ὡς εἴ τις ἐν βασιλικῷ σχήματι ὀρθὴν τιάραν ἔχον καὶ διάδημα καὶ τὰ ἄλλα ὅσα βασιλείας γνωρίσματα, &c.

The διάδημα was a white band encircling the royal tiara. So in *Inf. Dial.* 10, where Lampichus, tyrant of Gela, is being stripped of all his regal and moral characteristics, L. says, οὐκοῦν ἀλλὰ τὸ διάδημα ἔασόν με ἔχειν καὶ τὴν ἐφεστρίδα (robe)...Hermes, οὐδαμῶς ἀλλὰ καὶ ταῦτα ἄφες.

15 τὸν δέ τινα...τὸν δὲ, "some other too...while another," cf. p. 4, l. 26.

17 τὴν θέαν: notice from θέα, not θεά.

19 διαπομπεῦσαι, "to continue in the procession *up to the end*," "to go right through."

p. 15. 1 Κροῖσον. Conquered by Cyrus, he was condemned to death, but was pardoned, when already the pyre was being lighted, having touched the heart of his conqueror by his recital of a conversation he had had with Solon on the uncertainty of life. Lucian relates the whole story in *Charon* § 12, &c.

3 Μαιάνδριον...Πολυκράτους: a story again alluded to in *Charon* § 14, "*Hermes.* Well! there you see Polycrates, tyrant of Samos, who thinks himself the happiest of mortals; and yet he shall be betrayed to Oroetes the satrap by that attendant standing by, Maeandrius, and shall be impaled, poor wretch, being thrown down from his sovereignty in a moment of time."

4 μετενέδυσε. μετενδύω, causal sense, while μετὰ in composition implies change, "make a person change his dress," "to put other clothes on a person"; we have a similar use in *Inf. Dial.* 14. 4, κάνδυν (a short Persian robe), ὥς φασι, μετενέδυς καὶ τιάραν ὀρθὴν ἐπέθου.

8 μηδὲν would be οὐδέν in Attic Greek.

9 ἀγνωμοσύνης, "folly."

10 ἐπιστᾶσα ἡ Τύχη. For similar thought and phraseology cf. *Charon* § 17, "Expecting to enjoy their present blessings for ever, ἐπειδὰν ἐπιστὰς ὁ ὑπηρέτης καλῇ...ἀγανακτοῦσιν."

12 ἃ ἐχρήσαντο. "What they had had furnished to them," a rare usage; but as the active verb, in the signification of "lend," takes an acc., so the middle "to have lent to one" (i.e. to "borrow") might be expected to have the same construction.

13 τοὺς τραγικοὺς ὑποκριτάς. So in *Gallus* § 25 there is a passage very similar to this section. "And then when they fall, they seem to resemble *tragic actors* many of which you can see, who

are for the time Cecropses or Sisyphuses or Telephuses, wearing
diadems...and *gold-bespangled cloak*...and who cause much amusement to the spectators, when they trip up, as they often do, and
their rags are seen underneath and their bursting shoes, never made
to fit."

14 πρὸς τὰς χρείας, "according to the exigencies of the play." As,
even at its height, the Attic drama did not allow more than three
actors, each one had to sustain two or three parts, and thus the
characters had to be so arranged, that a man (for no women were
allowed to act) might have time to change his dress.

21 χρυσόπαστον, "gold-bespangled." The same word is used in a
like sense in the passage from *Gallus*, quoted just above ; cf. also
a very close parallel from *Icarom.* 29, ἐμφερεῖς μάλιστα τοῖς τραγικοῖς
ἐκείνοις ὑποκριταῖς, ὧν ἢν ἀφέλῃ τις τὰ προσωπεῖα καὶ τὴν χρυσόπαστον
ἐκείνην στολήν, τὸ καταλειπόμενόν ἐστι γελοῖον ἀνθρώπιον ἐπτὰ
δραχμῶν ἐς τὸν ἀγῶνα μεμισθωμένον.

22 ἐμβατῶν. In the parallel passage above the reading is ἐμβάδων
(*cothurnus*) which should perhaps be read here: "putting off that
fine gold-bespangled dress, and laying aside his mask, and coming
down from his stilts, he goes away, poor and lowly, no longer called
Agamemnon son of Atreus, but Polus, the son of Charicles, of the
deme of Sunium."

p. 16. 3 § **17.** στήλας, κ.τ.λ., = *columnas, imagines, titulos,*
"monuments, busts, inscriptions."

4 παρ' αὐτοῖς, i.e. in the nether world.
    ἰδιωτῶν, "than the *ordinary* dead," *Char.* 18, καιρὸς λογίζεσθαι
οἷα τὰ τῶν ἰδιωτῶν ἂν εἴη. "You may guess how great would be
those of *ordinary* mortals."

5 τὸν Μαύσωλον αὐτόν. "Mausolus himself—the Carian you
know, the man noted on all sides for his tomb." This tomb,
erected to the King of Caria by his wife Artemisia, was one of
the seven wonders of the ancient world. The "Mausoleum" gallery
in the British Museum is devoted entirely to the fragments discovered
of this magnificent erection.

6 τὸν ἐκ τοῦ τάφου περιβόητον. περιβόητος, "noised abroad."
L. uses the word in several other places.

7 ἐπαύσω. "You would never have stopped laughing."

8 ἐν παραβύστῳ που, "somewhere, away in a corner, not noticed
(λανθάνων) among the rest of the crowd." παράβυστος = "pushed

aside," "stuffed away," and τὸ παράβυστον was the little out-of-the-way law-court where "the eleven" sat.

9　ἐμοὶ δοκεῖν, see note § 10.

11　ἐπικείμενος, cf. note § 11. "Enjoying the monument erected to him, just in proportion to the burden he has to bear through having such a weight laid upon him."

13　οὐ πλέον ποδός. Cf. *Char.* § 24; though each of them should get the mastery even of the whole of Greece, yet scarcely will they get a square foot from Aeacus (ποδιαῖον τόπον).

The well-known passage in Shaks. *Henry IV.* Part 1. Act 5, Sc. 4, is similar in sentiment:

Prince Henry (over the corpse of Percy Hotspur):

"Ill-weav'd ambition, how much art thou shrunk!
When that this body did contain a spirit
A kingdom for it was too small a bound;
But now, *two paces of the vilest earth
Is room enough.*"

ἀγαπῶντα, "content," the ordinary usage of ἀγαπᾶν. Cf. *Timon* § 12, ἀγαπάτωσαν ἄθλιοι.

14　πρὸς τὸ μέτρον συνεσταλμένον. This last word is not in agreement with μέτρον, but with the dead man:—cf. Shak. *Jul. Caes.* III. 1,

"O mighty Caesar! dost thou lie so low?
Are all thy conquests, glories, triumphs, spoils,
Shrunk to this little measure?"

16　βασιλέας καὶ σατράπας, cf. note, § 14.

17　ταριχοπωλοῦντας. It is clear from the custom of the Egyptians alluded to in § 15, why they should be "selling spirits-of-wine." L. and S. say "engaged in the embalming of corpses," but give no parallel usage. In *Tox.* § 4 the noun appears in its common meaning of fish-seller: οὓς κατὰ τὸν αὐτὸν λόγον θεοὺς νόμιζε, καὶ ταῦτα καπήλους καὶ ταριχοπώλας, εἰ τύχοι, τοὺς πολλοὺς αὐτῶν ὄντας.

ἤτοι…ἤ. The τοι gives the more probable alternative; cf. below, p. 34, l. 15. So Thuc. II. 40, καὶ αὐτοὶ ἤτοι κρίνομέν γε ἢ ἐνθυμούμεθα. Cf. Aesch. *Choeph.* 497.

18　τοῦ τυχόντος, "any chance person," a very common use. Cf. *Vit. Auc.* 11. Cf. note on ἐντυγχάνοντες, *Timon* § 23.

19 **κατὰ κόρρης παιομένους,** a by no means uncommon phrase with
Lucian, e.g. *Tyran.* § 11, παρέτιλλέ τέ με καὶ κατὰ κόρρης ἔπαιε.
Inf. Dial. 20, § 2, τὸν Σαρδανάπαλλον...πατάξαι μοι κατὰ κόρρης
ἐπίτρεψον, "to smite on the cheek," "box the ears." Cf. Theoc.
XIV. 34.

20 **Φίλιππον γοῦν,** "*anyhow*, when I saw Philip...I *couldn't*
contain myself" (from bursting with laughter).

22 **γωνιδίῳ.** The diminutive increases the ridiculousness of the
picture; ἀκούμενος (ἀκέομαι) "mending."

23 **τὰ σαθρά.** So in *Catapl.* we have ὀττοτοῖ τῶν σαθρῶν ὑποδημάτων. τὰ σαθρὰ τῶν βαλαντίων (purse) in *Inf. Dial.* 11. 14.
So elsewhere in *Inf. Dial.* 10. 1 Charon says his boat is ὑπόσαθρον. σαθρὸς, "with holes in" connected with σήθω, as σαπρὸς,
"rotten" with σήπω. ·Cf. *de merc. cond.* § 37, χιτώνιον ὑπόσαθρον.
de Calumnia, § 19, "Just as the enemy in a siege attack the part of
the fortifications which is unprotected, low, and σαθρὸν, so do
calumniators make their attack on that part of a man's life which
they see to be easily assailable and ὑπόσαθρον."

24 **μεταιτοῦντας,** taking us back in thought to Irus, the μεταίτης, in
§ 15, q. v.

p. 17. 2 § 18. **μικροῦ δεῖν,** cf. note § 10.

4 **κἀκεῖ,** "there too," just as he did when on earth.

διελέγχων, "confute," "prove wrong." This art of dialectics
was that in which Socrates was the greatest proficient of antiquity—
the power not only of proving your adversary's argument wrong, but
convincing the adversary too. The opening book of Plato's *Republic,* where the true definition of justice is sought, is the most
celebrated "*locus classicus*" on the subject.

5 **Παλαμήδης,** the reputed inventor of dice, draughts, &c., and
supposed to have added four letters (φ, χ, θ, ξ) to the ancient alphabet. He was one of the Greek heroes in the siege of Troy.
The most celebrated story about him is that which tells how, when
Odysseus pretended to be mad, so as to avoid going to the war,
P. proved it to be a mere imposition by placing Telemachus, the
son of Odys., in the way of the plough which Odys. was driving.
Of course Odys. was sane enough to turn his plough aside, and
he never forgave Palamedes his trick, but in the end forged a letter,
implicating him in apparent treachery, so that he was stoned to
death by the whole army. It is clear, therefore, why the mention

of Palamedes here should at once suggest the name of Odysseus also.

6   **Νέστωρ,** the aged counsellor of the Greeks, who had seen three generations of men, and of whom Homer says: *τοῦδ' ἀπὸ γλώσσης μέλιτος γλυκίων ῥέεν αὐδή.*

7   **ἐπεφύσητο,** *τὰ σκέλη* is the subject.   Socrates' legs are amusingly represented as still retaining the effect of the draught of hemlock, which he had been forced to drink at Athens, B.C. 399.   This (from *φυσάω,* cf. § 12) and *διῳδήκει (διοιδέω,* to be swollen) are pluperfects.

8   **Διογένης,** the Cynic, see note on *κύων* at the very beginning of this dialogue.   In the *Sale of the Philosophers' Lives* he only fetches *4d.,* as against 2 talents, the price of Socrates.   Here, though on earth he hated mankind and shunned all show of luxury, he is bound to associate with such voluptuous and wealthy people as

9   **Σαρδανάπαλλος,** one of Lucian's favourite characters.   He was king of Assyria, celebrated for his luxurious mode of life.   Being defeated in civil war, he collected wives, treasures and all, and burned them together with himself in the flames of his palace, which he had set on fire 820 B.C. (?).   He is mentioned in *Inf. Dial.* 2. 1, also 20. 2, *Jup. Conf.* 16, *Char.* 23, and in other passages.

   Μίδας, King of Phrygia, who begged of Jove that all he touched might turn to gold, and so died of starvation.   Cf. *Inf. Dial.* 2. 1, "Midas here remembering his gold, and Sardanapallus his great voluptuousness."

12   **ὕπτιος,** cf. also note on *Timon* 5, *ὑπτίαν στήλην,* = Lat. *supinus:* "thrown backward," "on the back," &c.   Cf. *Dial. Mer.* 3. 3, *ὕπτιον καταβαλὼν ἑαυτὸν* : *Symp.* § 13, *μικροῦ δεῖν ὕπτιοι κατακείμενοι ἑστιᾶσθε* : § 20, *εἰς ὑπτίας τὰς χεῖρας* ("palms upward," "into the hollow of his hands ").

13   **ἀπηνεῖ.**   The word occurs again in *Timon* § 35, in a line quoted from Homer *(Il.* XV. 202); it is used by classical writers, but not frequently.   The derivation is doubtful, = "rough," "harsh."   This is another good instance of L.'s use of the predicate, cf. p. 2, l. 22.

15   **μετοικεῖν.**   There is here, of course, an allusion to one who is technically known as a *μέτοικος,* a "resident alien," "a foreigner who was allowed to settle in a state not his own" = "take up fresh quarters."   Translate, "so that these worthies are annoyed, and are contemplating a move, as they cannot endure Diogenes."

17   § 19.   **Ταυτὶ μὲν ἱκανῶς:** *ἐστί,* or *εἴρηται,* or *ἔλεξας* understood.

p. 18. 1 **ἐν ἀρχῇ ἔλεγες,** "which you mentioned when you began," i.e. at the beginning of § 2.

3 **Εὖ γε ὑπέμνησας,** "thank you for reminding me." The same phrase occurs in several other places; cf. also εὖ ποιεῖν: *Timon* § 30, εὖ ποιεῖς χειραγωγῶν, "Thank you for conducting me," and § 45, εὖ γε ἐποίησεν. Cf. also Hor. *Sat.* I. 4. 17, *Di bene fecerunt,* "Thanks to the gods."

οὐ γὰρ οἶδ' ὅπως. One of L.'s most favourite phrases, "somehow or other:" see note § 1.

5 **προύθεσαν οἱ πρυτάνεις ἐκκλησίαν.** προτίθημι is the usual formula for "summoning" an assembly. Here it is active, but in Soph. *Ant.* 159 (προύθετο λέσχην) the middle voice is used, because Creon called that assembly not for the people but for *himself* to issue an edict.

The Athenian Senate (βουλή) was composed of 50 from each of the 10 tribes = 500. The 50 of each tribe formed a committee which presided in the council in turn (ἐπρυτάνευε) for about 5 weeks. This period was a πρυτανεία; the presiding committee the πρυτάνεις. These πρυτάνεις summoned the ἐκκλησία at least four times during its πρυτανεία,— and, if necessary, more often. Cf. Gow, *Companion to School Classics,* pp. 115—118.

9 **διῳκήθη,** "other business was transacted, but at the end."

10 **αὐτῶν κατηγόρητο πολλὰ καὶ δεινά.** For the form of construction with κατηγορεῖν, cf. Thuc. II. 95 (see Arnold's note) ἀδικία πολλὴ κατηγορεῖτο αὐτοῦ, "much criminality was imputed to him." So too Herod. VII. 205. We find the passive form too in *Timon* § 38. Verbs of accusing, condemning, acquitting, &c. always take a *genitive* of the person. Trans. "many terrible charges had been brought forward against them."

§ 20. A similar kind of decree occurs in *Timon* § 51. The whole decree is written in a mock-heroic style, in imitation of the proper legal phraseology: cf. for instance the psephism in the *De Corona,* proposing to give Demosthenes a crown, ἐπειδὴ Δημοσθένης Δημοσθένους Παιανιεὺς πολλὰς καὶ μεγάλας χρείας παρέσχηται...δεδόχθαι τῇ βουλῇ καὶ τῷ δήμῳ ἐπαινέσαι Δημοσθένην...κ.τ.λ. εἶπεν Ἀριστόνικος ὁ Φρεάρριος. A more elaborate decree is to be found at the end of the *Concilium Deorum.*

19 **τὰς ψυχὰς καταδύεσθαι,** "their souls descend into asses," according to the Pythagorean doctrine of transmigration.

24 **Κρανίων Σκελετίωνος,** κ.τ.λ., all in regular legal order, name, father's name, deme, tribe. "Skull, son of Skeleton, of Corpse-deme, of the tribe of the dead."

25 **'Αλιβαντίς,** comically formed from ἀλίβας (ἀ...λιβάς, "sap-less"), a word used of the dead in Plat. *Rep.* 387 c, and of the river Styx in Soph. *Frag.* 751 ; cf. too note on ἠλιβάτων, p. 37, l. 5.

26 **ἐπεψήφισαν,** "put it to the vote:" so in *Timon* § 44, ἐπεψήφισε τῇ ἐκκλησίᾳ Τίμων ὁ αὐτός.

p. 19. 1 **ἐπεχειροτόνησε,** stronger than the simple word χειροτονέω, =to *confirm* or *ratify,* by show of hands, cf. Dem. *de Cor.* § 29 (235), ἡ εἰρήνη ἡ ἐπιχειροτονηθεῖσα. So at the end of *Conc. Deor.,* we have the simple verb after a similar decree: *Momus.* "This then is our decree." *Zeus.* "A very just one, Momus, and let all who favour it hold up their hand (ἀνατείνειν τὴν χεῖρα)—or rather, let it be held as passed—for I know that those who will *not* hold up their hands (χειροτονέω) will be in the majority,"—a ridiculous ending of a solemn assembly.

2 **Βριμώ,** an onomatopoeic word, as shown by the verb. It was a special title of Proserpine, or Hecate, given, because supposed to cause those horrors and terrors which the weak-minded and superstitious are subject to at night. Compare § 13, Χίμαιρα for a similar "bogey." We find the word in Propertius, II. 2. 12, "Mercurio et sanctis fertur Boebeidos undis | Virgineum Brimo composuisse latus."

5 § **21.** **οὗπερ ἀφίγμην ἔνεκα,** "my object in descending," which he had mentioned before in § 1 in a parody from Hom. *Odys.* XI.

7 **ποῖόν τινα,** more indefinite than ποῖος by itself; cf. Herod. III. 34, κοῖόν μέ τινα νομίζουσιν εἶναι; observe the graphic use of the present ἡγεῖται.

8 **τυφλόν τι γερόντιον,** κ.τ.λ., "a little old man, blind and sallow, with a thin little voice."

9 **αἰτίαν οἶδα,** κ.τ.λ., "I know the cause of your perplexity, that it arose from wise men disagreeing among themselves in their opinions." τὰ αὐτὰ...ἑαυτοῖς. The reflexive is commonly employed in a reciprocal sense, ἑαυτοῖς = ἀλλήλοις.

11 **οὐ θέμις λέγειν...μηδαμῶς,...μὴ,** exactly as in § 2 where Menippus says οὐ θέμις ἐκφέρειν and Philonides answers μηδαμῶς...μὴ: see note there, and p. 41, l. 10.

13 **περιίδῃς,** "allow me to wander about the world in a blinder state

than yourself." For the participial construc. after περιοράω cf. Herod. I. 89, οὐ περιείδον αὐτὸν ἀναρπασθέντα.

16 ὁ τῶν ἰδιωτῶν ἄριστος βίος. Notice the order; βίος goes with ἄριστος as part of the predicate, not with ὁ. "That of private individuals is the best life;" and cf. § 4 note χρυσὸν...τὸν τῶν ἰδιωτῶν βίον.

17 μετεωρολογεῖν, "to study sublime subjects," "to live up in the clouds."

τέλη καὶ ἀρχάς, "fines ac principia," "beginning and end," "whence and whither."

18 καὶ καταπτύσας, κ.τ.λ., "and eschewing these clever sophistries, and deeming such things to be rubbish, seek after this alone of all, viz. how," &c.

19 συλλογισμῶν. Technically συλλογισμός is a logical term, meaning an inference from certain premises (= Lat. ratiocinatio), as opp. to ἐπαγωγή, an argument by Induction (= Lat. inductio).

τὰ τοιαῦτα λῆρον ἡγησάμενος. Certainly Lucian himself is never tired of "deeming such things as humbug"—not *true* philosophy, remember, in any shape or form—but all the false shams prevailing in his time (see Introduction); so too of all the foolish stories and legends which many still professed to believe: cf. *Timon* § 9.

20 τὸ παρὸν εὖ θέμενος, a well-known Thucydidean expression, cf. I. 25, ἐν ἀπόρῳ εἴχοντο θέσθαι τὸ παρόν, and IV. 59, τὰ γὰρ ἴδια ἔκαστοι εὖ βουλόμενοι δὴ θέσθαι. The idea is that of *making a good investment of the present time*, e.g. by not wasting it, or by showing forbearance toward a foe, in case luck may turn (the common meaning in Thucydides), or, as here, spending your time on something which may be practically useful.

p. 20. 1 κατ' ἀσφοδελὸν λειμῶνα, see note § 11.

4 § 22. ἐς τὸν βίον. Hitherto we have had βίος in the sense of "manner of life." Here it manifestly refers to the earth, and means "the world," opposed to the nether-world. So in one of the *Inf. Dial.* of the gods we have Hercules boasting: ὃς Διὸς μὲν υἱός εἰμι τοσαῦτα δὲ πεπόνηκα, ἐκκαθαίρων τὸν βίον, i.e. *our* earth in opposition to the heaven where he is dwelling. So *Charon* (§ 15) says he sees τὸν βίον μεστὸν ταραχῆς.

6 ἀτραπόν. Cf. p. 10, l. 2.

καὶ δή, see note § 6.

9   **Τροφωνίου,** a king of Orchomenus and a celebrated architect,
supposed to have built Apollo's temple at Delphi. After his death,
Trophonius was believed to give oracles in a cave, to which the
Boeotians were led by a swarm of bees. He was then worshipped
as a god, and this cave was one of the most celebrated in Greece,
due especially to the peculiar rites, which the suppliant had to
perform. In the third *Dial. Inf.* we find Trophonius and Menippus
wrangling together, the latter declaring the former an impostor.
According to Menippus in that place, the preliminary rite required
the going down to Lebadeia (see below), putting on a ridiculous
costume, holding a sacrificial cake, and creeping through the narrow
mouth into the cave. So in *Conc. Deor.* § 12, among other things
which Momus refuses to believe, he names τὸν Τροφώνιον (μυστή-
ριον).

13   **οὐκ οἶδ' ὅπως,** cf. note at the end of § 1.

ἐν Λεβαδείᾳ, "goodness knows how, here I am in Lebadeia,"
a town of Boeotia, near Coronea, chiefly known for the shrine of
Trophonius.

TIMON.

p. 21. § 1. The Dialogue opens with a volley of abuse from Timon in a mock-heroic style, addressing Zeus in several of those epithets which suppliants were wont to use according to their several needs. "O Zeus, thou god of friendship, hospitality, fellowship, thou god of our homes, thou lightner, guardian of oaths, cloud-gatherer, thunderer."

1 φίλιε, so of Zeus in *Tox.* 11, ἆρ᾽ ἱκανὸς ὁ φίλιος; *Icarom.* 3, μηδὲ πρὸς φιλίου με περιίδῃς. Cf. Arist. *Ach.* 734, ναὶ τὸν φίλιον.

ξένιε. *Amor.* 6, πάντας ἐπιχωρίους θεοὺς προσκυνήσας καὶ Δία ξένιον...ἐπικαλεσάμενος, so also Aesch. *Agam.* 61 and 353, Δία τοι Ξένιον μέγαν αἰδοῦμαι, and Paley's note.

ἑταιρεῖε καὶ ἐφέστιε. Cf. Herod. 1. 44, where it says Croesus ἐκάλεε μὲν Δία καθάρσιον ἐκάλεε δὲ ἐπέστιόν τε καὶ ἑταιρήϊον τὸν αὐτὸν τοῦτον ὀνομάζων θεόν. For the latter see also Jebb, *Ajax* 492.

2 ἀστεροπητά, an Homeric epithet, *Il.* 1. 580. Cf. Soph. *Phil.* 1198, πυρφόρος ἀστεροπητής.

ὅρκιε, Soph. *Phil.* 1324, Ζῆνα δ᾽ ὅρκιον καλῶ.

νεφεληγερέτα and ἐρίγδουπε, not employed elsewhere by L., but common epithets of Zeus with Homer.

3 καὶ εἴ τι ἄλλο. At last,· getting exhausted, Timon ends up with, "and any other epithet which crack-brained poets are wont to apply to you, especially when they are hard up to make the line scan."

καὶ. This is the eighth καὶ in the first three lines. The whole section is a specimen of a paragraph overloaded with καὶ's, there being 18 in these few lines. Cf. Introd., section on "Menippus, the Dialogue," and also on "Lucian's style."

εἴ τι ἄλλο = *si quid aliud*, "whatever else."

ἐμβρόντητοι. So Heracles calls Asclepius in *Dial. Deor.* 13. 1, ὦ ἐμβρόντητε. Cf. *Phil.* 2, πόσοι ἐμβρόντητοι ποιηταί.

5 ὑπερείδεις τὸ πῖπτον, κ.τ.λ. "You help to prop up the weak parts of the metre, and to fill the gap in the rhythm."

6   ῥυθμὸς...μέτρον. The first is not exactly our "rhythm," which is only used of *sounds* with us, but ῥυθμὸς was applicable to *motion* as well as sounds, and to prose as well as verse. "*Time*" is nearer the word, and μέτρον is "*verse*."

7   ποῦ σοι νῦν, κ.τ.λ. "Where is now thy loud-crashing lightning? where thy deep-booming thunder, and thy flaming, white-hot, terror-bearing bolt?"

ἐρισμάραγος. For form cf. ἐρι-σθενής, ἐρί-τιμος, ἐρί-γδουπος (supra), &c.

9   ἅπαντα...λῆρος. L. is very fond of calling things "rubbish." λῆρος and its verb are continually occurring. In *Inf. Dial.* 20 § 2 we have a similar expression, κόνις πάντα καὶ λῆρος πολύς. Cf. § 9, and *Men.* 21.

12   οὐκ οἶδ' ὅπως, a phrase which Lucian can scarcely use often enough; cf. note on *Men.* § 19.

p. 22. 1   μηδὲ would be οὐδὲ in good Greek.

σπινθῆρα, "a spark of anger," used in its literal sense in *Dial. D.* 5. 5, οὐδ' οἱ σπινθῆρες οὐδὲ ἡ κάμινος ἀπέτρεπόν σε.

4   § **2**. ἕωλος, lit. "a day old," as we speak of "yesterday's bread." So in *Tyr.* 18, ἕωλον ἤδη νεκρὸν ἀπολιμπάνων, "leaving the corpse till to-morrow." Then = "stale," cf. *Rhet. Prec.* § 9, ἕωλα παραδείγματα παρατιθείς. *Char.* § 19, ἕωλός ἡ ψυχρολογία. *Pseud.* § 3, εἰ καὶ ἕωλα δόξω λέγειν. In this passage it means "the wick after the flame is put out," i.e. = "stinking wick."

The wick was called θρυαλλίς, ἐλλύχνιον, or φλόμος: so Hesych. φλόμος=πόα τις, ᾗ καὶ ἀντὶ ἐλλυχνίου χρῶνται. ἡ αὐτὴ δὲ καὶ θρυαλλίς. It was made in part of the woolly leaves of a plant, known as φλόμος λυχνῖτις. Cf. θρυαλλὶς διψῶσα, *Gall.* 29: so διψαλέον θρυαλλίδιον (§ 14 below), and *Philops.* § 21, ἐπειδὰν ἡ θρυαλλὶς ἀποσβῇ.

πανδαμάτορος: cf. Soph. *Philoc.*, ad fin., of Zeus, χὢ πανδαμάτωρ δαίμων, ὃς ταῦτ' ἐπέκρανεν.

5   κεραυνοῦ φλόγα: cf. Aesch. *Prom.* 1017, βροντῇ καὶ κεραυνίᾳ φλογὶ Πατὴρ σπαράξει, and Eur. *Med.* 144, διά μου κεφαλᾶς φλὸξ οὐρανία βαίη.

οὕτω δαλόν. δαλὸς is a "burnt-out torch." Cf. *Asin.* § 31, ἐκ τῆς ἑστίας κλέψας δαλὸν ἔτι θερμόν = "to such an extent do you seem to be holding out to them a smoky torch."

6   ὡς=ὥστε, see Introduction.

7 ἀπολαύσειν, lit. "to have a share in anything," usually in a good sense "enjoy" (§§ 14, 17); here, in a bad sense, "to get harm from"—"and only so far do they think they will get any harm from its wounding." Cf. *Jup. Conf.* § 15, οὐδὲ γὰρ τὸν κεραυνὸν αὐτὸν φαίην ἂν αἴτιόν μοι γενέσθαι τοῦ τραύματος.

9 Σαλμωνεὺς imitated lightning with burning torches, and thunder by driving his chariot over a brazen bridge. For which impious act he was hurled into Tartarus by a bolt from Zeus. Cf. *Philop.* § 4, ἢ ἀγνοεῖς ὡς τοὺς θεοὺς πάντας ἀπέρριψεν ἀπὸ τοῦ θεσπεσίου βηλοῦ καὶ τὸν Σαλμωνέα ἀντιβροντῶντα πρῴην κατεκεραύνωσε. Cf. also Verg. *Aen.* VI. 585, "Vidi et crudeles dantem Salmonea poenas | Dum flammas Jovis et sonitus imitatur Olympi."

10 οὐ πάντη, lit. "not quite" (ironical), much the same as οὐ πάνυ. Cf. § 4, οὐ πάνυ ἀναγκαῖα ποιεῖν δοκῶν. So *Dial. Inf.* 21. 1, οὐ πάνυ δεδιέναι δοκῶν. So here = "being by no means unlikely to persuade."

ἀπίθανος, here used in an active sense "non-persuasive;" cf. *Jup. Trag.* 27, σφόδρα πιθανὸς ὤν. *Bacc.* 2, πάνυ πιθανόν τινα συνταγματάρχην. *Adv. ind.* 22, ἀπίθανος ὢν ζωγράφος. More commonly ἀπίθανος and πιθανός are passive, "credible, incredible."

11 θερμουργὸς, in antithesis to the ψυχρὸν just applied to Zeus, "hot-headed:" cf. Aesch. *Eum.* 530, γελᾷ δὲ δαίμων ἐπ' ἀνδρὶ θερμῷ (v. l. θερμουργῷ).

πῶς γάρ; ὅπου γε. "And what wonder, when." See note on § 8, πόθεν γάρ;

12 μανδραγόρα. This is probably correct (i.e. genitive), not μανδραγόρᾳ (dative). The word is used by Lucian again in *V. H.* II. 33, where Jerram quotes Shak. *Othello*, III. 3, "Not poppy nor *mandragora* shall ever medicine thee to that sweet sleep which thou owedst yesterday." So *adv. indoc.* § 23, οἴει τοσοῦτον μανδραγόραν κατακεχύσθαι αὐτοῦ ὡς ταῦτα μὲν ἀκούειν, ἐκεῖνα δὲ μὴ εἰδέναι. "The mandrake (*Mandragora officinalis*) was anciently thought to possess miraculous properties. It was said to shriek when taken from the ground, and to cause the instant death of any one who heard its cries. The person who gathered it, therefore, always stopped his ears with cotton, and harnessed a dog to the root, who in his efforts to escape, uprooted the plant and instantly fell dead. The forked root was then trimmed so as to resemble the human form, a berry being left to represent the head." Johns, *Flowers of the Field*, p. 443. Lord Bacon also (vol. I. p. 454) speaks of enchanters and

sorcerers using this plant to frighten people, cutting the head into fantastic shapes, and letting the fibrous part serve as a beard. The plant is allied to *Atropa Belladonna* (Deadly Nightshade). Cf. also Shakspere's "insane root that takes the reason prisoner," and Cleopatra says: "Give us to drink mandragora, | That I may sleep out this great gap of time."

14 λημᾷς. Cf. *Inf. Dial.* 9. 2, γέροντά με καὶ φαλακρὸν ὄντα καὶ λημῶντα, and Hor. *Sat.* I. 3. 25, Cum tua pervideas oculis mala *lippus* inunctis.

ἀμβλυώττεις πρός. The same construction (with πρὸs) occurs in *Char.* § I, ἀμβλυώττω πρὸs τὸ φῶs, "be dazzled at the light;" so here, "you are blind to what is happening." In § 27 we have the plain accusative. In *Char.* § 7 it is used absolutely.

15 ἐκκεκώφησαι, so Dind. Most read ἐκκεκώφωσαι, and so Dind. reads in *Philop.* I, δυσχεραίνεις καθ' ἡμῶν ἢ ἐκκεκώφωσαι. ἐκ-κωφεῖν seems the more classical word. The word is *passive* not middle, "and as for your ears, why, you are as deaf as a man in his dotage."

οἱ παρηβηκότες, "those past their prime." In *Lexiph.* 13 the word is applied to οἶνos. In *Tyran.* I it is opposed to ἀκμάζειν:— τὸν μὲν ἤδη παρηβηκότα, τὸν δὲ ἀκμάζοντα.

19 § 3. ἦγες...ἐκεχειρίαν. ἐκεχειρίαν ἔχειν, ἄγειν, ποιεῖσθαι="to make a truce," "hold out terms."

20 αἰγίς. Cf. *Sat. Epis.* 3, ἀλλὰ τὴν αἰγίδα ἐπισείων καὶ τὸν κεραυνὸν ἐπανατεινόμενος. The "aegis," or shield, of Zeus is described Hom. *Il.* v. 738, &c.

21 συνεχὲς προηκοντίζετο, "was continually being hurled, as in a skirmish." I am not sure what L. means by this. Dr Abbott says, "Zeus threw his lightning so freely that he was not careful whether it hit or missed," which can hardly be, when the passage is about the way in which Zeus in his earlier days punished the *wicked*. The German editors say either "jaculorum in morem densissime et edito loco devolantium" ("like darts hurled from higher ground in clouds"), or "in morem velitaris pugnae," as I have taken it. The εἰς needs noting. Wheeler compares *Inf. Dial.* 27. 3, ἐs τὸ βαρβαρικὸν ἤχθετο, "he was annoyed, as barbarians are wont to be." Cf. *Jup. Trag.* 33, οὐδέπω, ἀλλ' ἐν ἀκροβολισ-μοῖs ἔτι ἦσαν ἀποσφενδονῶντες ἀλλήλοις.

22 οἱ σεισμοί, κ.τ.λ. "Your earthquakes were as though in a

sieve," i.e. "Zeus shook the earth, as though it were a mere sieve,"
"your snow came in heaps," "your hail was like rock."

p. 23. 1 κοσκινηδὸν, σωρηδὸν, πετρηδὸν, a favourite form of
adverb, cf. βοστρυχηδὸν, ποταμηδὸν, ἀκτινηδὸν, ταυρηδὸν, ἑλικηδόν.

2 καὶ ἵνα, κ.τ.λ. "And, to use a slang term," seems to be the
meaning. Cf. *Pisc.* 5, εἰ μὴ φορτικὸν εἰπεῖν.

3 ῥαγδαῖοι, akin to ῥήγνυμι, a post-classical word, "violent."

4 ἐν ἀκαρεῖ χρόνου, "in a moment," either with or without
χρόνου. Cf. *Fug.* § 21, "Whatever I weave, τοῦτο ἐν ἀκαρεῖ αὖθις
ἀναλύεται." *Jup. Conf.* 8, ἐκ πλουσιωτάτων πενέστατοι ἐν ἀκαρεῖ
γίγνεσθε.

ἐπὶ τοῦ Δευκαλίωνος, "in the days of D.," a common use of ἐπὶ
with gen., cf. ἐπὶ Κύρου, ἐπὶ Καμβύσεω in Herodotus. Cf. the
spurious *Philopatris* § 1, ἠκηκόεις τὸν κόσμον κλυσθῆναι ὥσπερ ἐπὶ τοῦ
Δευκαλίωνος. Ovid tells the story *Met.* 1. 318.

5 ὑποβρυχίων...καταδεδυκότων, "all things being sunk under
water." ὑποβρύχιος, "under water." In *Dips.* § 3 we have it
in opposition to ἐπιπολάζων: v. note on latter word, § 9.

6 προσοκεῖλαν. Neut. part. aor. agreeing with κιβώτιον.

7 Λυκωρεῖ. Lycoreus was one of the peaks of "the two-peaked
Parnassus." Lycorea was a small town on its summit, whither
(Pausanias says) the people vainly fled, being drawn thither by the
howling of *wolves*, hence its name.

9 § 4. ἀκόλουθα governs τῆς ῥαθυμίας, "commensurate with"
or "as a natural consequence of your apathy." Cf. Arist. *Ach.*
438, κἀκεῖνά μοι δὸς τἀκόλουθα τῶν ῥακῶν, "give me the things
that go with the rags." In *Hermot.* 74 we have the dative, ἀκόλουθα γὰρ τῇ ἀρχῇ, "these things are the natural consequence of
his power." For τἀπίχειρα cf. Aesch. *P. V.* 318, τοιαῦτα...τῆς
ἄγαν ὑψηγόρου | γλώσσης, Προμηθεῦ, τἀπίχειρα γίγνεται. "The ἐπὶ
gives the sense of reciprocity," Paley. Trans.:—"You get paid
out as your laziness deserves."

11 πάρεργον, evidently an accusative in apposition to the whole
sentence; "unless perhaps by way of appendage to the Olympic
games." Same sentiment in *Icarom.* 24, ἐμὲ δὲ ὥσπερ παρηβηκότα
ἱκανῶς τετιμηκέναι νομίζουσιν, ἢν διὰ πέντε ὅλων ἐτῶν θύσωσιν ἐν
'Ολυμπίᾳ, and cf. παρέργως, *Men.* § 3 and note. For this well-
known idiom, cf. Eur. *Orest.* 1105, Ἑλένην κτάνωμεν Μενελάῳ λύπην
πικράν. Soph. *Ajax* 559, τέως δὲ κούφοις πνεύμασιν βόσκου, νέαν |

98   *TIMON.*   [§ 4—

ψυχὴν ἀτάλλων, μητρὶ τῇδε χαρμονήν. Cf. *Aen.* III. 305, "Tu-
mulum viridi quem cespite inanem | Et geminas, *caussas lacrimis,*
sacraverat aras."

Lucian uses the same phrase in several other places, cf. *Jup.
Trag.* 21, ὁ Θησεὺς ἐκ Τροιζῆνος εἰς ᾿Αθήνας ἰὼν ὁδοῦ πάρεργον
ἐξέκοψε τοὺς κακούργους. Herod. VI., ἀπῆλθε γῆμας καὶ αὐτός, πάρεργον
τῶν ᾿Αλεξάνδρου γάμων.

A verb from the previous sentence is easily supplied to τις,
"offer a sacrifice or a garland to you."

13   συντελῶν, "conforming to a kind of old custom."
      κατ᾽ ὀλίγον. For the distributive force cf. note on *Men.* § 15.

14   ἀποφανοῦσι, "they will render," in which sense the word occurs
      again a few lines down in § 5, and end of § 32. Here="They will
      make a Kronos of you."

15   ἐῶ λέγειν, *praetermitto dicere,* a phrase continually recurring.

17   ὑψιβρεμέτης, so Homer styles him often.
      ἀναστῆσαι τοὺς κύνας, "to set the dogs loose." A dog was
      usually placed at the door of large houses, in the absence of the
      porter; hence "cave canem." Cf. Theoc. XV. 43, τὰν κύν᾽ ἔσω κά-
      λεσον, and Arist. *Lysist.* 1215, εὐλαβεῖσθαι τὴν κύνα. In the same
      way the temples were guarded, which is the point in question here.
      So in *Vit. Auc.* 7 Hermes says of Diogenes the Cynic, with a play
      on his name (κυνικὸς), that he is as good as a watchdog, ἢν θυρωρὸν
      αὐτὸν ἐπιστήσῃς, πολὺ πιστοτέρῳ χρήσῃ τῶν κυνῶν.

18   τοὺς γείτονας ἐπικαλέσασθαι, "to call out for your neighbours'
      help," very likely alluding to the well-known story of Cyclops and
      "Οὗτις."

19   συσκευαζομένους, note the present, "while in the act of packing
      up," a word very often employed by Xen. e.g. *Cyr.* I. 4. 25.

20   Γιγαντολέτωρ. Cf. *Philop.* 4, παρὰ δὲ τῶν ποιητῶν Τιτανοκράτωρ
      καὶ Γιγαντολέτης ἀνυμνεῖται ὡς καὶ παρ᾽ ῾Ομήρῳ. Cf. Hor. *Od.*
      III. 1. 6, "Reges in ipsos imperium est Jovis | Clari Giganteo
      triumpho."

21   Τιτανοκράτωρ, cf. *Od.* III. 4. 42, "Scimus, ut impios | Titanas
      immanemque turmam | Fulmine sustulerit caduco."

22   περικειρόμενος, "letting them cut your hair, though you held a
      15-foot thunderbolt in your hand." Here used passively. The hair
      was thought to contribute greatly to the nobility and bearing of a
      man; cf. also § 8, for the simple verb. The story of Samson,

and how he was shorn of his strength naturally recurs to one's mind.

23 **ὦ θαυμάσιε.** Abbott says "strange god." But why not in an ironical sense as in Dem. *de F. L.* 113, αὐτὸς ὢν οἶμαι θαυμάσιος στρατιώτης, ὦ Ζεῦ, in some such sense as "your serene highness"? Other places where the word occurs rather make for this sense, e.g. Momus uses it to Apollo, Damon to Timocles (*Jup. Trag.* §§ 30, 39, 49), Solon to Anacharsis (§ 28).

πηνίκα παρορώμενα, "When will these things cease to be over-looked in so careless a fashion?" παρορᾶσθαι implies a passing over either from contempt or wilful neglect. Cf. Dem. *de Cor.* § 161, παρορῶντας καὶ οὐδὲ καθ᾽ ἓν φυλαττομένους, "*shutting their eyes to the fact,* &c."

25 **πόσοι Φαέθοντες, κ.τ.λ.** Concrete for abstract. "How many conflagrations and floods," in allusion to the well known story given in full *D. D.* 25, of Phaethon, who upset the chariot of his father, the Sun. For Deucalion see above, § 3.

26 **ὑπέραντλον,** a nautical expression, occurring again in § 18, μὴ ὑπέραντλος εἰσπεσὼν ἐπικλύσω αὐτόν; "water-logged," "overflow-ing," the condition of a ship in which the water is too much for the pumps to pump out. The passage in *Nav.* § 16 shows the metaphor well: ὁρᾷς ὡς ἐρυθριᾶν Ἀδείμαντον ἐποίησας πολλῷ τῷ γέλωτι ἐπι-κλύσας τὸ πλοῖον, ὡς ὑπέραντλον εἶναι καὶ μηκέτι ἀντέχειν πρὸς τὸ ἐπιρρέον.

§ **5.** The two following short passages from Shakspere are ap-posite enough to this section to deserve quotation. *Timon* IV. 3. 259:

"But myself,
Who had the world as my confectionery,
The mouths, the tongues, the eyes and hearts of men
At duty, more than I could frame employment,
That numberless upon me stuck, as leaves
Do on the oak, have with one winter's brush
Fell from their boughs and left me open, bare
For every storm that blows."

Ib. I. 1. 83:

"When Fortune in her shift and change of mood
Spurns down her late beloved, all his dependants,
Which labour'd after him to the mountain's top

Even on their knees and hands, let him slip down,
Not one accompanying his declining foot."

p. 24. 1 Ἵνα γὰρ...εἴπω, "Passing over public misfortunes, and speaking of my own."

3 πενεστάτων, *poverty* as distinguished from *beggary:* cf. § 11, and *Men.* § 14 note. Cf. Aristophanes on the same, *Plut.* 553,

πτωχοῦ μὲν γὰρ βίος, ὅν σὺ λέγεις, ζῆν ἐστιν μηδὲν ἔχοντα,
τοῦ δὲ πένητος ζῆν φειδόμενον καὶ τοῖς ἔργοις προσέχοντα.
ἀποφήνας, see § 4.

4 ἀθρόον, *en masse*, "all at once." Cf. note on ἀθρόως, § 23.

6 οὐδὲ...οὐδὲ = "not even"..."nor." Cf. p. 26, l. 12.

γνωρίζομαι. The universal story, "he that is rich hath many friends," &c. Cf. Eur. *Med.* 561, πένητα φεύγει πᾶς τις ἐκποδὼν φίλος, and Soph. *Frag.* 773, φίλου κακῶς πράξαντος ἐκποδὼν φίλοι.

7 οἱ τέως ὑποπτήσσοντες, "those who formerly toadied." Cf. *Prom.* § 13, ᾿τὸ τέως ἀκίνητον ἐς κίνησιν ἤγαγον.

8 νεῦμα, Lat. *numen*, Lucr. III. 145, and *nutus, Aen.* IX. 106, "nutu tremefecit Olympum."

ἀπηρτημένοι, see note on *Men.* § 5.

10 ὑπτίαν, cf. *Men.* § 18, = Lat. *supinus*, "thrown backwards" or "lying on the back." Cf. Hor. *Sat.* I. 5. 19, "stertitque supinus."

11 μηδὲ ἀναγνόντες. μηδὲ for οὐδὲ of good Greek—"without even recognizing me" (or "it").

12 ἑτέραν. Understand ὅδον, the dative is more common.

δυσάντητον, "unlucky to meet." ἀποτρόπαιον "ill-omened;" cf. in *Gall.* 2, where, when the Cock speaks, it says, ἀποτρόπαιον ἡγούμενος τὸ ἄκουσμα. For δυσάντητον, cf. *Pseudol.* 8, ὥρα ἡμῖν ἐκτρέπεσθαι τὸ δυσάντητον τοῦτο θέαμα. *Trans.:*—"And moreover, if they catch sight of me at some distance, they turn their heads, as though they felt they would only see some ill-omened and terrible sight, though a little while ago I was their saviour and benefactor."

15 § 6. ἐπὶ ταύτην τὴν ἐσχατιὰν, "to this desolate spot." The word occurs also in §§ 30, 42.

16 διφθέραν. Cf. § 38, ταύτην τὴν διφθέραν...Πενία περιτέθεικεν, and § 12, διφθέραν παρ' αὐτῆς λαβόντες καὶ δίκελλαν. "The διφθέρα was a coat of skins used by herdmen and country folks. It could be drawn over the head." Becker, *Char.* p. 442.

17 ὑπόμισθος, "hired for pay;" apparently a word peculiar to Lucian. It occurs in *de merc. cond.* § 5, πένης καὶ ἐνδεὴς καὶ

ὑπόμισθος ὤν. *Apolog.* 5, γίγνονται ὑπόμισθοι τραγῳδοῦντες, and in two or three other places.

ὀβολῶν τεττάρων. Better pay than as a dicast; viz. 7½*d.* as against 5*d.*

τῇ ἐρημίᾳ καὶ τῇ δικέλλῃ, "on my solitude and my spade." A case of zeugma, for which cf., among many passages, Verg. *Aen.* I. 426 and II. 258. Tennyson, *Princess*, has a good example: "The sloping pasture murmured sown | With happy *faces* and with *holiday.*" So Dickens says: "She went home in a flood of tears and a sedan-chair," and "The girls were in tears and white muslin" (*Pickwick Papers*). I quote from memory.

18   προσφιλοσοφῶν, "making speculations on." For the preposition cf. Cic. *ad Attic.* II. 19, nimium τῷ καλῷ προσπέπονθα, "I am passionately devoted to the beautiful." ἐνταῦθα, so modern editors generally. The older editions put the stop after this word.

20   ἀνιαρότατον γάρ, "for this is most loathsome to me:" to find "the ungodly in such great power and flourishing like a green bay-tree" is much more a burden to him than his solitary digging. Cf. Shaks. *Timon* IV. I. 35, "Timon will to the woods, where he shall find | The unkindest beast more kinder than mankind."

22   νήδυμον, an Homeric word. *Il.* II. 2, Δία δ' οὐκ ἔχε νήδυμος ὕπνος. Cf. *bis acc.* 2.

Ἐπιμενίδην, "the Rip Van Winkle of classic story. He is said to have sought shelter in a cave from the heat of the sun while keeping his father's sheep, and to have slept there 57 years." *Collins.* He was held in such estimation by the ancients that in the time of Solon he was sent for by the Athenians to stay their great plague. S. Paul quotes from his works *Titus* i. 12. Plutarch (*Life of Solon*) says some placed him as the seventh Sage of Greece instead of Periander.

23   ἀναρριπίσας. The simple verb ῥιπίζω occurs in Arist. *Frogs* 360, στάσιν ἐχθρὰν...ἀνεγείρει καὶ ῥιπίζει = "fan into flame," though the connexion of the word with ῥίπτω suggests the idea of ignition by quick revolution. Cf. *Anacharsis* § 21, τὴν ψυχὴν μουσικῇ καὶ ἀριθμητικῇ ἀναρριπίζομεν.

24   ἐναυσάμενος, "having got your light from Aetna," or "having set fire to," as in *Mar. Dial.* 2. 2, where Cyclops telling his story of Odysseus says καὶ τὸ πῦρ ἀνέκαυσα ἐναυσάμενος ὃ ἔφερον δένδρον ἀπὸ τοῦ ὄρους. Collins takes the word with κεραυνόν, though it seems

better to keep it with φλόγα and take μεγάλην ποιήσας "having made it great." Αἴτνης is the reading adopted by Faber, Hemst., &c. though Dindorf has Οἴτης, a Thessalian mountain, where Heracles burnt himself. But we do not find it to have been volcanic.

p. 25. 1 τὰ ὑπὸ Κρητῶν. The story was that when Pythagoras visited the sepulchre of Minos in Crete, he found on it this inscription ΤΟΥΔΙΟϹ="the sepulchre of Zeus." So in *Conc. Deor.* § 6, Momus says to Z., 'Ἐν Κρήτῃ μὲν οὐ μόνον τοῦτο ἀκοῦσαί ἐστιν, ἀλλὰ καὶ ἄλλοτε περὶ σοῦ λέγουσι, καὶ τάφον ἐπιδεικνύουσιν. *Jup. Trag.* 45, also bears on this passage well: καὶ πῶς οὐ μέλλω βροντῆς ἀκούειν, ὦ Τιμόκλεις; εἰ δ' ὁ Ζεὺς ὁ βροντῶν ἐστί, σὺ ἄμεινον ἂν εἰδείης ἐκεῖθέν ποθεν παρὰ τῶν θεῶν ἀφιγμένος, ἐπεὶ οἵ γε ἐκ Κρήτης ἥκοντες ἄλλα ἡμῖν διηγοῦνται, τάφον τινὰ ἐκεῖθι δείκνυσθαι καὶ στήλην ἐφεστάναι δηλοῦσαν ὡς οὐκέτι βροντήσειεν ἂν ὁ Ζεὺς πάλαι τεθνεώς.

2 ἐκεῖ. This is Dindorf's reading. The older editors had τῆς σῆς ταφ. Hemst. τῆς ἐκεῖ σῆς ταφ.

§ 7. Zeus begins to wake up at last, and asks Hermes who the man is, bawling at him and abusing him thus. "He can only suppose it is some philosopher, as no one else would dare to do it." Hermes is amazed to think that Z. doesn't know Timon. It only shows how fast asleep he must have been.

4 Ὑμηττόν, the well-known mountain near Athens. In Hor. *Od.* II. 18. 3 we have "trabes Hymettiae," alluding to its white marble ; *Sat.* II. 2. 15 "Hymettia mella," alluding to its far-famed honey.

ὑπωρείᾳ, "foot of the mountain." So in *Char.* § 5, when they have piled Pelion on Ossa, Hermes says to Charon παπαῖ, κάτω ἔτι ἐσμὲν ἐν ὑπωρείᾳ τοῦ οὐράνου. In *Hermot.* 3 Luc. says to H. ποῦ σε φῶμεν τῆς ὁδοῦ τυγχάνειν ὄντα; and H. says, ἐν τῇ ὑπωρείᾳ κάτω ἔτι, ἄρτι προβαίνειν βιαζόμενον : so *Rhet. Praec.* 3, ἐν τῇ ὑπ. τῆς ἀνόδου.

5 ὑποδίφθερος, see note § 6 on διφθέρα.

6 ἐπικεκυφώς, cf. note § 54.

7 ἢ που φιλόσοφος...οὐ γὰρ ἄν, κ.τ.λ. For ἢ που cf. *Dial. Deor.* 8, ἢ που στρατόπεδον ... ἐλελήθεις ἔχων, "*surely* you've got" &c. In *Inf. Dial.* 27. 9 it is used interrogatively, ἢ που βασιλεύς τις ἦσθα; οὐδαμῶς. ἀλλὰ σατράπης; οὐδὲ τοῦτο : "*Of course* you were a king of some kind?" "Oh dear no!" "Well then, a satrap?" "No, not even that." So here it ="*of course* a philosopher."

οὐ γὰρ ἂν οὕτως. Cf. note *Menip.* § 1, and fuller note below, *Timon*, § 24.

11 καθ' ἱερῶν τελείων ἐστιάσας: "κατά with a genit. follows εὔχομαι, and similar verbs or phrases. ἐστιάω, as used of a sacrifice, may perhaps be classed with them, but it does not occur with this construction elsewhere," *Yonge*. Cf. Arnold Thuc. v. 47, and his note. "The victims were to be full-grown animals, and not the young, a bull, or ox, e.g. and not a calf or a lamb."

ὁ τὰς ὅλας ἑκατόμβας, with ellipse of θύων. This ellipse of a participle is common, so *Tyran.* § 13, ποῦ δὲ ὁ τὸ ξύλον (supply ἔχων). Cf. also *Conc. Deor.* 9, ὁ τὸν κάνδυν καὶ τὴν τιάραν. So ἡ τὸν μέγαν περίβολον *Char.* § 23, and cf. Heitland's note on *Char.* § 9, τὴν τὸ τριπλοῦν τεῖχος (περιβεβλημένην) where he cites several instances from Lucian.

12 παρ' ᾧ=*apud quem*. Cf. § 10, παρὰ τῷ Τίμωνι.

13 τὰ Διάσια, a festival in honour of Zeus Meilichius (Μειλίχιος). It was held at Athens twice a year, cf. Thuc. I. 126, ἔστι γὰρ καὶ Ἀθηναίοις Διάσια, ἃ καλεῖται Διὸς ἑορτὴ Μειλιχίου μεγίστη, ἔξω τῆς πόλεως, ἐν ᾗ πανδημεὶ θύουσι, and in *Icarom.* 24 Zeus asks *Men.* δι' ἣν αἰτίαν ἐλλίποιεν Ἀθηναῖοι τὰ Διάσια τοσούτων ἐτῶν.

14 Φεῦ τῆς ἀλλαγῆς. The genitive with interjections is very common, e.g. *Char.* § 13, ὢ πολλοῦ γέλωτος, § 23, παπαῖ τῶν ἐπαίνων, § 24, ὢ τῆς ἀνοίας. So lower down § 45, φεῦ τοῦ τάχους. § 48, ὢ τῆς ἀναισχυντίας.

15 τί παθών, a very common idiom, lit. "experiencing what, is he thus?" i.e. "what possesses him to be like this?" So in Arist. *Vesp.* 251, τί δὴ παθὼν τῷ δακτύλῳ τὴν θρυαλλίδ' ὠθεῖς; cf. τί μαθών.

16 αὐχμηρὸς=*squalidus*, "dirty."

σκαπανεύς, "digger," a less common word than σκαφεύς, cf. also *Vit. auc.* 7.

p. 26. 1 § 8. Οὑτωσὶ μὲν εἰπεῖν. The phrase is balanced by ὡς δὲ ἀληθεῖ λόγῳ (supply εἰπεῖν) two lines below:="ut ita dicam ...sed ut vere loquar."

This section is clearly aimed against the folly of those who have such little sense as to choose these worthless creatures to be their associates. Cf. Introd. "Timon, the Dialogue."

χρηστότης. So Shakspere, *Tim.* III. 1. "Every man has his fault, and honesty is his."

3 ὡς δὲ ἀληθεῖ λόγῳ, κ.τ.λ. "But to tell you the truth, it was his folly, and simpleness, and inability to judge of true friends."

4   ὃς οὐ συνίει κόραξ...χαριζόμενος, "Inasmuch as he couldn't see that he was bestowing favours on," &c.   The ὃς here is=*quippe qui*.

5   κόραξι καὶ λύκοις, "by carrion-crows and wolves."   Cf. Pers. v. 116, "et fronte politus *Astutam* vapido servas sub pectore *vulpem*." So λύκοι in the N. Test., S. Matt. vii. 15, Acts xx. 29.   The use of κόραξ as an expression of worthlessness is well known, cf. Hor. *Ep.* I. 16. 48.   See also § 12 λάροι.

ὑπὸ γυπῶν...τὸ ἧπαρ.   No doubt the story of Prometheus was in L.'s mind.

6   κειρόμενος, cf. note περικειρόμενος § 4.

8   χαίροντας τῇ βορᾷ.   Cf., among the many abusive words which Shakspere more or less justly puts into Timon's mouth, Act III. *ad fin.*:

> "You fools of fortune, trencher friends, time's flies,
> Cap and knee slaves, vapours, and minute-jacks."

10   ἐκμυζήσαντες, "squeezing, or draining out."   For the metaphor cf. Juv. VIII. 9, "Ossa vides regum vacuis exsucta medullis," Hor. *Epod.* v. 37, "Exsucta uti medulla et aridum jecur | Amoris esset poculum," and see Pretor's note on Pers. VI. 52, "Non adeo," inquis, "Exossatus ager juxta est."

εὖ μάλα ἐπιμελῶς.   The double duty which μάλα has to do is rather curious.   We are all but bound to make two adverbs of it, "right well and thoroughly."

11   τὰς ῥίζας.   Note the sudden change of metaphor.

12   οὐδὲ...οὐδὲ, cf. p. 24, l. 6.

πόθεν γάρ;   "How should they?"   Cf. πῶς γάρ; § 2.   Soph. *Elec.* 910, οὐκ ἔδρασα...οὐδ' αὖ σύ. πῶς γάρ;   "I never put it there, nor you—How could you?"   So Dem. *de Cor.* 312, ἐπ' ἔδωκας οὐδέν, οὐκ ἀπορῶν, πῶς γάρ; so in *Pseud.* 29, οὐ γὰρ ἂν ἅπαντες ὅμοιά σοι λέγειν δυναίμεθα. πόθεν; τίς οὕτως ἐν λόγοις μεγαλότολμος;

13   ἐν τῷ μέρει=à *leur tour* (*Anach.* 1, *Pisc.* 8); not quite synonymous with ἐν μέρει (*Symp.* 17, *Nig.* 3) which=*vicissim.*

15   ὑπ' αἰσχύνης.   ὑπὸ="owing to."   Cf. § 9, ὑπ' ἀσχολίας. § 10, ὑπὸ χρηστότητος.

μελαγχολῶν, "melancholy mad"—a superfluity of bile was supposed to be one of the causes of madness.   Cf. *Dial. Deor.* 13. 2, ἀλλ' οὐδὲ μελαγχολήσας ἀπέκτεινα τὰ τέκνα καὶ τὴν γυναῖκα.   "*I didn't kill my children and wife in a fit of madness,*" Asclepius retorts on

Heracles. And again *Dial. Marin.* 2. 4, Cyclops relating the story of Odysseus to Poseidon, his father, says his neighbours μελαγχολᾶν οἰηθέντες με ᾤχοντο ἀπιόντες. Cf. below § 34, ἀπίωμεν, ὦ Ἑρμῆ, μελαγχολᾶν γὰρ ὁ ἄνθρωπός μοι δοκεῖ.

16   **οἱ πλουτοῦντες παρ' αὐτοῦ.** πλουτεῖν is constructed here as though it were passive in form, "enriched at his hand." So in *Dial. Mar.* 8. 2, ὁ δὲ πλουτήσας παρὰ τοῦ τυράννου ἐπεθύμησε. In Dem. 576. 1 we have ὑφ' ὑμῶν πεπλουτηκότας.

19   **§ 9. Καὶ μὴν.** See note *Menip.* § 8.

20   **ἤγαν. δυστυχ.,** "for he would naturally be indignant if left to his misfortune."

     ἐπεὶ καὶ, "*since if we do otherwise,*" we shall act like," &c.

22   **τοσαῦτα μηρία, κ.τ.λ.** Nearly all the MSS. omit μηρία. The Cod. Reg. inserts it. Faber says it is a barbarism without the μηρία; to which Hemst. agrees, adding that αἰγῶν πιότατα is not Attic, only αἶγας πιοτάτας or αἰγῶν πιοτάτας being permissible; *de Sacr.* § 3 probably settles the point, τοσαῦτά σοι μηρία ταύρων τε καὶ αἰγῶν ἔκαυσα ἐπὶ τ. βωμῶν; cf. Thuc. 1. 5, τὸν πλεῖστον τ. χρόνου.

23   **ἔτι γοῦν,** "still at any rate."

24   **πλὴν ὑπ' ἀσχολίας,** "moreover, *through* being so busy." Cf. last section, note on ὑπ' αἰσχύνης.

p. 27.   2   **παρὰ τῶν ἱεροσυλούντων,** cf. Timon's complaint § 4, ἐῶ λέγειν ποσάκις ἤδη σου τὸν νεὼν σεσυλήκασιν.

3   **καταμύσαι.** Twice used in N. Test. in its shortened form καμμύω, S. Matt. xiii. 15, and Acts xxviii. 27, in reference to the prophecy of Isaiah, "their ears are dull of hearing, and their eyes *have they closed.*"

4   **πολὺν ἤδη.** "For a long time past I haven't even had a glance at Attica."

6   **ἐπεπόλασαν.** Lit. "lie on the surface," and in this sense used by Aristotle of eels, αἱ ἐγχέλεις οὐκ ἐπιπολάζουσι (*H. A.* VIII. 2. 7). Then used metaphorically in many ways: hence "to prevail," "to be insolent," &c. Here it means "to be all the fashion," "to be popular." Luc. seems to use the verb in this sense in *de Salt.* 34, πηδήματα καὶ νῦν ἔτι ταῖς ἀγροικίαις ἐπιπολάζοντα, certain steps in dancing "still in vogue."

     μαχομένων, *not* dependent on τῶν εὐχῶν or we should have the article, but genit. absolute.

8   **ἐπιβυσάμενον** (cf. *de imag.* 29, ἤδη ἀποσοβῶ παρ' αὐτὴν ἐπι-

βυσάμενος τὰ ὦτα. Arist. *Plutus* 379, τὸ στόμα ἐπιβύσας. Cf.
in *Men.* § 17, ἐν παραβύστῳ που), "stuffing up" one's ears, no doubt
in allusion to Odysseus, who stuffed his sailors' ears with wax, that
they might not hear the Sirens' song, as L. says in *Saturn. Epist.*,
§ 32, τοὺς γὰρ οἰνοχόους ὑμῶν ὥσπερ τοὺς Ὀδυσσέως ἑταίρους κηρῷ
βεβύσθαι τὰ ὦτα.

9   ἀσώματα, cf. note on the word, *Men.* § 4.

10   λήρους, cf. note on *Men.* § 21, and *Tim.* 1.

    μεγάλῃ τῇ φωνῇ. For the predicate see note on p. 9, l. 1, and
p. 2, l. 22.

    συνειρόντων, "stringing together." συνείρειν is often used in
this metaphorical sense by Lucian. So in *Jup. Trag.* 14 Hermes
advises Zeus to "string a few phrases from Demosthenes' *Philippics*
together, and change the words a little" (σύνειρε ὀλίγα ἐναλλάττων).
Cf. *Aen.* VI. 160, "Multa inter sese vario sermone serebant."

11   οὐ φαῦλον go closely together = "good."

16   § **10.** παρὰ τῷ Τίμωνι, so παρ' ᾧ § 7, = *apud Timonem* = *chez
Timon,* "in Timon's house." On this part of the section, cf.
Shaks. *Tim.* Act I. Sc. 1 (end).

> "Come, shall we in,
> And taste Lord Timon's bounty? He outgoes
> The very heart of kindness.
> He pours it out; Plutus, the god of gold,
> Is but his steward."

17   ὅτι μάλιστα go closely together = *quam maxime,* "ever so much."
χρηστότης, cf. § 8 (init.). So in § 46 T. is called χρηστός.

19   καὶ αὖθις μὲν answered by πλὴν (at end of section). "But
I'll think about these toadies another time," "meanwhile for the
present," &c. (πλὴν ἐν τοσούτῳ).

23   τὸν σοφιστὴν Ἀναξαγόραν. Anaxagoras was one of the early
Greek philosophers, born circ. B.C. 500. He came to Athens about
B.C. 456. Aristotle says that he appeared among the older philosophers as a sober man among drunkards. He·departed from his
predecessors in their attempt to explain the phenomena of nature,
and was the first to assume a non-material cause, viz. intelligence
(νοῦς), as the First Cause. Among his pupils were Pericles and
Euripides. He was accused by the faction hostile to Pericles
of atheism, and sentenced to death. By the interposition of

Pericles, however, the sentence was commuted to banishment. Hence the remark of Zeus here, that Pericles "put his hand in the way."

p. 28. 3 τὸ 'Ανάκειον, cf. *Pisc.* § 42. Castor and Pollux were called *Anakes* or *Anaktes* for their kindness toward Athens. So in *Sympos.* § 9 Hermon the Epicurean is called ἱερεὺς τοῖν ἀνάκοιν. Hence their temple was ἀνάκειον. Cf. *Symp.* 24, ἕωθεν ἐπὶ τῇ οἰκίᾳ καὶ ἐν τῷ ἀνακείῳ θύοντα ὕστερον.

4 ὀλίγου δεῖν. Cf. note on μικροῦ δεῖν, *Men.* § 10.

5 ἐν τοσούτῳ. For the sense of this sentence v. heading to the section.

7 **§ 11. Οἷον.** The few lines of Hermes' are spoken "aside." "What a grand thing bawling is!" The Imperfect seems to mean, "always was and still is."

τὸ μέγα κεκραγέναι. For the adverb cf. *Men.* §§ 4, 9. The absence of τὸ before ὀχληρὸν shows the whole expression is one— "loud bawling, importunity, and brazenfacedness."

8 τοῖς δικαιολογοῦσι, "advocates," i.e. in a law court. Cf. note on δικαιολογήσωμαι, § 37.

10 αὐτίκα μάλα. The very numerous places in which this collocation is found show that μάλα does not go with πλούσιος. Cf. § 34, αὐτίκα μάλα βάλλων. *Dial. Deor.* 1, αὐτίκα μάλα εἴσῃ.

πλούσιος...πενέστατος, cf. § 5.

11 βοήσας...παρρησιασάμενος, "*thanks* to his shouting and declamation" &c.

12 εἰ δὲ σιωπῇ, "whereas, had he gone on digging in silence."

13 ἐπικεκυφώς, cf. note § 54.

14 οὐκ ἂν ἀπέλθοιμι. Slightly more polite than a direct "won't." "I would rather not go, Zeus." Cf. Dem., ἡδέως ἂν ἔγωγε ἐροίμην Λεπτίνην, "I should just, please, like to ask Leptines."

16 καὶ ταῦτα. Cf. *Men.* § 4.

p. 29. 1 **§ 12.** νὴ Δία, a rather comical affirmation when he is addressing Zeus himself.

2 ἐς πολλὰ κατεμέριζε, "scattered me hither and thither in many fragments."

πατρῷον...φίλον, "though I was an old family friend."

3 μονονουχὶ, cf. note *Men.* § 12.

δικράνοις, "a two-pronged pitchfork," Lat. *furca.* Cf. Hor. *Ep.* 1. 10. 24, "Naturam expellas furca, tamen usque recurrit," and cf. Arist. *Pax* 637, δικροῖς ἐώθουν τὴν θεὸν κεκράγμασιν.

5 ἀπέλθω...παραδοθησόμενος, "Am I to go back again, then, (delib. subj.) to be given up" (purpose)?

7 τοὺς αἰσθησομένους, "those who will appreciate the gift, and will take care of me, and who esteem me as an object of worth and of great affection."

περιέψοντας, from περιέπω, imperf. περιεῖπον. The future is found in Herodotus, but in Attic prose only the pres. and imperf., as in *Inf. Dial.* 12. 4 we have τὴν Μακεδόνων ἀρχὴν περιέπων, "managing the government."

8 περιπόθητος. περὶ intensive, as in περίθυμος, περικαλλής, &c. Cf. *Inf. Dial.* 9. 2, οὔκ, ἀλλὰ τοιοῦτος ὢν περιπόθητος ἦν, and ib. 4. 2, πάνυ γὰρ περιπόθητά ἐστι ταῦτα.

9 λάροι. Greedy people he had called *crows* and *wolves* in § 8. He now likens the foolish to "cormorants," birds which were supposed to be easy of capture. Cleon in Arist. *Nub.* 591, is called λάρος because of his greed : ἦν Κλέωνα τὸν λάρον δώρων ἑλόντες καὶ κλοπῆς. Cf. our slang terms "fleeced," "gulled." "But as for these silly creatures, let them dwell with poverty, if they prefer her to us."

10 ἀγαπάτωσαν, cf. note *Menip.* § 17.

12 ἀμελητί. In § 3 was given a note, showing L.'s fondness for adverbs in -δόν. The following will no less show his partiality for the form in -τί : ἀσκαρδαμυκτί, ἀδακρυτί, ἀψοφητί, ἀπονητί, ἀκονιτί, ἀμισθί, ἀπνευστί, ἀμογητί, ἀμυστί, ἀναιμωτί, νεωστί, ἀμεταστρεπτί, τετραποδιστί, ἀγελαστί, ἀκροποδητί, μεγαλωστί, and for proper names Συριστί, Κελτιστί, Ἑλληνιστί.

13 § **13.** ἐργάσεται περί. ἐργάζεσθαι simply = ποιεῖν or δρᾶν, in which case the preposition is usually omitted, e.g. *Pisc.* § 4, ἅτινα εἴργασαι ἡμᾶς τὰ δεινά, and *Alex.* 56, μηδὲν ἡμᾶς δεινὸν ἢ κακὸν ἐργάσασθαι. Cf. however Plat. *Gorg.* 522 D, ἐργάζεσθαι περὶ θεοὺς ἄδικον.

14 πεπαιδαγώγηκεν, "has educated him," so in *de Salt.* 72, ὁρᾷς τὸ θέατρον...ὅλως τὰ ἤθη τῶν ὁρώντων παιδαγωγοῦν. S. Paul's phraseology is somewhat similar, in Gal. iii. 24, 25, where he says the Law "is our schoolmaster to bring us to Christ" (παιδαγωγὸς ἡμῶν γέγονεν εἰς Χριστόν).

15 εἰ μή, κ.τ.λ., "unless his loins are altogether impervious to pain."

16 ὡς = ὥστε, as just below.

17 μεμψίμοιρος, "querulous," "grumbling," cf. § 55 too. The word occurs not unfrequently in L.; in *Bis acc.* 2 Zeus says, try as

he will to listen to every one at once, still τὸ μεμψίμοιρον οὐδὲ οὕτω διαφυγεῖν ῥάδιον. *Cynic.* 17, καθάπερ οἱ νοσοῦντες δυσάρεστοι καὶ μεμψίμοιροι ὄντες.

18　**ἤφίει.** Observe the double augment, a form of ἀφίημι by no means uncommon. Cf. *Hermot.* § 74 (twice), Thuc. II. 49. So in N.T., S. Mk. xi. 16.

19　**περινοστεῖν,** "to wander about;" cf. fuller note § 24.
　　ζηλοτυπῶν, "showing jealousy," cf. § 14.

22　**μοχλοῖς, κλεισὶ, σημείων ἐπιβολαῖς.** So in the *Thesmophoriazusae,* the women complain: ταῖς γυναικωνίτισιν | σφραγῖδας ἐπιβάλλουσιν ἤδη καὶ μοχλούς.
　　ὡς = ὥστε.

24　**ἀποπνίγεσθαι λέγων ἐν πολλῷ τῷ σκότῳ.** So in *Plutus* 234 the sentiment is similar.

> *Plutus.*　"If I perchance took lodging with a miser,
> 　　　　　He digs a hole i' the earth, and buries me;
> 　　　　　And if some honest friend shall come to him,
> 　　　　　And ask a loan of me, by way of help,
> 　　　　　He swears him out, he never saw my face.
> 　　　　　Or if I quarter with your man of pleasure,
> 　　　　　He wastes me on his dice and courtesans,
> 　　　　　And forthwith turns me naked on the street."
> 　　　　　　　　　　　　　　　　　　COLLINS.

25　**ὠχρὸς,** "sallow:" cf. note on this word, *Men.* § 11. Cf. *Gall.* 22, Mikyllus says to Simon, οἰμώξε καὶ διαγρύπνει, καὶ ὅμοιος γίγνου τὸ χρῶμα τῷ χρυσῷ, προστετηκὼς αὐτῷ. So for **φροντίδος ἀνάπλεως** and **συνεσπακὼς τοὺς δακτύλους,** "full of care and with contracted fingers." Cf. *Gall.* 30, ὁρᾶς ἐπαγρυπνοῦντα καὶ τοῦτον ἐπὶ φροντίδων ἀναλογιζόμενον τοὺς τόκους, καὶ τοὺς δακτύλους κατεσκληκότα...ἐκτέτηκεν ὅλος ὑπὸ τῶν λογισμῶν.

27　**λογισμῶν.** So Dind. and Somm.; the MSS. have συλλογισμῶν. Gronovius suggested συλλογιστων.

p. **30.**　1　**καιροῦ λάβοιο,** "if you could snatch an opportunity."

3　**παρθενεύεσθαι,** "to be left untouched." For *Danaë,* cf. *Menip.* § 2.

§ **14.** The subject of this section, the love of a miser for his hoards, is one which satirists have always delighted in: e.g. cf. Hor. *Sat.* I. 1. 70—72:

"Congestis undique saccis
Indormis inhians, et tanquam parcere sacris
Cogeris, aut pictis tanquam gaudere tabellis,"

and *Sat.* II. 3. 109, I. I. 42, and Verg. *Aen.* VI. 610, *Georg.* II. 507.

6 **ἐρῶντας μὲν**, balanced by οὐ δὲ τολμῶντας, "enamoured, but not daring, though it was in their power to enjoy " (ἐξὸν, accus. absol. like παρόν, ὑπάρχον). Then the construction changes to φυλάττειν, instead of φυλάττοντας, the word being still governed by ἔφασκες.

8 **ἐπ' ἀδείας**. ἄδεια is the technical word for "immunity" or "indemnity" from war, taxation, &c. Hence τῶν σωμάτων ἄδειαν in Thuc. III. 58. So in Dem. *de Cor.* 286, ὧν ἐφρόνουν λαβόντας ἄδειαν ("secured impunity for their aims "). And so ἐν ἀδείᾳ became commonly used as =ἀδεῶς "fearlessly," "without fear of results," like ἐπ' ἀδείας in this passage, which is not so common.

9 **φυλάττειν ἐγρηγορότας**, so *Gall.* § 28, ὁρᾷς αὐτὸν ἀγρυπνοῦντα, and § 30 as quoted last section.

10 **ἀσκαρδαμυκτί.** Cf. *Tyran.* § 26, ῥᾴδιον γοῦν ἄν τις τὸν ἥλιον ἢ τοῦτον ἀσκαρδαμυκτὶ προσέβλεψεν: "without blinking;" v. § 12.

11 **τὸ...ἔχειν** go together: "deeming it sufficient enjoyment *not* to be able to enjoy them, *but* to keep others from sharing."

13 **ἐσθίουσαν τῶν κριθῶν.** Partitive gen., "eating of the barley." The same fable is mentioned in *adv. indoc.* 30: "You cannot use your library yourself, nor do you let any one else, ἀλλὰ τὸ τῆς κυνὸς ποιεῖς τῆς ἐν τῇ φάτνῃ κατακειμένης, ἣ οὔτε αὐτὴ τῶν κριθῶν ἐσθίει οὔτε τῷ ἵππῳ ἐπιτρέπει."

15 **τὸ καινότατον**, "what was most strange." This turn of phrase, which is to be explained grammatically as an accusative in apposition to the sentence (cf. note on πάρεργον § 4), is very commonly employed by Lucian, e.g. τὸ οἴκτιστον, τὸ παραδοξότατον, τὸ ὅλον, τὸ μέγιστον, &c.

16 **αὐτοὺς ζηλοτυπούντων**, "being jealous of themselves," being afraid lest even they themselves should touch it.

17 **πεδότριψ.** Hemst. following the MSS. reads παιδότριψ =a slave who had care of children; L. and S. say this is a fals. lect. for πεδότριψ. Dr Abbott has παιδοτρίβης, "a gymnastic master," a reading too easy to be probable; v. next note for translation.

18 **ἐμπαροινήσει**, "will revel," "will indulge himself." Earlier editors make it govern δεσπότην, in sense of "insulting" (ludibrio habiturus, *Hemst.*): but δεσπότην is governed by ἐάσας, and this word is

used absolutely. So we find it in *Sympos.* § 2, εἴτε γέροντες εἴτε νέοι ἐμπαρῴνησάν τι παρὰ τὸ δεῖπνον, and *Alex.* § 41, ἐμπαροινῶν πάντα τρόπον. Translate, "And not knowing that some cursed slave or rascally steward will creep in stealthily and make himself merry, leaving his luckless and loveless master to keep watch over his gains by the light of a dim and narrow-necked little lamp, and a small dried-up wick." The sarcastic diminutives are to be noticed ; the master would not afford himself even a decent lamp or a sufficiency of oil to count his treasures properly.

§ 15. For this section cf. Goldsmith, *Traveller, ad init.:*

"As some lone miser, visiting his store,
Bends at his treasure, counts, recounts it o'er—
Hoards after hoards his rising raptures fill,
Yet still he sighs, for hoards are wanting still."

24   Καὶ μὴν, cf. § 9.

εἰ γε...ἐξετάζοις...δόξω. Notice this. "If you were to examine" (which is very unlikely), "both sides of the question will turn out reasonable" (positive fact).

25   τὸ πάνυ τοῦτο ἀνειμένον. For πάνυ cf. *Charon* § 17, αἱ ἄγαν σπουδαί, "over-eagerness :" so here, "excessive wastefulness." So § 16, τοὺς πάνυ προχείρους, and § 35, τὸ πάνυ τοῦτο ἄγριον.

26   ὡς πρὸς ἐμέ. Faber would omit πρός and read εἰς: but for this reading cf. *Charon* § 7, Τυφλὸς ὁ Λυγκεὺς ἐκεῖνος ὡς πρὸς ἐμέ: *Hermot.* § 13, παῖδας εὖ ἴσθι οἰήσῃ ἅπαντας ὡς πρὸς σέ ("be assured you will deem all as children by the side of yourself"). Cf. § 42, ὡς πρὸς Τίμωνα. The phrase occurs again and again in L. Here it seems elliptical for *quod ad me attinet* = "as far as my opinion goes," "as far as I can see."

27   τούς τε αὖ κατάκλειστον, κ.τ.λ., cf. *Gall.* 28, οὐκοῦν τάλαντα μὲν ἑβδομήκοντα ἐκεῖνα πάνυ ἀσφαλῶς ὑπὸ τῇ κλίνῃ κατορώρυκται, τὰ δὲ ἑκκαίδεκα εἶδεν, οἶμαι, Σωσύλος ὁ ἱπποκόμος ὑπὸ τῇ φάτνῃ κατακρύπτοντά με.

p. 31.   2 πιμελὴς, "fat." Cf. *Sympos.* § 40, ἡ δὲ ὄρνις ἡ πρὸ τοῦ Ἑρμῶνος πιμελεστέρα, "but the bird placed in front of Hermon happened to be plumper." The noun πιμελὴ "fat" occurs in *Prom.* 7, ὀστᾶ κεκαλυμμένα τῇ πιμελῇ. ὑπέρογκος, "of vast bulk."

10   § 16. τούς, ὅπερ ἄριστόν ἐστι, μέτρον ἐπιθήσοντας, moderation once again inculcated, as in *Men.* § 4.

17   **οὐ σύ γε,** "You at least wouldn't say so, who have had so much experience in love."

19   **§ 17. Εἰ δέ τις.** The apodosis does not come till ἔσθ' ὅπως.

22   **καὶ ταῦτα,** as so often before, v. *Men.* § 4: "and that too, though he affirms he loves her, and clearly does so, judging by his pallor and wasted body and sunken eyes."

25   **παραπαίειν,** cf. note *Men.* § 1.
     καταμαραίνων, "causing to waste away."

27   **ἱέρειαν τῇ Θεσμοφόρῳ,** cf. *Dial. Meret.* 7. 4, οὐκοῦν ἀνέραστος σὺ μενεῖς διὰ τοῦτο καὶ σωφρονήσεις καθάπερ οὐχ ἑταίρα, τῆς δὲ Θεσμοφόρου ἱέρειά τις οὖσα = "priestess of Demeter," who was bound by vows like the Roman Vestal. Cf. Verg. *Aen.* IX. 58 for the epithet: "legiferae Cereri."

p. 32.   2   **λαφυττόμενος,** "swallowed up;" cf. *Asin.* 27, ἐώρων κύνας ...λαφύττοντας πολλά. ἐξαντλούμενος, v. l. 14 just below.

3   **στιγματίας.** Branding was a very common punishment, especially for runaway slaves or thieves; cf. Arist. *Aves* 759, εἰ δὲ τυγχάνει τις ὑμῶν δραπέτης ἐστιγμένος. Very often the mark was on the forehead, and many tried to conceal it under the hair, cf. Athen. VI. 225, ἀλλ' ἐστιγμένος | πρὸ τοῦ μετώπου παραπέτασμ' αὐτὴν ἔχει, "but being branded on the forehead he wears it (his hair) as a veil." There is an amusing story to the point in *Tyr.* 24.

5   **§ 18. διδόασι...ἄμφω,** "both get paid out grandly."

6   **οἱ μὲν ὥσπερ ὁ Τάνταλος ἄποτοι,** cf. Hor. *Sat.* I. 1. 68,

> "Tantalus a labris sitiens fugientia captat
> Flumina. Quid rides? Mutato nomine de te
> Fabula narratur."

Cf. *Men.* § 14; a somewhat similar passage occurs in *Char.* § 16, οἴχονται κεχηνότας αὐτοὺς ἀπολιποῦσαι, ὅπερ καὶ τὸν Τάνταλον κάτω πάσχοντα ὁρᾷς ὑπὸ τοῦ ὕδατος.

8   **ἐπικεχηνότες.** L. is very fond of using this word as expressing open-mouthed astonishment or expectation; e.g. below § 22, τοὺς μάτην κεχηνότας. *Pisc.* 34, πρὸς τὸ ἀργύριον κεχήνασιν. *Somn.* 12, κἄν πού τι λέγων τύχῃς, κεχηνότες οἱ πολλοὶ ἀκούσονται.

9   **Φινεὺς...Ἁρπυιῶν,** cf. *Aen.* III. 211,

> "Insulae Ionio in magno, quas dira Celaeno
> Harpyiaeque colunt aliae, Phineia postquam
> Clausa domus, mensasque metu liquere priores."

The story of Phineus and the Harpies is found in Apol. Rhod. II.
178, &c. For cruelty to his step-children he was tormented by the
Harpies, who carried off his food whenever it was brought on the
table (cf. Aeneas' experience Verg. *Aen.* III. 225, &c.). They were
slain by Zethus and Calais, two of the Argonauts. Translate, "and
the others, like Phineus, see their food snatched away from their
very mouths by the Harpies."

'Αρπυιῶν.   Cf. Dante, *Inf.* Canto XIII.

"Here the brute Harpies make their nest...
Broad are their pennons, of the human form
Their neck and countenance, armed with talons keen
The feet, and the huge belly fledge with wings."

10   σωφρονεστέρῳ παρὰ πολύ, "by far the more prudent." So
Char. § 20, σωφρονεστέρους ἂν γενέσθαι παρὰ πολύ.

12   Ἐκεῖνος γάρ ποτε. "Why! will he ever cease from emptying
me out with all his might, as if from a leaky tub, before I have
fairly run in, wishing to be first with my stream, that I may not
break in upon him with a flood, and wash him away?"   *Abbott.*

13   κοφίνου τετρυπημένου. The κόφινος was a small wicker-basket,
used for carrying provisions about. Cf. Juv. III. 14 of the Jews,
"Judaeis: quorum cophinus foenumque supellex," and the miracle
of the feeding of the 5000 in N. T. Here it seems used rather as
= πίθος, v. below, = "a tub with a hole in it." For τρυπάω cf.
Sat. Epis. 24, κοσκινηδὸν διατετρυπῆσθαι, "with holes in like a
sieve."

15   ὑπέραντλος, cf. note, end of § 4.

16   τὸν τῶν Δαναΐδων πίθον. The whole passage in *Inf. Dial.* 11. 4
is worth quoting, as showing how L. is always repeating himself, v.
Introd. "Menippus, the Dialogue."

Timon, 18.	*Inf. Dial.* 11.
παύσεται ὥσπερ ἐκ κοφί-	ὥστε εἴ ποτε καὶ ἐμβάλλοι τις ἐς
νου τετρυπημένου,...κατὰ	αὐτοὺς ἢ σοφίαν ἢ παρρησίαν, ἢ ἀλή-
σπουδὴν ἐξαντλῶν, ..."Ωστε	θειαν, ἐξέπιπτεν εὐθύς, καὶ διέρρει,
ἐς τὸν τ. Δαναϊδων πίθον	τοῦ πυθμένος στέγειν οὐ δυνα-
ὑδροφορήσειν μοι δοκῶ καὶ μά-	μένου· οἷόν τι πάσχουσιν αἱ τοῦ
την ἐπαντλήσειν, τοῦ κύ-	Δαναοῦ αὗται παρθένοι, ἐς τὸν
τους μὴ στέγοντος.	τετρυπημένον πίθον ἐπαντλοῦ-
	σαι.

μοι δοκῶ, cf. note § 34 and δοκεῖν μοι, *Men.* 17.

17 τοῦ κύτους μὴ στέγοντος, "inasmuch as the vessel won't hold." For στέγειν, "to be water-tight," cf. Thuc. II. 94 καὶ αἱ νῆες αὐτοὺς...οὐδὲν στέγουσαι ἐφόβουν. So metaphorically, Aesch. *Supp.* 127, δόμος ἄλα στέγων.

22 § 19. ἐς τὸ ἅπαξ ἀναπεπταμένον. There seems some difficulty here. Either these four words are taken together = "the continual, or complete aperture," *Hemst.*, or else εἰς τὸ ἅπαξ = εἰσάπαξ (§ 45) = "once for all," and would then go with ἐμφράξεται, the words being probably misplaced. Sommerbrodt and Dr Abbott take it in the latter way; in support of the former cf. *De Cor.* 197, οἱ καθάπαξ ἐχθροὶ τῆς πόλεως, = "out-and-out enemies." So τὸ ἀναπεπταμένον is used = "apertura" in *de domo* § 3, *de merc. cond.* 3, &c.; cf. τὸ ἀνεῳγός, *Inf. D.* 4.

23 ἐν βραχεῖ, "in a trice."

24 τῇ τρυγί, "the dregs."

25 ἐπανιών, present tense, "as you return."

p. 33. 1 τοὺς Κύκλωπας. The locus classicus for the Cyclopes making the thunderbolts of Zeus, is Verg. *Georg.* IV. 170—175, and the parallel lines in *Aen.* VIII. 418, &c.

2 ὡς...δεησόμεθα, "as we shall very soon (ἤδη γε) be wanting it, when it is sharpened." Zeus intends to take Timon's hint, after his strong language in §§ 1, 2.

4 § 20. τί τοῦτο; ὑποσκάζεις; "Why! how's this? are you a bit lame?" (ὑπὸ = "slightly"). So in *Char.* 1 Hermes says that Zeus cast him out of heaven, so that ὑποσκάζων γέλωτα καὶ αὐτὸς παρέχοιμι οἰνοχοῶν.

5 ἐλελήθεις με...οὐ τυφλὸς μόνον, κ.τ.λ. Lit. "you had escaped my notice being not merely blind but lame as well," i.e. "Then you have been lame as well as blind without my knowing it." Cf. note on *Men.* §§ 1, 4.

8 οὐκ οἶδ' ὅπως, cf. § 1.

9 ἀμφοτέροις, supply ποσί: in § 55 χερσί is understood. So in *Asin.* § 18 ἀπολακτίσας ἀμφοτέροις, § 28 ἀμφοτέροις εἰς ἐμὲ ἀπολακτίζοντες.

For the blindness of Plutus cf. Aristoph. *Plut.* 87:

"Jove wrought me this, out of ill-will to men.
For in my younger days I threatened still
I would betake me to the good and wise

And upright only: so he made me blind,
That I should not discern them from the knaves."

COLLINS.

12 ἡ ὕσπληγξ, the bar drawn across the racecourse; Dr Abbott says "the winning tape" which is surely a mistake, as it must mean, "the moment *the starting tape* is dropped I am announced as victor," flying so fast, as he says in the next line, that the spectators could not see him. A passage from *de Calumnia* § 12 settles this: κἀκεῖ γὰρ ὁ μὲν ἀγαθὸς δρομεὺς τῆς ὕσπληγγος εὐθὺς καταπεσούσης μόνον τοῦ πρόσω ἐφιέμενος καὶ τὴν διάνοιαν ἀποτείνας πρὸς τὸ τέρμα κἂν τοῖς ποσὶ τὴν ἐλπίδα τῆς νίκης ἔχων τὸν πλησίον οὐδὲν κακουργεῖ, and cf. *Tyr.* 4, καὶ ὥσπερ ἀπὸ ὕσπληγγος θέοντες κατελαμβάνομεν αὐτὸν ἤδη ἐν Ταινάρῳ.

16 χθὲς μὲν οὐδὲ ὀβολόν...βρόχον. Cf. Hor. *Sat.* II. 2. 99, "Te tibi iniquum, | Et frustra mortis cupidum, cum deerit egenti | *As, laquei pretium*," and Plaut. *Pseud.* I. 1. 86, "*P.* Sed quid de drachma facere uis? *C.* Restim uolo mihi emere. *P.* Quamobrem? *C.* Qui me faciam pensilem." Here, "yesterday not having even so much as a penny to buy a yard of rope to hang themselves."

18 ἐπὶ λευκοῦ ζεύγους, "driving out with a pair of greys." From earliest times white horses were highly esteemed (Hom. *Il.* X. 437, ἵπποι λευκότεροι χιόνος), cf. Eur. *Phoen.* 172, ἅρμα λευκὸν ἡνιοστροφεῖ. So again *Sat. Epis.* 29, ἢν ἴδητέ ποτε ἐξελαύνοντας ἐπὶ λ. ζεύγους, κεχήνατε καὶ προσκινεῖτε, and *Gall.* 12, ἐξήλαυνον ἐπὶ λευκοῦ ζεύγους ἐξυπτιάζων.

19 οἷς οὐδὲ κἂν ὄνος. In later times κἄν came to be used as a stronger form of καί: cf. *D. D.* 5. 2, πλὴν ἀλλ' ἐκεῖναι μέν σοι κἂν ἐν γῇ μένουσι. *Tyr.* 20, κἂν μικρόν τι ἐπιστέναξον. Here="to whom not even so much as an ass belonged before." Notice also ὑπῆρξε not ἐγένετο.

20 χρυσόχειρες, i.e. with rings on their fingers. A Greek usually wore one ring, if only to serve as a signet, but of course fops, as now, were often bedizened with them. Thus in *Icarom.* § 18 a man has eight, and in *Gall.* 12 even more: ἔχων δακτυλίους βαρεῖς, ὅσον ἑκκαίδεκα, ἐξημμένους τῶν δακτύλων. With this last compare the well-known passage of Juvenal (1. 28):

"Crispinus, Tyrias humero revocante lacernas,
Ventilet aestivum digitis sudantibus aurum,
Nec sufferre queat majoris pondera gemmae."

8—2

21 ὄναρ πλουτοῦσιν, cf. note on § 41, p. 45, l. 19. μὴ would be οὐκ in good Greek.

p. 34. 1 § 21. Ἑτεροῖον, that is, *the other* side, the reverse side of the picture, ἑτεροῖος can be only like ἕτερος=either of two: so παρ' ἑτέρου πρὸς ἕτερον just below, "from the first to the second."

3 Πλούτων. Avoid confounding Pluto with Πλοῦτος, the speaker.

5 μετοικισθῆναι, "to *change* my residence." Cf. § 16, μετέβαλε, μεταμφιέσασα, μετενέδυσε.

6 ἐς δέλτον ἐμβαλόντες με, "having thrown me into a will, sealed me *down*, and wrapped me up in a parcel, they carry me away." A δέλτος is properly a writing-tablet; here it means the "will" inscribed on the tablet.

7 φορηδὸν, cf. κοσκινηδὸν § 3 and note there.

8 ὁ μὲν νεκρὸς, κ.τ.λ. This whole passage is quoted by Becker, *Char.* 165. L. here represents the will as being publicly opened; we see, however, by *Nigr.* 30, that it was usually done in private before witnesses. Moreover, the will often contained directions about the burial, so that it was bound to be opened at once.

9 πρόκειται (passive of προτίθημι) is the technical word for the corpse being "laid out." πρόθεσις is the laying out: cf. Eur. *Alc.* 1012, Soph. *Aj.* 1059. The 'locus classicus' is Luc. *de Luctu* 12.

παλαιᾷ...σκεπόμενος. Ordinarily the corpse was laid out on a couch (κλίνη) and was lamented over by females round the couch (cf. the virgins at Agamemnon's fate, Aesch. *Choeph.* 20—28); it was also covered with a splendid garment (προτίθενται λαμπρῶς ἀμφιέσαντες, *de Luc.* 11). But here it is put away in a dark corner, just covered with an old sheet, and left a prey for cats, while the should-be mourners go after the money.

10 σκεπόμενος, a less common form for σκεπαζόμενος, used frequently by L. but not often elsewhere. I have noted the following forms: Active, σκεπάσαντες (*Asin.* 4. 2), σκεπουσῶν (*Cynic.* 9). *Pass.* σκεπόμενος (adv. ind. 23), σκεπόμενα (*Inf. Dial.* 10. 8), τὸν σκεπόμενον (*Cynic.* 4), σκεπέσθω (*Rhet. Praec.* 18). In *Pisc.* 29 the form σκεπόμενος is *middle*. The article τῇ is generic, i.e. *the* sheet usually employed for such purposes. Cf. *Men.* 3, τοὺς νομοθέτας.

11 κεχηνότες. For this word v. note § 18.

ὥσπερ τὴν χελιδόνα, κ.τ.λ. The open-mouthed nestlings are a very good illustration of the gaping fortune-mongers. Cf. Juv. x. 231, "Hiat tantum, ceu pullus hirundinis, ad quem | Ore volat pleno mater jejuna."

12   **τετριγότες,** "twittering," cf. Hom. *Il.* II. 314; and note *Men.*
§ 11.

13   **§ 22. τὸ σημεῖον ἀφαιρεθῇ.** Note the four steps here, in due
order: (1) The breaking of the seal, (2) The cutting of the string,
(3) The unfolding of the will, (4) The chief inheritor published.

15   **ἤτοι...ἤ.** See note, p. 16, l. 17.

17   **αὐτῇ δέλτῳ,** "will and all." This use of αὐτὸς is well-known,
cf. αὐτοῖσι συμμάχοισι, Aesch. *Prom.* 229. *Alect.* 25, τοῦ προσωπείου
μὲν συντριβέντος αὐτῷ διαδήματι. *Mar. Dial.* 8. 1, αὐτῇ σκευῇ καὶ
κιθάρᾳ, "robe, lyre and all."

ἀντὶ τοῦ τέως Πυρρίου. Pyrrhias was a common name for a
slave; so in *de merc. cond.* 23 and *Philops.* 24. Pyrrhia, Hor. *Ep.* I.
13. 14, and the cook *Men.* 15. Dromo is equally common, *de merc.*
cond. 25, *dial. meret.* X. 2. 4. Tibius also, *de merc. cond.* 25, *dial.*
meret. 9. 5. For ἀντὶ τοῦ τέως Πυρρίου, "the quondam Pyrrhias,"
cf. *Men.* 16, τὸν δὲ Μαιάνδριον τέως ἐν τοῖς οἰκέταις πομπεύοντα.

19   **μετονομασθείς.** For μετὰ=change, cf. μετοικισθῆναι, last
section. For a similar sentiment, Yonge well compares Pers.
Sat. v. 78: "Verterit hunc dominus, momento turbinis exit | Marcus
Dama." "'Dama' is his original name, but with a twirl he comes
out 'Marcus Dama.'" Cf. *Gall.* 14, εἴπατε τῷ πτωχῷ μὴ κατα-
σμικρύνειν μου τοὔνομα, οὐ γὰρ Σίμων ἀλλὰ Σιμωνίδης ὀνομάζομαι.

τοὺς μάτην κεχηνότας: cf. § 18, and Hor. *Sat.* II. 5. 56: "Scriba
ex quinqueviro corvum deludet hiantem."

21   **ἀληθὲς ἄγοντας,** " And unfeigned is their grief, (when they think)
what a fine fish &c.!" Their grief was feigned before, now there is
no doubt of it.

οἷος=ὅτι τοιοῦτος, a not uncommon idiom: cf. Xen. *Cyr.* VII. 3.
14, Κῦρος ἀπῄει κατοικτείρων τήν τε γυναῖκα, οἵου ἀνδρὸς στέροιτο,
καὶ τὸν ἄνδρα, οἵαν γυναῖκα καταλιπὼν οὐκέτ' ὄψοιτο=ὅτι τοιούτου
ἀνδρός...ὅτι τοιαύτην γυναῖκα. *Tyr.* 16, κἀμαυτοῦ ἔτι μᾶλλον κατεγέλων οἷον κάθαρμα ἐτεθήπειν.

ὁ θύννος. So Horace, *Sat.* II. 5. 44, likens credulous and
foolish old men to the tunny: "Plures adnabunt thunni et cetaria
crescent." The tunny-fish is still caught in the Mediterranean, being
very common round Sicily. It is a large fish of the mackerel species.
A looker-out for the shoal was posted on some conspicuous spot, as
in the case of the pilchard fishery now round S. Michael's Mount.
The watchman was called **θυννοσκόπος,** and he gave the signal to

lower the nets. Cf. Theoc. III. 26, ὥπερ τὼς θύννως σκαπιάζετα. Ὄλπις ὁ γριπεύς. In Aesch. *Pers.* 426 the defeated Persians are likened to the tunnies caught in a net and beaten to death, as seems to have been the custom : ὥστε θύννους ἤ τιν' ἰχθύων βόλον. So in Arist. *Eq.* 300, Cleon is said τοὺς πόρους θυννοσκοπεῖν. L. refers to the tunny in not a few passages, the best being *Jup. Trag.* 25.

22   **τὸ δέλεαρ καταπιών.** οὐκ ὀλίγον go closely together, "after swallowing the bait so finely." *Inf. Dial.* 6. 4, ὁ δὲ τοσοῦτόν μοι δέλεαρ καταπιὼν ἐφειστήκει θαπτομένῳ πρῴην ἐπιγελῶν. Mart. VI. 63. 5, "Munera magna quidem misit, sed misit *in hamo*," and Hor. *Sat.* II. 5. 24, "si vafer unus et alter | Insidiatorem *praeroso* fugerit *hamo*."

p. 35.   1   **§ 23.** 'Ο δὲ, subject of οὐκέτι φορητός ἐστι.

ἐμπεσὼν ἀθρόος. The use of ἀθρόος of a single person is not uncommon in Plutarch, e.g. *Themist.* 12. 1, αὐτός τε βασιλεὺς... ἀθρους ὤφθη: *Lucullus* 27, ὑπερβαλὼν τὸν Ταῦρον ἄθρους κατεφάνη, though these are not quite parallel to L.'s usage here, because there were armies with these individuals, while the legacy-gainer was alone. Theoc. XIII. 50 is a better instance, κατήριπε δ' ἐς μέλαν ὕδωρ ἀθρόος "in a heap:" and in XXV. 252, of a lion ἀπόπροθεν ἀθρόος ἆλτο.

ἀπειρόκαλος καὶ παχύδερμος, "unrefined and thick-skinned," i.e. stupid. In *de domo* 2 we find ἀπειροκαλία in company with ἀγροικία καὶ ἀμουσία. Cf. *Nigr.* 21, "How ridiculous do the wealthy make themselves, as they sport their fine purple, and air their rings, πολλὴν κατηγοροῦντες ἀπειροκαλίαν."

2   **ἔτι τὴν πέδην πεφρικὼς,** "Still shuddering at the fetters" he had been wont to wear as a slave. For the general sentiment, cf. Hor. *Epod.* IV. 2 and 11, "Ibericis peruste funibus latus, | Et crura dura compede... | ...Sectus flagellis hic Triumviralibus."

3   **εἰ...μαστίξειέ τις,** "if anyone cracked his whip as he went by;" so Hor. *Sat.* I. 2. 42, "Ille flagellis | Ad mortem caesus."

ὄρθιον ἐφιστὰς τὸ οὖς, "pricking his ears *up*." Cf. Aesch. *Theb.* 569, τριχὸς δ' ὄρθιος πλόκαμος ἵσταται ="stands *on end*," and Soph. *Elec.* 27, ὀρθὸν οὖς ἵστησιν.

4   **τὸν μυλῶνα...προσκυνῶν.** μυλὼν =*pistrinum*, a mill-house, in which the grinding-pole was generally worked by asses (cf. *Asin.* 42), but refractory slaves were often threatened with it, as a punishment; cf. Eur. *Cycl.* 240, πέτρους μοχλεύσειν, ἤ 's μυλῶνα καταβαλεῖν,

and so *detrudere* (*tradere*) *in pistrinum* is a common expression in Lat.
comedy: Terence, *Andria* I. 2. 28; Plautus, *Mostel.* I. I. 16; *Bacc.*
IV. 6. II. This man is so used to the treadmill that he looks upon it
as his peculiar temple. For προσκυνεῖν cf. l. 27 below, and *Men.* 12.

5   οὐκέτι φορητός ἐστι. His behaviour is unsufferable.

τοῖς ἐντυγχ., anybody that he comes across. Cf. *Tyr.* 16,
ἑαυτὸν ἐξυπτιάζων, καὶ τοὺς ἐντυγχάνοντας ἐκπλήττων, and
Thuc. IV. 132.

9   ὀμνύουσιν is dative, agreeing with κόλαξι.

ἦ μὴν, commonly used in introducing oaths and asseverations;
cf. Thuc. IV. 118 fin., σπείσασθαι ἦ μὴν ἐμμενεῖν ἐν ταῖς σπονδαῖς,
and VIII. 81, ὑπεδέξατο ἦ μὴν...μὴ ἀπορήσειν αὐτοὺς τροφῆς.

10   Νιρέως, cf. *Men.* 15, note. In *Inf. Dial.* 25 Nireus adapts Hom.
Il. II. 672, and describes himself as Τὸν ᾿Αγλαΐας καὶ Χαρόπου | ὃς
κάλλιστος ἀνὴρ ὑπὸ ῎Ιλιον ἦλθον, carefully stopping short of the next
line, τῶν ἄλλων Δαναῶν μετ᾿ ἀμύμονα Πηλείωνα.

11   Κέκροπος...Κόδρου. The former, the most ancient king of Attica, founder of Athens, cf. *Men.* 16. The latter, the last king
of Athens, who by devotion defeated Sparta; in honour of his
patriotism, the citizens discontinued the title of 'king.'

12   Κροίσων, "sixteen Croesuses taken together." The famous king
of Sardis, conquered by Cyrus, whose wealth was a proverb.

13   τὰ κατ᾿ ὀλίγον...συνειλεγμένα, "what he has accumulated bit by
bit" (for κατ᾿ ὀλίγον=*paulatim*, cf. note § 4) "through a long course
of perjury, and rapine, and knavery."

16   § **24.** Αὐτά που, κ.τ.λ., "You're not very wide of the mark, in
what you say." "However, when you go on your own account," &c.

17   αὐτόπους, "on your own feet," in contradistinction to οὐχὶ τοῖς
ἐμαυτοῦ ποσὶ βαδίζω τότε of § 21. Is αὐτόπους purposely used as a
play on αὐτά που σ | χεδόν? The Greeks were very fond of this.

20   Οἴει γάρ. The same interrogative γάρ occurs again at beginning
of § 27, = "*videlicet*" or "*nimirum*." "Why! surely you don't
suppose," &c. Cf. *D. D.* 4. 2, where Ganymede says to Zeus, Τί
λέγεις; οὐ γὰρ κατάξεις με ἤδη ἐς τὴν ῎Ιδην τήμερον;

21   οὐ γάρ...προσῄειν, "No, by Zeus, not at all: *for if I did*, I
shouldn't leave Aristeides in the lurch, and go to such fellows
as Hipponicus and Callias," &c. So too in § 7, οὐ γὰρ ἂν οὕτως
q. v., and *Men.* § 1.

24   Πλὴν ἀλλά, cf. note, *Men.* §§ 2, 9.

25   περινοστῶν, often used by L. of an aimless sort of wandering.
Our slang term of "hanging about" often expresses it.   Cf.
§§ 13, 30 ; Arist. *Plut.* 121 (Ζεὺς) νῦν δ' οὐ τοῦτο δρᾷ, ὅστις σε
προσπταίοντα περινοστεῖν ἐᾷ; and 494, ἣν γὰρ ὁ Πλοῦτος νυνὶ βλέψῃ
καὶ μὴ τυφλὸς ὢν περινοστῇ.

26   ἄχρι ἂν λάθω, "I wander up and down listlessly, until I unex-
pectedly fall into somebody or other's hands."

ὅστις—πρῶτος—περιτύχῃ, not "whoever *first* comes across me
(πρῶτον)," but "whoever *is the first to*," &c.   Cf. *ille primus fecit*
=*ille* (*erat*) *primus* (*qui*) *fecit.*

27   σὲ...προσκυνῶν, "Blessing you, Hermes, for such an unexpected
godsend."   So in Soph. *Antig.* 397, ἀλλ' ἔστ' ἐμὸν θοὔρμαιον οὐκ
ἄλλου τόδε.   Hermes was the god of gain: hence any lucky wind-
fall was attributed to him.   So below in § 41, and in *Navig.* 18
he is addressed as Ἑρμῆ κερδῷε: in *Jup. Trag.* 33 as ἀγοραῖος: in
Arist. *Plut.* 1156 as παλιγκάπηλος.

For Latin passages, cf. Hor. *Od.* I. 10, Ov. *Fasti* v. 671, and
"saliva mercurialis " in Pers. v. 112.

p. 36.   1   ἐπὶ τῷ π. τ. κ.=ἐπὶ τῷ παραλόγῳ κέρδει.

6   **§ 25.**   Καὶ μάλα δικαίως, "aye, and rightly so, my good sir,
inasmuch as he sends a fellow to seek out...though he knows he is
blind," &c.   There is no μὲ expressed in the Greek purposely, therefore avoid the first person in translating.   καὶ μάλα is one of the
many forms of affirmation in Greek: cf. *Jup. Conf.* § 2, ληρεῖν δηλαδὴ φήσομεν τότε αὐτόν;...καὶ μάλα.   *Herm.* 17, οἱ δ' ἄρα ἰδιῶται
ταῦτα ἔλεγον; καὶ μάλα.   For ὦγαθέ cf. note, *Menip.* § 2.   ὅς γε
=*qui,* causal.

7   δυσεύρετον οὕτω χρῆμα, "a creature so hard to find," cf. § 55.
χρῆμα is a very interesting word in its wide usage: e.g. Herod. I. 36,
ὑὸς χρῆμα μέγιστον, "a great monster of a boar."   Arist. *Nub.* 1,
τὸ χρῆμα τῶν νυκτῶν ὅσον ἀπέραντον, "What an interminable length
of a night!"   *Frogs* 1278, τὸ χρῆμα τῶν κόπων ὅσον, "What a lot of
toils there are!"   *Achar.* 150, ὅσον τὸ χρῆμα παρνόπων προσέρχεται, "What a heap of locusts are coming!"   So L. again in *V. H.*
I. 8, ηὕρομεν ἀμπέλων χρῆμα τεράστιον, "We found a marvellous
monster of a vine!"

8   πρὸ πολλοῦ ἐκλελοιπὸς, "long ago has left this earth."   πρὸ πολ.
=*jamdudum.*   βίος, here, as often,=the upper air, opposed to the
world below.

9   **Λυγκεύς.** Lynceus was one of the Argonauts, so keen of sight
as to be able to see through the Earth. Cf. *Hermot.* 20, σὺ δὲ ὑπὲρ
τὸν Λυγκέα ἡμῖν δέδορκας καὶ ὁρᾶς, ὡς ἔοικε, τὰ ἔνδον.
ἀμαυρὸν, cf. end of *Menip.* and *T.* § 14.

13   **σαγηνεύομαι**, "caught in a net."

16   **'Οξυδερκὴς** instead of τυφλὸς, and ἀρτίπους instead of ὑποσκάζων :
cf. opening line of § 20.

17   **πρὸς μόνον τὸν καιρὸν**, "just for the time of my flight."

19   **§ 26. εἰρήσεται γάρ**, "By your leave," "Excuse my saying so,"
or some such apologetic phrase. Cf. *Zeux.* § 2, πλὴν ἐμέ—εἰρήσεται
γάρ—οὐ μετρίως ἤνία ὁ ἔπαινος αὐτῶν. In *Mar. Dial.* 13. 1 the subject is expressed : Οὐ καλὰ ταῦτα, ὦ Πόσειδον. εἰρήσεται γὰρ τἀληθές.
ὠχρός. Cf. § 13 note.

20   **ἔχεις.** This is the general reading of modern editors with the
weight of MSS. Earlier editions have ἔχοις, "How is it you should
have?"

p. 37. 1 **τυχόντας μὲν**, counterbalanced by εἰ δὲ ἀποτύχ. which is
equal to ἀποτυχόντας δὲ, "if they possess you," "if they do not."

3   **ζῶντας**, part. construc. after ἀνέχεσθαι.

4   **δυσέρωτας**, "miserably in love."

ὥστε...ἔρριψαν. Three lines above ὥστε has the *infinitive* (ἀποβλέπειν) ; here the *indicative*, which it takes when a positive actual
fact is stated—"that they cast themselves (have done so, and will
do it again) into the sea,"—a *fact*.

βαθυκήτεα πόντον. In *Apolog.* 10 Lucian tells us this is taken
from Theognis (175), τὸ μὲν γὰρ τοῦ Θεόγνιδος κἂν ἐγὼ μὴ λέγω, τίς
οὐκ οἶδεν, οὐκ ἀπαξιοῦντος καὶ ἐς βαθυκήτεα πόντον σφᾶς αὐτοὺς ῥίπτειν
καὶ κατὰ κρημνῶν γε ἠλιβάτων, εἰ μέλλοι τις οὕτως ἀποδράσεσθαι τὴν
πενίαν; **βαθυκήτεα.** Hemsterhuis, in his note on this passage,
classes this word with μεγακήτης and κητώεις; and says κῆτος,
though originally meaning a huge sea-monster, came eventually to
have the sense of any vast depth, space, gulf. Hence βαθυκήτης
merely = "vast and deep."

5   **ἠλιβάτων.** The derivation very doubtful. Perhaps D. B.
Monro's explanation, connecting it with ἀλίβας, "dry" (Plato *Rep.*
387 C), as ἀκάματος with ἀκάμας, is the best; see Edwards' note on
Hom. *Od.* x. 88. Then it will mean "craggy," "hard;" "inaccessible" was the old rendering, cf. Eur. *Hipp.* 732, ἀλιβάτοις ὑπὸ
κευθμῶσι γενοίμαν, and p. 18, l. 25.

6 οὐδὲ τὴν ἀρχήν, lit. "not even to begin with"=*omnino non:* then "not at all;" cf. *Icarom.* 9, οὐδὲ τὴν ἀρχὴν εἶναι θεούς τινας ἐπίστευον. So *Tyr.* 21, ἀρχὴν δὲ οὐδὲ οἶδα="in fact I do not even know."

7 πλὴν ἀλλά, cf. *Men.* §§ 2, 9, &c. &c.

εὖ οἶδα ὅτι, a common parenthetic phrase, like οὐκ οἶδ' ὅπως, § 1. It occurs, as here, between ἂν and its verb in *Alex.* 4, παῖς ἂν εὖ οἶδ' ὅτι...ἔδοξε. *Mar. Dial.* 23, οὐ γὰρ ἂν εὖ οἶδ' ὅτι ἐδυνήθη.

8 εἴ·τι συνίης σαυτοῦ, "if you are at all conscious of yourself," i.e. "if you know who and what you are."

κορυβαντιᾶν αὐτούς, "that they are mad," "frenzied;" lit. "to play the Corybant," something similar to our "living like a Bohemian," or Lat. *Graecari* = "merry as a grig" (i.e. a Greek). The Corybantes were priests of Cybele, whose religious services were noisy music and wild dances, cf. Verg. *Aen.* III. 111, "Hinc mater cultrix Cybelae Corybantiaque aera | Idaeumque nemus." Cf. in Lucian *D. D.* 12. 1, τοὺς Κορύβαντας ἅτε μανικούς.

9 ἐρώμενος, here as in Xen. *Symp.* VIII. 36 "the beloved object." In Hdt. III. 31 we have ἡ ἐρωμένη; and Pind. *Ol.* I. 128, ἐρῶν, as "*a lover.*"

ἐπιμεμηνότας, "being so desperately enamoured of such an object."

10 § 27. Οἴει γάρ, cf. note § 24.

ὁρᾶσθαι is not the same as δοκεῖν, as it implies actual sight, which δοκεῖν does not necessarily.

13 Ἀλλὰ πῶς, "Well! but how could it be otherwise?"

19 λιθοκόλλητον, "set with gems," cf. *Prom.* § 4, λιθοκόλλητος χαλινός, and *Tyran.* § 16, τὸν χρυσὸν καὶ τὰ λιθοκόλλητα ἐκπώματα.

20 αὐτοπρόσωπον, i.e. without any mask on, as in *pro Imag.* 3, φανῆναι αὐτοπρ. Cf. also *Jup. Trag.* § 29, λέγειν αὐτοπρόσωπον, "face to face." For αὐτὸς in composition v. § 54 note.

23 ἀμβλυώττοντες, cf. § 2. It is to be taken closely with κατεγίνωσκον ἄν, "would blame themselves for being so blind." Dindorf inserts πρὸς before the accusative.

p. 38. 1 § 28. Τί οὖν ὅτι, "Why then is it that...?" cf. S. Luke ii. 49, Τί ὅτι ἐζητεῖτέ με;

4 πρόοιντο, "surrender," "give up," cf. l. 18, below.

5 ἐπίχριστος in nearly all the MSS. is certainly preferable to ἐπί-χρυσος (Faber with 2 MSS.), ="smeared over." Cf. the Ciceronean

word "fucatus," e.g. *de Amic.* 95, "omnia fucata et simulata a sinceris atque veris."

11   **συμπαρεισέρχεται.** Note the force of each preposition, σὺν, παρὰ, ἐς, "there enters *in with* me *at my side.*"

15   **θαυμάζει τε τὰ οὐ θαυμαστά.** Cf. Hor. *Ep.* i. 6, "Nil admirari prope res est una, Numici, | Solaque, quae possit facere et servare beatum."

17   **τέθηπε,** "admire." Cf. § 56 *ad init.;* so *Tyr.* § 16, κάμαυτοῦ ἔτι μᾶλλον κατεγέλων, οἶον κάθαρμα ἐτεθήπειν.

23   § **29. ἐγχέλεις,** cf. *Anach.* § 1, ὥσπερ αἱ ἐγχέλεις ἐκ τῶν χειρῶν διολισθάνοντες. No MSS. appear to have the αἱ which D. inserts.

     δραπετεύεις. So in Lucian's *Dream* Education says of Socrates, δραπετεύσας παρ᾽ αὐτῆς ηὐτομόλησεν ὡς ἐμέ.

p. 39.   1   **ἰξώδης,** "sticky," opposed to ὀλισθηρὸς (supra), "oily," as εὐλαβὴς, "easy to keep hold of," is to δυσκάθεκτος. It is quite a late word, though ἰξός (=viscum, "birdlime" or "mistletoe") is found in Eur. in the former sense (*Cyc.* 433). Cf. *Tyr.* § 14, οὐ γὰρ οἶδ᾽ ὅπως καθάπερ ἰξῷ τινι προσέχεται τοῖς τοιούτοις ἡ ψυχή.

2   **ἄγκιστρα,** "fish-hooks." Cf. *Pisc.* 47, τὸ ἄγκιστρον δελεάσας ἰσχάδι καθῆκεν, "having baited the hook, he lowered it down." The idea of the word is that of "feelers" or "hooks" or "tendrils," anything which is likely to cling to what it touches; another good instance of Lucian's favourite predicate, p. 9, l. 1.

10   § **30. τούτου γε ἕνεκα,** "as far as *this* is concerned:" cf. Xen. *Cyr.* v. 5. 20, τόδε γε εἰπέ, "at any rate tell me *this.*"

11   **ἐπισκήψας,** "having straitly charged him." Cf. *Tyran.* § 8, ἄχρις ἄν τι ἐπισκήψω τῇ γυναικὶ περὶ τῶν χρημάτων.

15   **ἐχόμενος τῆς χλαμίδος.** The genitive naturally follows after the idea of "clinging to" (partitive).

     This whole scene is very amusing. Picture the blind god of riches, holding on to Hermes' coat-tails, and creeping slowly along. Suddenly he hears the noise of Timon digging, and then when he finds who are keeping him company, he wants to slip off by the shortest cut.

17   **Εὖ ποιεῖς.** Cf. *Men.* § 19 and note there: "you are very good," "it is very kind of you." Cf. § 45, εὖ γε ἐποίησεν ἀφικόμενος.

18   **Ὑπερβόλῳ ἢ Κλέωνι,** the two much-abused Athenian demagogues, whom Grote has shown to be not quite so black as they had been painted. *Cleon* was a tanner; *Hyperbolus* a lamp-maker; the

former is especially noted for his strange capture of the Spartan nobles at the siege of Sphacteria; the latter gained considerable power and influence after Cleon's death, but was eventually banished by ostracism. Each was the continual butt of Aristophanes.

22 § **31.** γήδιον, dimin. of γῆ, as *agellum* of *ager* = "a farm." παπαῖ, "Hullo!"

Πενία. Poverty has such a body-guard as Plutus never could gather, a body-guard of virtues, Labour, Perseverance, Wisdom, Fortitude. So with these around Timon, what good can Plutus do? Had he not better be gone? So in Arist. *Plutus* 469 where Πενία pleads against Chremylus: ἀγαθῶν ἁπάντων οὖσαν αἰτίαν ἐμέ. Cf. also 558.

24 ὑπό, "under," not "by."

p. 40. 1 τὴν ταχίστην, understand ὁδόν. For similar instances of suppressed substantives cf. below, note on § 40, βαθείας.

6 § **32.** Ἀργειφόντης. The old Argus legend is believed by some philologists to be due to a misunderstanding of this epithet, which they say is from ἀργός and φαίνω and means, "bright-shining one;" for further note see Edwards on *Odys.* X. 302.

10 Νῦν. This is very emphatic, by its position. "What! Plutus been sent to Timon after all I've done for him?" ἐπέμφθη is easily supplied from the lines above.

11 κακῶς ἔχοντα, "treated ill," is equal to a passive construction, and so is naturally followed by ὑπό of the agent; cf. § 8, πλουτεῖν παρά τινος. For the sentiment, cf. Ar. *Plut.* 575–6.

13 εὐκαταφρόνητος "despicable," a very favourite word of L. εὐαδίκητος, "easy of injury."

15 ὃ μόνον κτῆμα. The antecedent, as often, is here put in the relative sentence, = τὸ μόνον κτῆμα ὃ εἶχον.

18 ἀποφήνας. Cf. note on § 4.

19 ῥάκος ἤδη γεγενημένον. Cf. *de merc. cond.* 39, καὶ τὸ ἀκμαιότατον τοῦ σώματος ἐπιτρίψας καὶ ῥάκος σε πολυσχιδὲς ἐργασάμενος..., and *Pseud.* 18, ἄχρι δή σε, τὸ τοῦ λόγου, ῥάκος πολυσχιδὲς ἐργασάμενος ἐξέωσε. It is clear by this latter passage that the phrase had passed into a proverb.

21 § **33.** Ἀπέρχομαι, a vivid present, "Then, I'm off!"
καὶ ὑμεῖς δὲ, "aye and you;" cf. for καὶ...δὲ, p. 51, l. 11.

23 οἵαν με οὖσαν ἀπολείψει. οἷος is rather a complicated word when attracted, as here and often, into the case of the ante-

§ 34]

NOTES.

125

cedent. Here the full meaning is τάχα εἴσεται οἴα ἐγὼ εἰμί, ἥν ἀπολείψει, "He will soon find out how great a friend he loses in losing me." Faber says ἀπολείψῃ should be read, which Solanus and others deny, inasmuch as innumerable passages in L. would have to be altered for the same reason.

24 ᾗ συνών. Avoid taking this after διετέλεσεν. συνών, ζῶν, ἀποβλέπων are part of the subject; ὑγιεινός and ἐρρωμένος part of the predicate. "For so long as he associated with me, he had a 'mens sana in corpore sano,' while he lived a manly and independent life."

p. 41. 1 πρὸς αὐτὸν ἀποβλέπων, i.e. depending on none but himself. The sentiment is exactly the same as in § 36, ἐξ αὐτοῦ ἐμοῦ τὰς ἐλπίδας ἀπαρτήσασά μοι τοῦ βίου (v. note).

τὰ δὲ περιττά, κ.τ.λ., "deeming these many superfluous things foreign to himself as indeed they are." The ὥσπερ ἐστὶν modifies ἀλλότρια not περιττά. Notice we say "many good," "many great" &c. Gk. "many and good," &c.

7 § **34.** οὐ χαίροντες, "unrequited," "without due reward."

8 ταῖς βώλοις καὶ τοῖς λίθοις. Note the article, "*the* clods, and *the* stones" [lying about]. Cf. *Pisc.* § 1, βάλλε τοῖς λίθοις...ἐπίβαλλε τῶν βώλων and § 32, παίων τοῖς ξύλοις.

10 Μηδαμῶς...μὴ, cf. 19. 12.

οὐ...ὄντας βαλεῖς. A good instance of the common Greek idiom, by which the more important thought is found in the participle not the finite verb; "for we are not *men*, at whom you will be pelting." Cf. *Men.* § 6, ὃν ἂν...φρονῶν.

13 ἀγαθῇ τύχῃ, a common expression = Lat. *quod bene vortat* or *quod felix faustumque sit.* So Thuc. IV. 118, at the beginning of the form of ratification by the Athenians, Λάχης εἶπε τύχῃ ἀγαθῇ τῇ Ἀθηναίων ποιεῖσθαι τὴν ἐκεχειρίαν. So too the heading of the Psephism in the *Conc. Deor.*, &c.

15 καίτοι would be καίπερ in good Greek. Note καίπερ in prose always is constructed with a participle.

17 τουτονί. οὑτοσὶ &c. are stronger forms of the demonstrative, denoting a pointing of the finger or a wave of the hand; cf. the Lat. *hic-ce* and French *celui-ci.*

18 μοι δοκῶ, cf. § 18, "I seem to myself," i.e. "I've got it in my mind." Cf. *Pisc.* § 29, προσθήσειν μοι δοκῶ: so in Arist. *Plut.* 1186, μοι δοκῶ καταμενεῖν.

20   μελαγχολᾶν, cf. note § 8.

21   μή τι κακόν, to be taken after ἀπίωμεν.

22   § **35.** Μηδὲν σκαιόν. Cf. p. 43, l. 11; p. 49, l. 5.
τὸ πάνυ, κ.τ.λ., "this exceeding boorishness," cf. note § 15.

p. 42. 1   τὼ χεῖρε. Cobet (*V. L.* 69, 70, 85; *N. L.* 695) says there
is only one form of the dual for all genders, i.e. the masculine.
Good Gk. forms are only τώ, τοῖν, τούτω, τούτοιν, λέγοντε, -τοιν &c.,
and this is the case with all adjectives, pronouns and participles.
The fem. forms, given in grammars, τά, ᾶ, λεγούσα &c. are wrong.
Hence τώ here, not τά. Cf. Thuc. IV. 23. 2 where the true reading
is δυοῖν νεοῖν ἐναντίοιν, and I. 93, δύο ἅμαξαι ἐναντίαι ἀλλήλοις
(not -αις).

2   τὰ πρῶτα = ὁ πρῶτος. Supply ὦν after ἴσθι. For similar usage
of the neuter cf. § 55, κολάκων ἐστὶ τὰ πρῶτα. Sommerbrodt quotes
Hipp. § 3, ὁ δὲ μηχανικῶν τε ὢν τὰ πρῶτα καὶ γεωμετρικῶν. So in
Eur. *Med.* 916, οἶμαι γὰρ ὑμᾶς τῆσδε γῆς Κορινθίας | τὰ πρῶτ' ἔσεσθαι,
and Lucr. I. 87, "prima virorum."

7   ὦ τᾶν, "my friend." The form, accent, and derivation of the
word are all equally doubtful, though it is of common occurrence.
Sometimes it is used in addressing several persons. It carries with
it generally a touch of inferiority or contempt.

8   τόνδε φέρω, κ.τ.λ. (deliberat. subjunctive) from Hom. *Il.* xv.
202.

9   ἦν for ἐστί, just as we say "it *were* natural" for "it *is.*"

12   § **36.** Ἀλλά, modifying his previous statement of hatred.
"Very well, then, I'm much obliged to you for your kind attention;
but I'll have none of this Plutus."

18   ἡδυπαθεία, "luxury."

19   ἀποφήνας, cf. § 4.

24   ἐξ αὐτοῦ ἐμοῦ…ἀπαρτήσασα. Cf. note on πρὸς αὐτὸν ἀποβλέπων
§ 33. Cf. Plat. *Menex.* 20, ὅτῳ γὰρ ἀνδρὶ εἰς ἑαυτὸν ἀνήρτηται πάντα
τὰ πρὸς εὐδαιμονίαν φέροντα. So in Hor. *Sat.* II. 7. 86, "In se ipso
totus, teres atque rotundus, | In quem manca ruit semper fortuna."

p. 43. 1   ἐκκλησιαστής, an assembly-man, a member of the Athenian
ἐκκλησία. The word occurs in *Men.* § 19; cf. note there.

6   § **37.** ἱκανὰ καὶ διαρκῆ. ἱκανός sufficient in quantity;
διαρκής sufficient in length of time, as we talk of provisions
"lasting out." Cf. *de hist.* § 21, ἀπόσιτοι δὲ καὶ εἰς ἑβδόμην διαρκοῦσιν
οἱ πολλοί, "hold out till the 7th day."

9 ἦν, "it *was* sufficient;" that *was* my only object when I first set out here.

ἡβηδὸν, to be taken closely with πάντες=omnes omnipo; so Faber and Hemst.; L. and S.'s "from the youth upwards" is unsatisfactory. Cf. the capture of Sybaris in Her. VI. 21, Μιλήσιοι πάντες ἡβηδὸν ἀπεκείραντο τὰς κεφαλάς, and *Vit. auc.* 14, ἐγὼ κέλομαι πᾶσιν ἡβηδὸν οἰμώζειν.

11 Μηδαμῶς, cf. p. 19, l. 12, and p. 49, l. 5.

ὦγαθέ, § 25, and *Men.* § 2.

13 οὗτοι ἀπόβλητα, adapted from Hom. *Il.* III. 65, οὔτοι ἀπόβλητ' ἐστὶ θεῶν ἐρικυδέα δῶρα.

15 Βούλει δικαιολογήσωμαι, so Hemst. followed by Dind. and Somm. and other editors. The MSS. give the future -σομαι. Grammarians tell us that after βούλει the aor. subj. and not the future must be used, cf. Goodwin, *M. and T.* §§ 287, 8; but it seems very probable that the MSS. are right and the editors wrong, and the ἐθέλεις ἐγὼ αὖθις ἐπάνειμι quoted by Heitland, note *Char.* § 9, shows Lucian at least is not tied down to this rule.

17 μὴ μακρὰ μέντοι, κ.τ.λ. Observe the alliteration. Cf. Eur. *Med.* 476, ἔσωσά σ', ὡς ἴσασιν Ἑλλήνων ὅσοι. *Aen.* VI. 833, "Neu patriae validas in viscera vertite vires." All MSS. but one have μακράν. Hemst. first restored μακρά.

18 ἐπίτριπτοι. Cf. Soph. *Ajax* 103, ἦ τοὐπίτριπτον κίναδος ἐξήρου μ' ὅπου; where Prof. Jebb says "accursed" not "knavish" is the proper meaning. Cf. also Arist. *Plut.* 619, αὕτη μὲν ἡμῖν ἡ 'πίτριπτος οἴχεται; The word occurs also in § 46 below, and in *Inf. Dial.* 13. 5, ὁ σοφός; ἁπάντων ἐκεῖνος κολάκων ἐπιτριπτότατος ὤν.

20 § **38.** Ἐχρῆν. For the imperfect, cf. ἦν § 35. "It were fitting that," "I ought to *have* replied," not "I ought to reply." For πολλὰ ...κατηγορηθέντα cf. note *Men.* § 19, ἐπεὶ γὰρ κ.τ.λ.

p. 44. 3 προεδρίας καὶ στεφάνων, the natural concomitants of the τιμή. The former means front seats, the best places, in the games and theatre; the latter the garlands or crowns of honour given to distinguished citizens, e.g. to Demosthenes.

4 περίβλεπτος, "the cynosure of neighbouring eyes." So Education says τῶν ὁρώντων ἕκαστος τὸν πλησίον κινήσας δείξει σε τῷ δακτύλῳ "οὗτος ἐκεῖνος" λέγων, which exactly expresses the notion of περίβλεπτος (*Somn.* 11).

ἀοίδιμος. So again in *Somn.* § 12, ὁ δὲ Σωκράτης...ἀκούεις ὡς παρὰ πάντων ᾄδεται.

128   *TIMON.*   [§ 38—

5   περισπούδαστος, a man much sought after, in a social sense, a man whose acquaintance is cultivated; corresponding to the words ἐπὶ τοῖς ἀρίστοις εὐδοκιμῶν καὶ ὑπὸ τῶν γένει καὶ πλούτῳ προὐχόντων ἀποβλεπόμενος, in *Somn.* § 11.

12   ἐπὶ κεφαλὴν ἐξωσθείς. So in *Rhaet. Prec.* § 25, ἐξωσθεὶς δὲ ἐπὶ κεφ. Cf. § 44 below, and *D. D.* 13. 2, σε ῥίψω ἐπὶ κεφαλὴν ἐκ τοῦ οὐρανοῦ, = "turned out headlong," or "neck and crop." Cf. Catullus XVII., "Ire praecipitem in lutum per caputque pedesque."

13   χλανίδος. This reading was first suggested by Hemst. and is adopted by most editors; the MSS. have χλαμύδος. The epithet μαλακῆς is far more applicable to the former; and the two words are often confused in the MSS.

14   διφθέραν, cf. note § 6.

16   προσενηνεγμένον, "who had behaved in so unfriendly a manner toward me," so προσφέρεσθαι with or without an adv. is used not uncommonly; cf. Thuc. V. 111, τοῖς δὲ κρείσσοσι καλῶς προσφέρονται, Id. ibid. 105, ὡς προσφέρονται.

19   § 39. θαρρῶν συνδιάτριβε. Cf. *D. D.* 8. 1, κατένεγκε μόνον, ὦ Ἥφαιστε, θαρρῶν.

σὺ μὲν σκάπτε...σὺ δὲ ὑπάγαγε. The first is addressed to Timon, "Go on with your digging" (continuous), the second to Plutus, "Summon Treasure to his spade" (single action). Cf. the tenses in next section, when P. does summon Treasure, παῖε, ὑπάκουσον, παράσχες, σκάπτε. For ὑπακούσεται, "will answer," cf. our "answering" a door.

23   τί γὰρ ἂν καὶ, κ.τ.λ. Cf. note on *Men.* § 3 for this phrase and the attracted optative; so in *Char.* § 2 the same words occur. The MSS. seem to have had ὅποταν, which violates all grammar; modern editors reject the ἂν.

24   πράγματα, "trouble," as so often.

25   ἄχρι νῦν. ἄχρι with πρὸς, or μεχρὶ πρὸς, is common enough (cf. *usque ad*), but a plain adverb following is not usual: L. and S. give ἄχ. πόρρω and ἄχ. δεῦρο. ἄχρι τοῦ νῦν is found, but that is a very different phrase. Cf. μεχρὶ τότε, Thuc. VIII. 24.

p. 45.   2   φροντίδας, "cares," "anxieties."

3   § 40. Ὑπόστηθι, "Endure it for my sake, Timon, even though," &c.

4   οἰστόν, verbal of φέρω.

5   διαρραγῶσιν, a word very commonly used in this sense. Cf. Arist. *Plut.* 279, διαρραγείης. Cf. also Verg. *Ecl.* VII. 26, "Invidia

rumpantur ut ilia." Juv. VII. 117, "Rumpe miser tensum jecur,"
and Dem. to Aesch. in *de Cor.* 21, οὐδ' ἂν σὺ διαρραγῇς ψευδόμενος.
So Shak. *T.* IV. 3,

Timon. Choler does tell me that thou art alive : I swoon to see thee.
Apem. Would thou woulds't burst !

8   τῇ εἰρεσίᾳ τ. π., "winged oars." Cf. *Aen.* VI. 19 and I. 301,
"remigio alarum." For a similar phrase see also Soph. *Elec.* 19,
ἄστρων εὐφρόνη = "a starry night ;" where Prof. Jebb gives other
instances and says, "This seems to be a genitive of material, like
οἴκημα λίθων."

10   παῖε... σκάπτε, "go on striking," "dig away ;" cf. note on
these tenses in last section.

12   βαθείας καταφέρων. Supply πληγὰς, a word commonly omitted,
e.g. § 53 with ἄλλην and τρίτην. Cf. δευτέραν πεπληγμένος in Aesch.
Agam. 1316. In § 44 μοῖραν or δίκην is suppressed with τὴν ἴσην.

13   ὑπεκστήσομαι, so Dindorf. The majority of MSS. read ὑποστή-
σομαι (=ὑποχωρεῖν); Hemst., Faber, Somm. read with a few MSS.
ἀποστήσομαι: the first-named thinking ὑπεκστήσομαι a too common
form to have been altered. ὑμῖν ὑπεκστήσομαι means "I will with-
draw for you" (i.e. in your favour).

16   § **41**. προκαλουμένη. For similar construction with προσκα-
λεῖσθαι cf. note § 46.

17   'Ερμῆ κερδῷε. Cf. note on § 24, end.

19   ἄνθρακας εὕρω. "Surely it is all a dream! I fear I shall wake,
and find only ashes." Cf. *Gall.* § 1, σὺ δὲ ὅρα, ὅπως μή, ὄναρ πλουτῶν,
λιμώττης ἀνεγρόμενος: v. § 20 end. Suidas says ἄνθρακες ὁ θησαυρὸς
ἦσαν was a Greek proverb for disappointed hopes. The wealth
possessed in dreams is referred to in Theoc. IX. 16, ἔχω δέ τοι ὅσσ'
ἐν ὀνείρῳ | φαίνονται, πολλὰς μὲν ὄϊς, πολλὰς δὲ χιμαίρας. Cf. Plato,
Theaet. 208 B, ὄναρ ἐπλουτήσαμεν.

20   ἐπίσημον, "stamped," "coined," opposed to ἄσημος, "bearing
no stamp or inscription," as in *Char.* § 10, Croesus speaks of his
offerings to the Delphic Temple : εἶδες γάρ μου τὸν πλοῦτον καὶ τοὺς
θησαυροὺς καὶ ὅσος ἄσημος χρυσός ἐστιν ἡμῖν. The words are contrasted
in Thuc. II. 13, ὑπαρχόντων δὲ ἐν τῇ ἀκροπόλει ἔτι τότε ἀργυρίου
ἐπισήμου ἑξακισχιλίων ταλάντων...χωρὶς δὲ χρυσίου ἀσήμου καὶ
ἀργυρίου...οὐκ ἐλάσσονος ἢ πεντακοσίων ταλάντων.

ὑπέρυθρον, so gold is described in *Char.* § 11, τὸ ὕπωχρον μετ'
ἐρυθήματος, "that pale substance with a ruddy glow" (Heitland).

M. L.   9

22   **Ὦ χρυσέ**, κ.τ.λ. from the fragments of Eur. (*Danae* 326), here
quoted correctly, but in *Gall.* § 14 Lucian writes ὦ χρυσέ, δεξίωμα,
κάλλιστον κτέρας. Cf. Shak. *Tim.* IV. 3,

> "Gold? yellow, glittering, precious gold?......
> Thus much of this will make black, white; foul, fair;
> Wrong, right; base, noble; old, young; coward, valiant."

23   **αἰθόμενον γὰρ πῦρ ἅτε**, quoted from the opening lines of Pindar's
first *Olymp.*: ἄριστον μὲν ὕδωρ, ὁ δὲ χρυσὸς αἰθόμενον πῦρ | ἅτε
διαπρέπει νυκτί. The ἅτε is of course misplaced, the order being
διαπρέπεις ὅτε αἰθ. π., = "as" in poetry, not "inasmuch as" as in
Men. 6, &c.

p. 46. 1   **Δία...χρυσόν.** L. is never tired of satirizing this story
of Danae, cf. § 13 supra, and note on *Men.* § 2.

5   **§ 42. τὰ ἐν Δ. ἀναθ.**, the offerings made by Croesus are referred
to in *Char.* § 11, πλίνθους τῷ Πυθίῳ χρυσᾶς ἀνατίθησι μισθὸν τῶν
χρησμῶν. Notice the use of the article with the vocative.

6   **ὡς...ὡς πρὸς...**"*how* were ye nothing *by the side of* Timon." Unless the ὡς be taken as repeated, "ye were *as* nothing (as) compared
with."

ἄρα = "it seems," "after all," especially with the impfct., cf.
Soph. *Aj.* 926, *Elec.* 935, and Jebb's note.

8   **τῷ Πανὶ...ἀναθεῖναι**, "dedicate to Pan," the presiding genius of
agriculture. It was customary on retiring from any business or
occupation to dedicate the discarded tools to the tutelar deity of that
particular handicraft. Thus the *gladiator* in Hor. *Ep.* I. 1. 4,
"Veianius, armis | Herculis ad postem fixis, latet abditus agro,"
and the *soldier* in *Od.* III. 26. 3, "Nunc arma defunctumque bello
Barbiton," &c. Cf. the epigram ascribed to L.,

> Σαμόθρηξι θεοῖς
> σωθεὶς ἐκ πελάγους Λουκίλλιος ὧδε κέκαρμαι
> τὰς τρίχας ἐκ κεφαλῆς· ἄλλο γὰρ οὐδὲν ἔχω.

10   **τὴν ἐσχατιάν.** Cf. § 6.

12   **ἕξειν μοι δοκῶ**, §§ 18, 34.

δεδόχθω. He now proposes a bill, himself being proposer, de-
fender, assembly, chairman and all; see heading in the text. He
starts in due legal phraseology, see *Men.* 20, and end of § 44.

15   **Ἐλέου βωμός.** Athens was the first to raise an altar to Compassion. The Schol. on Soph. *Oed. Col.* 258 says Ἐλέου βωμὸς ἐν

'Αθήναις ἵδρυται. So Pausanias, 'Αθηναίοις δὲ ἐν τῇ ἀγορᾷ τὰ ἄλλα ἐστιν...εἰς ἄπαντας ἐπίσημα, καὶ ἐλέου βωμός. Lucian mentions it again in *Vit. Demon.* 57, μὴ πρότερον ταῦτα, ὦ 'Αθηναῖοι, ψηφίσησθε, ἢν μὴ τοῦ 'Ελέου τὸν βωμὸν καθέλητε.

16   ὕθλος = *nugae,* "fudge," often occurring. Cf. *Inf. Dial.* 10. 8, λῆρον οὐκ ὀλίγον καὶ ὕθλους καὶ μικρολογίαν.

17   κατάλυσις τῶν ἐθῶν = "subversion of custom;" so καταλύειν of "annulling" laws.

18   μονήρης...λύκοις. Apparently the ancients thought that wolves were non-gregarious: so Luc. says in *Sat. Ep.* 34, ἡδὺ μόνον ἐμπίπλασθαι, ὥσπερ τοὺς λέοντάς φασι καὶ τοὺς μονίους τῶν λύκων.

20   § **43.** Οἱ δὲ ἄλλοι, κ.τ.λ. Continue to supply ἔστωσαν or ἔστω from last section.

21   ἤν τινα ἴδω, "If I so much as set my eyes on any one."

p. **47.** 1 ἀποφρὰς ἡ ἡμέρα. There is much about this in L.'s *Pseudologistes.* In § 12 it is described as a day ὅταν μήτε αἱ ἀρχαὶ χρηματίζωσι μήτε εἰσαγώγιμοι αἱ δίκαι ὦσι μήτε τὰ ἱερὰ ἱερουργῆται μήθ' ὅλως τι τῶν αἰσίων τελῆται, a day of ill-luck, on which no public business of any kind could be transacted, corresponding to the *nefastus dies* of the Romans. Cf. Ovid, *F.* I. 47.

"The last three days but one in each month were 'unlucky' days, and belonged to the dead and the gods of the infernal regions." Gow, *Comp. to Sc. Classics,* p. 84.

2   λιθίνων...διαφερέτωσαν. He is turning the tables on them now. In § 5 he complains of men treating *him* like some overturned moss-eaten pillar; now they shall be as stone monuments to him.

5   φυλέται, φράτορες, δημόται. So the MSS. and earlier editors with Somm. followed by Abbott and others. Dind. and Herm. and some others read φράτερες here and in other places (e.g. *Conc. Deor., ad fin.*). φυλ. "tribesmen" = *tribules* = of same φυλή:—10 φυλαὶ after Cleisthenes, B.C. 509. φράτ. "clansmen" = *curiales.* Three to each φυλή. These two are genealogical divisions, while δῆμος is a territorial division. Cleisthenes made 10 to each φυλή. Cf. passage at end of *Conc. Deorum,* mentioned above, where the gods are bidden at the summons of Hermes to bring clear proofs of their divinity: πατρὸς ὄνομα καὶ μητρός, καὶ φυλήν, καὶ φράτορας.

11   ἑκαστάτω τῶν ἄλλων. So Sommerbrodt; Faber, followed by Hemst. and Dindorf, reads ἕκας ὢν τ. ἄλλων. Abbott ἐκσείων τὰ τ. ἄλλων. Yonge the same, omitting τὰ the reading of the earliest

editors. The whole passage is in confusion. Somm. reads καθάπαξ
for καὶ ἅπαξ, and αὐτῷ for καὶ ἑαυτῷ. The reading in the text is as
likely as any.

δεξιώσασθαι, usually to "greet," e.g. Arist. *Plut.* 753, αὐτὸν
ἠσπάζοντο καὶ ἐδεξιοῦνθ' ἅπαντες ὑπὸ τῆς ἡδονῆς, and Aesch. *Agam.*
825, θεοῖσι πρῶτα δεξιώσομαι. Here it apparently refers to the
custom of holding a dying person's hand; so the editors explain it.
Cf. Xen. *Cyr.* VIII. 7. 28 at the death of Cyrus, ταῦτ' εἰπὼν καὶ πάντας δεξιωσάμενος συνεκαλύψατο καὶ οὕτως ἐτελεύτησεν, and *Alcestis*
191, δεξιὰν προὔτειν' ἑκάστῳ. The ἑαυτῷ στέφ. ἐπενεγκεῖν refers to
the well-known custom of crowning the dead with garlands. Cf. *de
Luc.* § 11, στεφανώσαντες τοῖς ὡραίοις ἄνθεσι, "with the flowers in
season." Parsley was, however, in common use on such occasions.
Hence the proverb mentioned by Plut. *Timol.* 26 (Beck. *Char.* 135),
παροιμία τις ἐκ τούτου γέγονε, τὸν ἐπισφαλῶς νοσοῦντα Δεῖσθαι τοῦτον
τοῦ σελίνου ("the patient would have no need of any other herb but
the parsley").

14   **§ 44. ὁ Μισάνθρωπος.** Shak. *Tim.* IV. 3,
    " I am Misanthropos, and hate mankind.
        For thy part, I do wish thou wert a dog
        That I might love thee something."

Cf. the passages from Cicero, and the epigrams of Callimachus given
in Introduction under "Timon the Misanthrope."

15   **δυσκολία**, "moroseness," opposed to εὐκολία, an easy-going tem-
perament, such as is ascribed to Sophocles in Arist. *Ranae*, 82, ὁ δ'
εὔκολος μὲν ἐνθάδ', εὔκολος δ' ἐκεῖ.

20   **ἀντιλαβέσθαι**, "to give him a helping hand."

21   **ἐπὶ κεφαλὴν**, v. note § 38.

22   **τὴν ἴσην**, scil. μοῖραν or δίκην.

εἰσηγήσατο...ἐπεψήφισεν, "moved," "put to the vote." Cf.
Thuc. IV. 76, Πτοιοδώρου...ἐσηγουμένου τάδε αὐτοῖς παρεσκευάσθη.
For ἐπεψήφισεν cf. *Men.* § 20, and for the order of the names T.
'Εχ. Κολ. cf. note in that place.

25   **ἐμμένωμεν**, "abide by them." Cf. *Anab.* IV. 4. 16, Thuc. IV.
118 &c.

26   **§ 45. περὶ πολλοῦ ἂν**, "I should deem of first importance,"
with a suppressed protasis; περὶ π. ποιεῖσθαι is a common idiom=
magni facere. Sometimes, but rarely, the preposition is omitted,
and the genit. becomes one of price.

p. 48. 1 διότι here=ὅτι, "that," a very common usage in Aristotle: e.g. *Pol.* I. 2. 10, διότι δὲ πολιτικὸν ὁ ἄνθρωπος ζῷον πάσης μελίττης καὶ παντὸς ἀγελαίου ζῴου μᾶλλον, δῆλον.

2 ἀγχόνη. Cf. Soph. *Oed. Tyr.* 1374, ἔργ' ἐστὶ κρείσσον' ἀγχόνης εἰργασμένα ("hanging is too good for such deeds"), and Arist. *Achar.* 125. Here="It will be as good (or bad) as hanging to them," i.e. they will hang themselves from envy.

καίτοι τί, κ.τ.λ. "Hullo! but what's this? Shame on their hastiness!" For φεῦ c. gen. cf. § 7.

3 πανταχόθεν, κ.τ.λ. Cf. what Apemantus says. Shak. *Tim.* IV. 3, "I'll say thou hast gold, | Thou wilt be throng'd to shortly."

4 κεκον. καὶ πνευστ., "covered with dust and out of breath." So *Tyr.* § 3, οὐχ ὁρᾶς δὲ καὶ τὸν Ἑρμῆν αὐτὸν ἱδρῶτι ῥεόμενον καὶ τὼ πόδε κεκονιμένον καὶ πνευστιῶντα; μέστον γοῦν ἄσθματος αὐτῷ τὸ στόμα.

5 τὸν πάγον τοῦτον means some rocky knoll, or peak close by, probably the same thing as that on which T. *does* climb at the very end of the book.

6 ἀπελαύνω is subj. mood.

ἐξ ὑπερδεξίων. Abbott takes it in its primary sense, and translates, "pelting them from the right hand." It would seem rather to mean "from higher ground" (locally): cf. § 58, ἐπιχαλαξῶ πόρρωθεν αὐτούς. For this sense of ἐξ ὑπ. cf. Xen. *Hell.* VII. 4. 13, and *Anab.* III. 4. 7, ὑπερδέξιον χωρίον. It may also have the meaning of "from a vantage-ground" i.e. "at an advantage."

7 ἀκροβολιζόμενος. Cf. ἀκροβολισμός § 3 and note; apparently quite literally, *eminus jacere* as opp. to *comminus pugnare*.

ἢ τό γε τοσοῦτον. The γε helps to point this second one out as the better of the two alternatives: "or rather, shall I just for this once break my own law?" He means, of course, the serio-comic law he has just passed, forbidding him to speak with any man.

12 ἔρανον αἰτήσαντί μοι, "when I asked a loan." Technically, at Athens ἔρανοι were clubs or friendly-societies and ἔρανος was the club-feast, usually monthly. The societies lent charitable loans to those in need, on the understanding that any money advanced was to be repaid when the borrower's circumstances allowed of it. Timon says here, then, that he only borrowed a loan.

The parallel scenes in Shak. are worth noticing. Timon there sends his servants to borrow of his friends. The first gives the man a "tip," to say he was out! The second says he unfortunately spent all his money yesterday, or he would have been very pleased to oblige. The third pretended to be very much aggrieved because Timon did not ask him first and says: "Who bates mine honour shall not know my coin."

πίθους ὅλους, κ.τ.λ. He has "returned" this quantity. How much therefore must he have gorged himself with, and yet he cannot spare a penny.

13　**παρ' ἐμοί**, *apud me, chez moi* = "when dining at my house." Cf. §§ 7, 10.

ἐμημεκώς is no doubt put παρὰ προσδοκίαν for ἐκπεπωκώς.

εὖ γε ἐποίησεν, cf. note § 30.

15　§ **46.** **ΓΝΑΘΩΝΙΔΗΣ**, from γνάθος, the man celebrated for the exercising of his "jaw," either in flattery or gluttony, a perfect type of the true parasite, or toady. Cf. *Fugit.* § 19, κολακείας ἕνεκα τὸν Γναθωνίδην ἢ τὸν Στρουθίαν ὑπερβαλέσθαι δυνάμενοι.

17　**συμποτικώτατε**, "most convivial." In *Cronosolon* §§ 17, 18 we have the νόμοι συμποτικοί or "laws of drinking." The superlative does not seem common. It occurs again in *Sat. Epist.* § 32, τὸ γοῦν ἥδιστον καὶ συμποτικώτατον ἡ ἰσοτιμία ἐστί.

18　**Νηδὶ καὶ σύ γε** is Dindorf's emendation. The MSS. read νὴ καὶ σύ γε. But νὴ requires some god's name after it. One MS. has νὴ Δία, and from that Dind. restores νηδὶ = νὴ Δία. He also thinks this is the true reading at Arist. *Equit.* 319, νηδὶ κἀμὲ τοῦτ' ἔδρασε ταὐτόν. So apparently *Ran.* 164, νηδὶ καὶ σύ γε ὑγίαινε.

γυπῶν. He has called his late friends appropriately "wolves," "crows," "gulls;" he now adds "vultures."

22　**διθυράμβων.** Arion was its reputed inventor. It was a free kind of composition, sung to the flute. The chorus of ten responded to these recitations; hence the first beginnings of the Drama.

23　**Καὶ μὴν.** Cf. *Men.* 8, *Tim.* 9, 15. "I'll make you sing something beside dithyrambs. You shall chant dirges."

25　**μαρτύρομαι**, used absolutely, "I protest." Cf. Thuc. VI. 80. 3, δεόμεθα δὲ καὶ μαρτυρόμεθα ἅμα, εἰ μὴ πείσομεν, ὅτι ἐπιβουλευόμεθα ὑπὸ Ἰώνων. Cf. too Lysias 97. 40, βοῶντα καὶ κεκραγότα καὶ μαρτυρόμενον.

p. 49. 1 **προσκαλοῦμαι**, another technical word "to challenge" anyone to anything, εἰς ὅρκον, εἰς ἀντιδόσιν, εἰς μαρτυρίαν. Here, as usual, the genit. is used of the charge. "I summon you for assault and battery before the Areopagus." The present implies: "I'm on my way to do it." Cf. for exactly similar phraseology, *Vit. Auct.* § 7, εἶτα οὐ δέδιας μὴ προσκαλέσηταί σε εἰς Ἄρειον πάγον.

4	προσκεκλήσομαι. "I'll give you reason to indict me" (Abbott). The MSS. and some editors read προ(σ)κέκλησει με, "You shall very soon bring a charge of murder against me,"—said, of course, ridiculously.

5	Μηδαμῶς, cf. p. 43, l. 11.

7	ἴσχαιμον (ἔχω αἷμα), "a marvellous stancher of blood."

9	οὐ χαιρήσεις, almost invariably used with the future tense in this sense, "thou shalt not get off scot free" i.e. "thou shalt pay dearly" (= κλαύσει). The γενόμενος is probably a causal participle, "*for having changed* your disposition." Cf. Arist. *Plut.* 64, οὔ τοι μὰ τὴν Δήμητρα χαιρήσεις ἔτι.

10	χρηστοῦ. Remember it was this virtue which had ruined Timon, § 8, χρηστότης ἐπέτριψεν αὐτὸν, and which made Zeus fear that Timon would refuse to house Plutus § 10, κἂν ὅτι μάλιστα ὑπὸ χρηστότητος αὖθις ἐκδιώκῃ αὐτοὺς τῆς οἰκίας.

11	§ 47. ὁ ἀναφαλαντίας, "the man with the bald-head." Cf. *Navig.* § 6, ἐδείχθη γάρ μοι ἀναφαλαντίας τις, and *Herac.* § 1, γέρων ἐστὶν αὐτοῖς ἀναφαλαντίας.

12	Φιλιάδης, the friendly man.

13	οὗτος δέ. The verb to this subject is the last word of the section; from παρ' ἐμοῦ to κύκνων may be bracketed.

14	προῖκα, "as a dowry." It was considered a very essential part of the marriage, for the bride to have a dowry (προῖξ or φερνή). In Dem. *adv. Boeot.* 1016, the unseemliness of the marriage of the plaintiff's mother, who was ἄπροικος, is dwelt upon. To such a pitch did these dowries come that Solon passed a law to restrict the amount, lest the independence of the husband might be endangered. Cf. Andoc. *con. Alcib.* 14, λαβὼν δὲ τοσαύτην προῖκα ὅσην οὐδεὶς τῶν Ἑλλήνων.

16	ᾠδικώτερον εἶναι τῶν κύκνων. The wild swan's song was proverbial. Cf. Verg. *Ecl.* VIII. 56, "Certent et cycnis ululae." So too Hor. *Od.* IV. 3. 19, "O mutis quoque piscibus donatura cycni, si libeat, sonum," and II. 20. 15, "canorus ales." Cf. Tennyson's beautiful ode on *The Dying Swan.* Lucian mentions the subject again in *Elect.* § 6, χρύσος αὐτὸς ἀποστάξει των λόγων, πολὺ τῶν κύκνων τῶν ποιητικῶν λιγυρωτέροις.

19	Ὦ τῆς ἀναισχ., cf. § 43. The first few words are addressed to Gnathonides, as he goes off to seek redress.

23　§ **48**. μετριάζομεν, "We keep within bounds" (are not too impetuous), "lest we may seem to intrude."

24　ὅπως. βλέπε or ὅρα being supplied, as commonly. Cf. Arist. *Nub.* 824, ὅπως δὲ τοῦτο μὴ διδάξεις μηδένα, "take care not to tell any one," i.e. *don't* do so. So here, "mind you keep off."

25　τοὺς...τραπέζης, "trencher-friends," Shak. *Tim.* III. *ad fin.*

p. 50.　2　τὰ κατεπείγοντα, a phrase used also by Isoc. and Polyb. for "urgent necessity." The sing. τὸ κατέπειγον occurs in Xen. *Mem.* II. 1. 2.

3　καθ᾽ ὁδόν = *in itinere*, "on my way here."

6　Νέστορι. Cf. *Men.* § 18 where we have his garrulousness alluded to. Here of course it is his wisdom, "You could give the needful advice even to N."

8　Ἔσται ταῦτα, i.e. "Thank you, I shall be very pleased to have your advice."

9　καὶ φιλοφρονήσομαι. The MSS. seem to have ὡς before καὶ, which editors agree in omitting. If it is retained, we must read -ήσωμαι.

10　τοῦ κρανίου. The accusative is more usual, but the gen. is not uncommon: e.g. Ar. *Ach.* 480, τῆς κεφαλῆς κατέαγε.

11　ἐνουθέτουν, the imperfect of "intention," "was for advising him."

12　§ **49**. Δημέας. As the first was from γνάθος and the second from φιλία, so this character is from δῆμος, "the public character."

14　ἑκκαίδεκα, if a talent = £240, the sum would be £3840.
　　παρ᾽ ἐμοῦ, "(borrowed) from me."

15　κατεδεδίκαστο, "for he had been condemned and thrown into chains for not paying."

17　ἔλαχε διανέμειν, "it was his lot to distribute." Cf. S. Luke, i. 9 of Zacharias, ἔλαχε τοῦ θυμιᾶσαι "it fell to his turn to burn incense."

　　Ἐρεχθηῖδι. There seems to be some mistake here. Timon was of the deme of Colyttus (§§ 44, 50), which was in the tribe of Αἰγηῖς, not Ἐρεχθηῖς. Faber would alter the word. Hemst. Dind. Somm. retain the text. It seems most probable that the mistake was Lucian's own.

　　There were 10 tribes, named after 10 famous Attic heroes (Herod. v. 66), viz. Aeneus, Aegeus, Acamas, Ajax, Antiochus, Cecrops, Erechtheus, Hippothoon, Leo, Pandion.

18　τὸ θεωρικόν. The fund, from which money was given to the poorer citizens to pay for their seats in the theatre at the great festi-

§ 50]   *NOTES.*   137

vals. The ticket was 2 obols (3¼*d.*). Note the humorous contrast between this which D. refused T., and what T. had given to D.

19 τὸ γιγνόμενον, "what was coming in to me:" "my proper share." Cf. *Somn.* § 1, ἀποφέρων ἀεὶ τὸ γιγνόμενον "when from time to time I brought home my earnings," where Heitland quotes *Tox.* § 18, τὸ γιγνόμενον ἐκ τούτου ἀποφέρων. Cf. also *de merc. cond.* § 23, λάβῃς ἐκεῖνο ὁτιδήποτε ἦν τὸ γιγνόμενον.

21 § **50**. τὸ ἔρεισμα τ. 'Αθ., so Theron is called ἔρεισμ' 'Ακραγάντος, Pind. *Olym.* II. 6.

22 ὁ δῆμος συνειλεγμένος, "The people in assembly, and the two Councils." The first is the Ecclesia, or assembly of all male citizens. The other two are the Areopagus and the Senate of 500. The *Areop.* sat only at night, was a religious and moral council, composed of the highest and most approved in the state, who were life-members. The *other* sat every day; they were chosen annually.

p. 51. 1 γέγραφα, "I have drawn up."

5 πὺξ, πάλην, κ.τ.λ., boxing, wrestling, racing, and a double chariot race; the first with four horses, full grown, the latter with only a pair, and those colts.

8 οὐδὲ ἐθεώρησα, "But I've never been there, even as a *spectator,* let alone a competitor."

11 ἠρίστευσε, "distinguished himself." So in *Inf. Dial.* 10. 7, the strategus says: ἐνίκησα, καὶ ἠρίστευσα καὶ ἡ πόλις ἐτίμησέ με. Cf. Soph. *Ajax*, 435, τὰ πρῶτα καλλιστεῖ' ἀριστεύσας στρατοῦ. For καὶ...δὲ, "and...too," cf. p. 40, l. 21; so Thuc. II. 36, δίκαιον γὰρ αὐτοῖς καὶ πρέπον δέ.

12 πέρυσι, "last year" opp. to ἐς νέωτα, "next year" (cf. § 52, note). Cf. *Bacc.* 7, ἐς νέωτα πιὼν αὖθις ἐκεῖνα συνάπτει ἃ πέρυσιν αὐτὸν λέγοντα ἡ μέθη κατέλιπε.

πρὸς 'Αχαρναῖς, "near Acharnae," so Somm., Dind., Abbott. The MSS. have 'Αχαρνέας, "against the Acharnians:" but these people were not likely to be at enmity with Athens, being themselves of Attica. Hemsterhuis suggested 'Αχαρνᾶνας. Faber περὶ 'Αχάρνας referring to Thuc. II. 19, 20.

13 μόρας. MSS. vary between this and μοίρας. The "mora" was according to Xenophon the largest division of the Lacedaemonian army = 4 λόχοι = about 2000 men. Others make it only from 400 to 1000.

14 **§ 51. Πῶς,** "What *do* you mean? Why, I wasn't even enrolled
with the rest because I had no arms." He means his name was not
even on the κατάλογος, or muster-roll of the citizens liable for service,
and which was kept by the ταξίαρχος of each tribe (Gow, p. 121).

20 **δεδόχθω,** so modern editors, though the MSS. seem to have
δέδοκται. For such legal formulae, cf. Dem. *de Cor.* §§ 54, 84,
115.

τῇ Ἡλιαίᾳ κατὰ φυλάς. "The great majority of cases in
Athens, both criminal and civil, were tried before ἡλιασταί, a body
of jurymen so called because they had a special meeting-place called
ἡλιαία, 'the sunny Hall'" (Gow, p. 125). There were 6000 of
them, 600 from each of the 10 tribes. Every citizen over 30 was
eligible. The whole number "was divided into 10 groups, num-
bered with the letters of the Ionic Alphabet from A to K, and
each ἡλιαστής received a bronze ticket bearing his name and the
letter of his group."

None of the commentators take note of the strange use of κατὰ
φυλὰς with τῇ Ἡλιαίᾳ except Wheeler, who thinks καὶ ταῖς φυλαῖς
may have been what L. wrote. As it stands, it is either (1) used
in reference to the fact of their being chosen 600 from each tribe : or
(2) it means "according to their (10) groups" mentioned above, or
(3) it is one of L.'s mock-heroic expressions, having no particular
meaning. To me it seems that (3) is the most likely.

21 **χρυσοῦν...παρὰ τὴν Ἀθηνᾶν.** Cf. *Anacharsis* § 17 where a
parallel passage occurs: ὥστε εὐεργέτης ὑμῶν ὁ ἀνὴρ ἀναγεγράφθω
καὶ χαλκοῦν αὐτὸν ἀναστήσατε παρὰ τοὺς ἐπωνύμους ἢ ἐν πόλει
παρὰ τὴν Ἀθηνᾶν.

23 **κεραυνὸν...δεξιᾷ,** a symbol of power, being the special weapon of
Zeus.

ἀκτῖνας ἑπτά. The best editors place the ἑπτὰ here, instead of
after στεφάνοις, which the MSS. read. The object of seven golden
crowns is not easy to discover, but the statues of the sun had commonly seven (or 12) rays, so that the text is a fairly certain emendation. Cf. Verg. *Aen.* XII. 163, where Latinus's descent from the
sun is shown by the crown of 12 rays: "cui tempora circum | Aurati
bis sex radii fulgentia cingunt, | Solis avi specimen."

26 **Διονυσίοις τραγῳδοῖς καινοῖς,** "at the great Dionysia, at the
time of the new tragedies" (lit. "tragedians"). Τὰ ἐν ἄστει, τὰ κατ'
ἄστυ, τὰ ἀστικά, or τὰ μεγάλα Διονύσια or sometimes simply τὰ

Διονύσια were celebrated between the 8th and 18th of Elaphebolion (March—April)..."It was then that the new tragedies were brought out, and the great annual contest took place" (Donaldson, *Theat. of Gks.* p. 102). Cf. Dem. *de Cor.* 243, ὡς ἄρα δεῖ στεφανῶσαι Δημοσθένην καὶ ἀναγορεῦσαι ἐν τῷ θεάτρῳ Διονυσίοις τοῖς μεγάλοις, τραγῳδοῖς καινοῖς, ὅτι στεφανοῖ ὁ δῆμος. So § 265, &c.

p. 52. 2 **συγγενὴς αὐτοῦ ἀγχιστεὺς,** "being his nearest of kin." ἀγχιστεὺς is only a connexion (by marriage); συγγενὴς a "blood-relation" in strict law. But the two together denote the nearest blood-relation, and consequently the heir-at-law; a polite hint to Timon that τὰ ἀγχιστεῖα (Soph. *Ant.* 174), or "the rights of inheritance," are legally due to Demeas.

4 **ὁπόσα ἂν ἐθέλῃ,** for MSS. ἐθέλοι. Cf. Hor. *Sat.* II. 3. 94, "Sapiensne? Etiam: et rex, *Et quicquid volet.*"

8 **§ 52. ὅσα γε καὶ ἡμᾶς εἰδέναι,** "At least so far as I am aware." "The acc. with inf. in some places stands without a governing word, expressing merely the thought present to the mind in the form of an indefinite sentence...so also an acc. with infin. is added in a qualifying or restricting sense to a statement with ὡς or ὅσον." Madv. *G. S.* § 168. Cf. Plat. *Theaet.* 145, ἦ οὖν ζωγραφικὸς Θεόδωρος; οὐχ, ὅσον γ᾿ ἐμὲ εἰδέναι. So in poetry: Ar. *Nub.* 1252, οὐκ ἄρ᾿ ἀποδώσεις; οὐχ, ὅσον γέ μ᾿ εἰδέναι: Soph. *O. C.* 150, ὡς (ὅσ᾿ alii) ἀπεικάσαι.

10 **ἐς νέωτα,** "when the new year comes." Cf. § 50, note on πέρυσι.

13 **εἰ γαμεῖς ἔτι,** "whether you will *any longer* have a chance of marrying."

15 **τυραννίδι ἐπιχειρεῖς,** not "make an attack upon" (as in Herod. v. 46, τῇ τυραννίδι ἐπιχειρεῖν) but "set your hand to," "aim at." To aim at despotism, it need hardly be said, was in the eyes of an Athenian a most heinous offence: cf. the boast of the tyrannicide in L.'s dialogue so called (*passim*).

16 **καθαρῶς,** cf. Τίμων καθαρός, quoted in Introd. p. xxii. note 2.

17 **τὴν δίκην,** the *proper* penalty; note the article.

18 **τά τε ἄλλα καὶ ὅτι,** "among other reasons, because."

20 **§ 53. δῆλος εἶ συκοφαντῶν,** "You are clearly acting the sycophant."

21 **ὀπισθόδομον.** "A private chamber like the modern sacristy, built at the back of a temple," Rich. Here it evidently refers to the treasury of Athens in the rear of Athena's Temple in the Acropolis,

cf. *de Pereg. morte* § 32, ἐπεὶ δὲ ἐς τὴν Ὀλυμπίαν ἀφικόμεθα, μεστὸς
ἦν ὁ ὀπισθόδομος τῶν κατηγορούντων, and Arist. *Plut.* 1191,

> ἱδρυσόμεσθ᾽ αὐτίκα μάλ᾽, ἀλλὰ περίμενε
> τὸν Πλοῦτον, οὖπερ πρότερον ἦν ἱδρυμένος
> τὸν ὀπισθόδομον ἀεὶ φυλάττων τῆς θεοῦ.

p. 53. 1 **διώρυκται,** shortened for the more common διορώρυκται.

5 **ἄλλην—πληγὴν** (so with τρίτην below) supplied, as commonly;
cf. note § 40.

8 **γελοῖα...πάθοιμι,** "I should be in a very ridiculous position."
See note on ἔπασχον...ὅμοιον, *Men.* § 4, and exx. given there.

δύο...μάρας, v. note at end of § 50.

11 **Ὀλύμπια πὺξ καὶ πάλην.** For the construction cf. § 50, and
coronari Olympia of Hor. *Ep.* I. 1. 50.

13 **§ 54.** **οὐ μὲν οὖν ἄλλος,** "Surely, none other," cf. *Men.* § 1.

Thrasycles makes the fourth type. Thus we have had Gnathonides, the κόλαξ, who offered him a rope when he asked for a
loan ; Philiades, the κολάκων βδελυρώτατος, who struck Timon when
sick and in sore need of help ; Demeas, the important man of state,
who refused T. a *4d.* ticket, though he had received thousands of
pounds from him in his better days, and now Thrasycles, the typical
philosopher, with cloak, beard, stick and wallet, ever greedy after
gain, called κολάκων τὰ πρῶτα.

14 **πώγωνα.** For the great importance which attached to a beard
cf. note on *Men.* § 6, and a passage in *Inf. Dial.* 10. 8, very similar
to this: ὁ σεμνὸς δὲ οὗτος ἀπό γε τοῦ σχήματος, καὶ βρενθυόμενος,
ὁ τὰς ὀφρῦς ἐπηρκώς...τίς ἐστιν ὁ τὸν βαθὺν πώγωνα καθειμένος; φιλόσοφός τις, ὦ Ἑρμῆ.

τὰς ὀφρῦς ἀνατείνας (the phrase occurs in *Tyran.* § 4 of Aeacus),
"lift up the eyebrows," as opp. to "knitting them:" which helped
to increase the air of grave importance. ἀνασπᾶν is the word in
more common use, e.g. Ar. *Ach.* 1069, τὰς ὀφρῦς ἀνεσπακώς: *Eq.* 631,
τὰ μέτωπ᾽ ἀνέσπασεν.

βρενθυόμενος, v. passage from *Inf. Dial.* 10, quoted above. The
noun βρένθος is used by Athenaeus of "conceit," a pompous bearing.
The verb therefore means to "carry one's head high" which seems to
be the meaning in *Dial.* 10, *Lexiph.* 24, and also in Arist. *Nub.* 362,
ὅτι βρενθύει τ᾽ ἐν ταῖσιν ὁδοῖς καὶ τὠφθαλμὼ παραβάλλεις. But in
our passage it rather means "muttering," or "grumbling" to him-

§ 54]   *NOTES.*   141

self; cf. Ar. *Lys.* 887, χἆ δυσκολαίνει πρὸς ἐμὲ καὶ βρενθύεται, and in Luc. *de mer. cond.* § 37 that sense is certain; ἅπαντες δ' οὖν ἀπαλλάττονται λαβόντες τι καὶ βρενθυόμενοι ὅτι μὴ πλείω ἔδωκας

15 **τιτανῶδες βλέπων.** Cf. Ar. *Eq.* 631, κἄβλεψε νᾶπυ ("looked mustard!"); *Vesp.* 454, βλεπόντων κάρδαμα ("garlic"); Luc. *Icarom.* § 23, ὁ δὲ Ζεὺς μάλα φοβερῶς δριμύ τε καὶ τιτανῶδες εἰς ἐμὲ ἀπιδών. Theoc. XIII. 45, ἔαρ ὁρόωσα, and cf. our "looking daggers."

ἀνασεσοβημένος τὴν κόμην, L. and S. say "with hair on end' through fright," and quote this passage; which is surely wrong. In *Jup. Trag.* § 30, κόμη ἀνασεσ. certainly seems to mean this: for he is speaking there of Phoebus' eyes rolling, and colour changing and hair standing on end, before he utters his oracular prophecy (cf. the passage of the frenzied Sybil in *Aen.* VI. 48, "non comptae mansere comae," &c.); but here it must mean "having his hair thrown back," brushed back from his forehead, and so standing up high in front. Dr Abbott thinks it is "dishevelled," but see note on εὐσταλής below l. 17.

16 **Αὐτοβορέας,** "a veritable Boreas." Cf. *Praec. Rhet.* § 12, Αὐτοθαΐς, "Thais herself;" *Philops.* 18, αὐτοανθρώπῳ ὅμοιον, "the very image of a man," and cf. note § 27 on αὐτοπρόσωπον.

17 **ὁ τὸ σχῆμα εὐσταλής,** "neat in his dress and orderly in his gait." Cf. *Pisc.* § 12, τὰ σχήματα εὐσταλῶν. This rather tells against ἀνασοβεῖν being "dishevelled," or "on end."

18 **σωφρονικὸς τὴν ἀναβολὴν,** "seemly in the way he wears his cloak." ἀναβολὴ is not the cloak, but the way it hangs: cf. *Somn.* § 6, τὸ σχῆμα εὐπρεπὴς καὶ κόσμιος τὴν ἀναβολήν, and a good example in *Gall.* 9, ἀπέρχομαι, κοσμίως μάλα ἐσχηματισμένος, ἀντιστρέψας τὸ τριβώνιον, ὡς ἐπὶ τοῦ καθαρωτέρου γένοιτο ἡ ἀναβολή.

19 **μυρία ὅσα,** "ever so many." So too *bis acc.* § 3, μυρία ὅσα ἔχοντας πράγματα. Cf. *Halcyon.* § 6, θαυμαστὴν ὅσην ἔχει τὴν διαφοράν. *Prom.* § 12, ὀλίγον ὅσον τοῦ πηλοῦ λαβεῖν. So in Arist. *Plut.* 750, ὄχλος ὑπερφυὴς ὅσος, "prodigiously large."

20 **ὀλιγαρκὲς** (avoid confusing with ὀλιγαρχία), "contentment with little." Cf. § 57.

21 **λουσάμενος...δεῖπνον.** The hour before δεῖπνον was in the better period always the time for going to the baths, though some bathed as often as five times in the day. Cf. Menander (Athen. IV. 166), καίτοι νέος ποτ' ἐγενόμην κἀγώ, γύναι· | ἀλλ' οὐκ ἐλούμην πεντάκις τῆς ἡμέρας.

22 **κύλιξ.** The most frequent drinking-vessel depicted on monuments, having a double handle; there are many exx. to be seen in the vase rooms of the Brit. Museum. For the predicate, cf. p. 9, l. 1.

23 **ζωροτέρῳ.** Among the Greeks wine was always drunk diluted. To drink οἶνος ἄκρατος was a barbarism. Hence ζωρότερον πίνειν was to drink *purer* wine than usual, i.e. less proportion of water (the proportion of water to wine was about 6 : 3 or 4), and so in time came to mean "to drink hard," "be a drunkard." So in a somewhat similar passage in *Inf. Dial.* 7, we have πριάμενος γὰρ φάρμακον ἀνέπεισα τὸν οἰνοχόον...(πίνει δ᾽ ἐπιεικῶς ζωρότερον) ἐμβαλόντα ἐς κύλικα ἕτοιμον ἔχειν αὐτὸ καὶ ἐπιδοῦναι αὐτῷ, and *Epis. Sat.* § 7, ζωρότερον πίνων τὸ νέκταρ.

καθάπερ...ἐκπιών, i.e. just as though he had drunk up the water of Forgetfulness, and so no longer remembered his teaching in the morning.

This whole passage is very similar in thought to *Men.* §§ 4, 5.

p. 54. 3 **τὸν πλησίον παραγκωνιζόμενος,** "elbowing his neighbours;" *Piscat.* § 34, περὶ τὰς τῶν πλουσίων θύρας ἀλλήλους παραγκωνιζόμενοι : *de Cal.* § 10, πρῶτος αὐτὸς ἕκαστος εἶναι βουλόμενος παρωθεῖται καὶ παραγκωνίζεται τὸν πλησίον.

καρύκης τὸ γένειον ἀνάπλεως, "getting his beard full of soup." καρύκη was properly a savoury sauce of blood and rich spices.

4 **κυνηδὸν ἐμφορούμενος,** "stuffing himself like a dog." So again *Pisc.* § 34, φορτικῶς καὶ πέρα τοῦ καλῶς ἔχοντος ἐμφορούμενοι. For form of adverb v. note § 3.

ἐπικεκυφώς. So of T. stooping over his work §§ 7, 11.

6 **τῷ λιχανῷ,** "carefully wiping the plates round with his forefinger." λιχανὸς is properly an adjective like "sinistra," "dextra," &c., δάκτυλος being understood, i.e. the "licking" finger.

8 **§ 55. Μεμψίμοιρος,** "grumbling," "discontented," as in § 13 q. v. **τὸν πλακοῦντα ὅλον,** a round flat cake. Cf. Arist. *Eq.* 1191,

> ΚΛ. λαβέ νυν πλακοῦντος πίονος παρ᾽ ἐμοῦ τόμον.
> ΑΛ. παρ᾽ ἐμοῦ δ᾽ ὅλον γε τὸν πλακοῦντα τουτονί.

So *Achar.* 1125, κἀμοὶ πλακοῦντος τυρόνωτον δὸς κύκλον. Cf. Hor. *Sat.* II. 8. 24, "Porcius infra | Ridiculus totas simul obsorbere placentas." The mss. have ὡς...λάβοι for κἂν...λαβῇ.

9 **ὅ τι περ λιχνείας καὶ ἀπληστίας ὄφελος.** In Xen. *Hell.* v. 3. 6

we have ὅ,τι περ ὄφελος στρατεύματος "the flower of the army,"
and in Arist. *Eccles.* 53, ὅ,τι πέρ ἐστ' ὄφελος "all that is good
for anything." So it would mean "whatever is serviceable to
luxury and greed." Abbott translates, "which is the very crown
of his gluttony and greed." L. and S. curiously make it refer to
Thrasycles = ὁ πάντων ἀπληστότατος. The ἤ was first suggested by
Hemst. and helps to simplify the passage. Somm. adds it.

10 πάροινος...ἄχρι...ὀρχηστύος. "To dance was always thought
a symptom of the highest state of transport that could be induced by
wine; cf. the epithet παρο νιοι ὀρχήσεις." Beck. *Char.* 103.

11 λοιδορίας καὶ ὀργῆς προσέτι. So Eubulus (Athen. II. 36) says
with regard to the number of goblets drunk, "that wise men go
home after their third:"

> ὁ δὲ τέταρτος οὐκ ἔτι
> ἡμέτερός ἐστ', ἀλλ' ὕβρεως· ὁ δὲ πέμπτος βοῆς·
> ἕκτος δὲ κώμων· ἕβδομος δ' ὑπωπίων·
> ὁ δ' ὄγδοος κλητῆρος· ὁ δ' ἔνατος χολῆς·
> δέκατος δὲ μανίας, ὥστε καὶ βάλλειν ποιεῖ.

12 ἐπὶ τῇ κύλικι, *inter pocula.*

14 ὑπὸ τοῦ ἀκράτου, cf. ζωροτέρῳ § 54.

15 ὑποτραυλίζων. I cannot find another instance of the use of this
compound. The simple verb is not uncommon. Cf. Ar. *Vesp.* 44 of
the "lisping" of Alcibiades: εἶτ' Ἀλκιβιάδης εἶπε πρός με τραυλίσας, |
"ὁλᾶς; Θέωλος τὴν κεφαλὴν κόλακος ἔχει," for ὁρᾷς, Θέωρος, κόρακος.

17 ἀμφοτέραις, χερσὶν understood; cf. note § 20.

18 πλὴν ἀλλά, § 25 note. καὶ νήφων, "*even* when sober."

τῶν πρωτείων. The singular is occasionally used, e.g. Dem. *de
Cor.* § 321, τὴν τοῦ γενναίου καὶ τοῦ πρωτείου τῇ πόλει προαίρεσιν
διαφυλάττειν, but more commonly the plural. Cf. Id. ibid. § 66, ἀεὶ
περὶ πρωτείων ("primacy") καὶ τιμῆς καὶ δόξης ἀγωνιζομένην τὴν
πατρίδα. Here it means "the first prize," "the palm."

παραχωρήσειεν ἄν, "would yield the palm to none." The word
has its ordinary classical construction, a *genitive* of the place or thing
from which one retires, and a *dative* of the person to whom you
yield: e.g. Dem. 63. 16, Φιλίππῳ Ἀμφιπόλεως παρακεχωρήκαμεν.

20 τὰ πρῶτα = ὁ πρῶτος. Cf. note § 35.

21 γοητεία, "jugglery," "quackery," always a concomitant of Lucian's pseudo-philosophers.

23 **πάνσοφόν τι χρῆμα,** "it is a wondrously learned creature, on all points perfect, and of finished versatility." For χρῆμα v. full note § 25 : as applied to human beings, cf. *Vit. Auct.* § 12, πολυτελές τὸ χρῆμα καὶ πλουσίων δεόμενον.

24 **οὐκ ἐς μακρὰν,** "shortly."

25 **χρηστὸς,** ironical, "being such a fine fellow," cf. §§ 8, 10.

χρόνιος, "late arriving." Cf. *pro laps.* 6, ὦ δέσποθ᾽, ὑγίαιν᾽, ὡς χρόνιος ἐλήλυθας.

p. 55. 2 § **56.** **οἱ...τεθηπότες.** This word and κέχηνα are L.'s two stock words for expressing open-mouthed astonishment: cf. *Pisc.* § 34, τοὺς πλουσίους τεθήπασι, "are amazed at."

5 **πρὸς ἄνδρα οἷον σὲ ἁπλοϊκὸν** = πρὸς τοιοῦτον ἄνδρα, οἷος σὺ εἶ, attrac. of the relative, more common with gen. and dat.

τῶν ὄντων κοινωνικόν, "ready to share your goods." Cf. *Pisc.* § 35, πολὺς ὁ περὶ τοῦ κοινωνικὸν εἶναι δεῖν λόγος.

6 **μᾶζα.** "A staple article of diet with the Gks., something similar to the Roman *puls.* It was made of flour, oil and wine, and continued to be the food of the lower classes till a late period," *Becker.*

8 **ἐννεάκρουνος,** cf. Thuc. II. 15. It was a celebrated spring in Athens originally called Callirhoë, when it was open; but it was afterwards covered by Pisistratus, and made to run through *nine pipes.* In the days of Thuc. it was still used for sacred purposes, esp. for marriage ceremonies.

9 **τρίβων,** a short mantle of coarse texture worn by the Spartans, affected too by the Stoic and Cynic schools; while the πορφυρὶς was a bright-coloured garment worn by those of higher rank; it seems to have been used by dandies, cf. *Bis acc.* § 17.

10 **τὸ χρυσίον...ψηφίδων,** cf. *Pisc.* § 35, τί γὰρ τὸ χρυσίον ἢ ἀργύριον οὐδὲν τῶν ἐν τοῖς αἰγιαλοῖς ψηφίδων διαφέρον;

11 **σὴν δὲ αὐτοῦ χάριν ἐστάλην,** "for *thy* special sake." Cf. Lat. *mea, tua gratia,* and Soph. *Trach.* 485, κείνου τε καὶ σὴν...χάριν, v. p. 56, l. 1.

12 **ἐστάλην,** "I have come." Cf. Soph. *Ajax* 328, τούτων γὰρ οὕνεκ᾽ ἐστάλην and Ar. *Vesp.* 487, ὅστις ἡμῶν ἐπὶ τυραννίδ᾽ ὧδ᾽ ἐστάλης.

14 **εἰ γάρ...ἐμβαλεῖς.** Cf. *Vit. Auc.* § 9, where Diogenes, on being put up for sale, says: τὰ δὲ χρήματα, ἢν ἔχῃς, ἐμοὶ πειθόμενος ἐς τὴν θάλατταν φέρων ἐμβαλεῖς. Cf. Hor. *Od.* III. 24. 47.

17 **μὴ μέντοι,** a common form of ellipsis (μὴ ἐμβαλῇς); so μόνον and

μόνον μὴ, of which S. Paul is so fond, e.g. Gal. ii. 10, vi. 12; 2 Thess. ii. 17. "Don't fling it into the deep, my good fellow, but go in as far as your waist, and (throw it) a little beyond the line where the waves break, with me as your sole witness."

19 κυματωγῆς. Fab. Hemst. Dind. &c. with the Reg. Codex; other MSS. read κυματώδους. Cf. *Hermot.* 84, ἔφη γὰρ ἄνθρωπόν τινα ἐπὶ τῇ ἠόνι καθιζόμενον πρὸς τὴν κυματωγὴν ἀριθμεῖν τὰ κύματα.

20 § 57. **Εἰ δὲ μὴ...σὺ δὲ.** Notice the δὲ in apodosis, which occurs not uncommonly: cf. Herod. I. 112, ἐπεὶ οὐ δύναμαί σε πείθειν, σὺ δὲ ὧδε ποίησον. *D. D.* 6. 2, εἴποτε πιοῦσα παραδοίην τῷ Γανυμήδει τὸ ἔκπωμα, ὁ δὲ ᾔτει ἐν αὐτῷ πιεῖν.

23 **δραχμάς, μνᾶν, τάλαντον.** 6 obols = 1 drachma (9*d*.), 100 drachmae = 1 mina (£4), 60 minae = 1 talent (£235).

24 **διμοιρίαν, τριμοιρίαν,** "double or triple share."

p. 56. 4 **δύο μεδίμνους...Αἰγινητικούς.** The medimnus was the largest Attic dry measure = 11½ gallons. The Aeginetan was even larger; so that this man's wallet was pretty capacious, holding some 25 gallons. The πήρα, ostensibly provided for the carrying of a few bare necessaries, was much worn by philosophers: cf. *Piscator* (the beginning) where the philosophers pelt Lucian, and Socrates calls on Plato, Chrysippus, &c. to help; ὡς πήρη πήρηφιν ἀρήγῃ, βάκτρα δὲ βάκτροις. In *Inf. D.* 11. 3 the wallet of Diogenes has only two choenikes of beans χοίνικας δύο θέρμων ἔχουσαν, i.e. not half a gallon.

χωροῦσαν, "holding," often used of measures in this sense; cf. Ar. *Nub.* 1238, ἐξ χοᾶς χωρήσεται. Dem. 579, ἡ πόλις αὐτὸν οὐ χωρεῖ.

8 **φέρε,** "come."

9 **κονδύλων,** lit. "knuckles," hence the "blows" received. Cf. Aris. *Vesp.* 254, εἰ νὴ Δί' αὖθις κονδύλοις νουθετήσεθ' ἡμᾶς......ἄπιμεν οἴκαδε. So in *Char.* § 2, ὁρῶ γοῦν ἤδη τὸν μισθὸν τῆς περιηγήσεως οὐκ ἀκόνδυλον παντάπασιν ἡμῖν ἐσόμενον ("will not be without blows").

ἐπιμετρήσας, "giving you full measure."

11 **ἐλευθέρᾳ τῇ π.,** for the predicate v. p. 9, l. 1.

12 **μῶν παρακέκρουσμαί σε;** παρακρούειν, "to cheat," the metaphor being prob. from striking the balance unfairly. Cf. Dem. *de Cor.* 276, φυλάττειν ἐμὲ ἐκέλευον, ὅπως μὴ παρακρούσομαι μηδὲ ἐξαπατήσω. So in Arist. *Pol.* VI. 12. 6, ἐν τῷ παρακρούεσθαι τὸν δῆμον. Here "Have I given you false measure?" "Have I cheated you?"

Then here's an extra gallon above your due." So *Pisc.* § 9, ὡς
παρακρουσάμενος τοὺς δικαστὰς ἀπέλθῃς.

15   § **58**. **Βλεψίας**. There is a Blepsias in *Inf. Dial.* 27. 7, a well-
known usurer, who may be the man in L.'s mind (Βλεψίας ὁ δα-
νεισ τικὸς). **Λάχης**, a wealthy man of this name is mentioned in *dial.
meret.* 7. 2, belonging to the same deme as Timon, Λάχης ὁ Κολυττεύς.
Γνίφων, Gnipho too was a rich money-lender, mentioned again
in *Tyr.* 17, τὸν δανειστὴν Γνίφωνα ἰδὼν στένοντα.

17   **ἐπὶ τὴν πέτραν ταύτην**. This was the plan he had first proposed
to himself : § 45, ἐπὶ τὸν πάγον τοῦτον ἀναβάς.

19   **αὐτὸς δὲ**, placed intentionally in a very emphatic position.
Hitherto the δίκελλα has done all the work, § 46 with Gnatho, ἄσει
ὑπὸ ταύτῃ τῇ δικέλλῃ: § 48, with Philiades, σὲ φιλοφρονήσομαι τῇ
δικέλλῃ: § 53 with Demeas. Now that it has worked so hard
(πάλαι πεπονηκυῖαν), it shall rest awhile, αὐτὸς δὲ ἐπιχαλαξῶ.

20   **ἐπιχαλαξῶ αὐτοῖς**. αὐτοὺς is the more general reading, so
Hemsterhuis, Somm., Abbott, &c. Dindorf reads αὐτοῖς. Anyhow,
whether acc. or dat. the word refers to the new arrivals, not the
stones. "I will hail them down upon them." Cf. *Gall.* § 21, κἄν
σοι δοκῇ, κατεχαλάξῃσας αὐτῶν ἀφθόνους τοὺς λίθους. But the compound verb there is no help to fixing the construction of the simple
verb.

22   **οὐκ...γε**. "Anyhow" if you do go off at once, "it shall not be
without loss of blood." Cf. Shak. *Tim.* IV. 3,

> *Tim.* (*to Apemantus.*)   "Away,
>   Thou tedious rogue; I am sorry, I shall lose
>   A stone by thee!"

The last words that Timon utters according to Shakspere will be
a fitting close :—The Senators, and Flavius his ever-faithful servant
have come to beseech him to return with them to Athens,

> "And of our Athens (thine, and ours) to take
>   The captainship."

But all words are useless :—

> "Come not to me again : but say to Athens
>   Timon hath made his everlasting mansion
>   Upon the beachèd verge of the salt flood;

Which once a day with his embossèd froth
The turbulent surge shall cover; thither come,
And let my gravestone be your oracle.—
Lips, let sour words go by, and language end:
What is amiss, plague and infection mend!
Graves only be men's works; and death their gain!
Sun, hide thy beams! Timon hath done his reign."

[Exit.

INDEX A. ENGLISH.

M. = Menippus; T. = Timon. The numbers refer to the section.

Hesiod (quoted) M. 4
Homer (quoted) M. 1 *et passim*
Hymettus T. 7
Hyperbolus T. 30

Irus M. 15
Ixion M. 14

Lebadaea M. 22
Lycoreus T. 3
Lynceus T. 25

Maeandrius M. 16
Mausolus M. 17
Midas M. 18
Minos M. 11, 12
Misanthrope T. 44
Miser (the) T. 14
Mithrobarzanes M. 6
Moderation (inculcated) M. 14;
  T. 15

Nestor M. 18; T. 48
Nireus M. 15; T. 23
Noun (suppressed) T. 5, 20, 31,
  40, 44, 53, 55

Odysseus M. 1, 8
Optative (by attraction) M. 1;
  T. 39
Orpheus M. 1, 8

Palamedes M. 18
Pan T. 42
Participle (w. main idea) M. 6; T.
  34
— (ellip. of) T. 7

Penia T. 31
Peripatetics M. 4
Persephone M. 9
Phaethon T. 4
Philiades T. 47
Philip M. 17
Phineus T. 18
Pluto T. 21
Polycrates M. 16
Predicative adjective M. 2, 9; T.
  9, &c.
Pyrrhias M. 15; (another) T. 22

Salmoneus T. 2
Sardanapallus M. 18
Shakspere Introd Sect. on "T.
  the Dialogue."
Sisyphus M. 14
Stoics M. 4
Subjunctive (delib.) T. 35
— (w. βούλει) T. 37

Tantalus M. 14; T. 18
Teiresias M. 16
Thersites M. 15
Thesmoph. T. 17
Tityus M. 14
Tmesis M. 9
Trophonius M. 22
Tunny-fishing T. 42

Verb (ellipse of) T. 56
Vote M. 20

Zeugma T. 6
Zoroaster M. 6

INDEX B. GREEK.

154 *INDEX B.*

For EU product safety concerns, contact us at Calle de José Abascal, 56–1°,
28003 Madrid, Spain or eugpsr@cambridge.org.

www.ingramcontent.com/pod-product-compliance
Ingram Content Group UK Ltd.
Pitfield, Milton Keynes, MK11 3LW, UK
UKHW020315140625
459647UK00018B/1894